WITHDRAW
PRINT

Turning | Points
IN WORLD HISTORY

The Rise of Islamic Fundamentalism

Phillip Margulies, *Book Editor*

Bruce Glassman, *Vice President*
Bonnie Szumski, *Publisher*
Helen Cothran, *Managing Editor*

GREENHAVEN PRESS
An imprint of Thomson Gale, a part of The Thomson Corporation

Detroit • New York • San Francisco • San Diego • New Haven, Conn.
Waterville, Maine • London • Munich

For more information, contact
Greenhaven Press
27500 Drake Rd.
Farmington Hills, MI 48331-3535
Or you can visit our Internet site at http://www.gale.com

Cover credit: © Hazem Bader/AFP/Hulton Archive by Getty Images. Islamic militants stab and point a gun at a defaced picture of Israeli prime minister Ariel Sharon in 2005.

LIBRARY OF CONGRESS CATALOGING-IN-PUBLICATION DATA

The rise of Islamic fundamentalism / Phillip Margulies, book editor.
    p. cm. — (Turning points in world history)
Includes bibliographical references and index.
ISBN 0-7377-2985-6 (lib. : alk. paper)
    1. Islamic fundamentalism. 2. Islam and civil society. I. Margulies, Phillip, 1952– . II. Turning points in world history.
BP166.14.F85R57 2006
297'.09'04—dc22
                                                                      2005046336

Printed in the United States of America

Contents

Chapter 1: The Roots of Islamic Fundamentalism

Throughout the twentieth century, Islamic leaders and writers helped to shape the view of history accepted by many Islamic fundamentalists today. According to their perspective, Islamic history has been a struggle between the treacherous infidels of the West and the righteous Muslims who must ultimately triumph.

The transition to a modern economy has caused social upheaval wherever it has occurred, giving strength to violent utopian movements. As a result, fundamentalism has gained many followers in the Middle East and South Asia.

In the early 1920s, influential Islamic organizations developed in Egypt and India and spread the message of Islamic fundamentalism throughout the Middle East and South Asia.

Israel's many triumphs in wars against other Middle Eastern countries have frustrated many Muslims and caused them to reject the secular regimes they blame for military ineffectiveness. These Muslims are turning to Islamic fundamentalism in hope of gaining power.

Religious schools in the Middle East and South Asia focus on teaching fundamentalist interpretations of the

Koran to thousands of extremely poor students in
Pakistan.

Chapter 2: Islamic Fundamentalism Achieves State Power

Chapter 3: Islamic Terrorism

a theological justification for suicide attacks, a tactic that
Islamic fundamentalists in many countries began to use.

Chapter 4: The Future of Islamic Fundamentalism

Foreword

Certain past events stand out as pivotal, as having effects and outcomes that change the course of history. These events are often referred to as turning points. Historian Louis L. Snyder provides this useful definition:

> A turning point in history is an event, happening, or stage which thrusts the course of historical development into a different direction. By definition a turning point is a great event, but it is even more—a great event with the explosive impact of altering the trend of man's life on the planet.

History's turning points have taken many forms. Some were single, brief, and shattering events with immediate and obvious impact. The invasion of Britain by William the Conqueror in 1066, for example, swiftly transformed that land's political and social institutions and paved the way for the rise of the modern English nation. By contrast, other single events were deemed of minor significance when they occurred, only later recognized as turning points. The assassination of a little-known European nobleman, Archduke Franz Ferdinand, on June 28, 1914, in the Bosnian town of Sarajevo was such an event; only after it touched off a chain reaction of political-military crises that escalated into the global conflict known as World War I did the murder's true significance become evident.

Other crucial turning points occurred not in terms of a few hours, days, months, or even years, but instead as evolutionary developments spanning decades or even centuries. One of the most pivotal turning points in human history, for instance—the development of agriculture, which replaced nomadic hunter-gatherer societies with more permanent settlements—occurred over the course of many generations. Still other great turning points were neither events nor developments, but rather revolutionary new inventions and innovations that significantly altered social customs and ideas, military tactics, home life, the spread of knowledge, and the human condition in general. The developments of writing, gunpowder, the printing press, antibiotics, the electric light, atomic energy, television, and the computer, the last two of which have recently ushered in the world-altering information age, represent only some of these innovative turning points.

Each anthology in the Greenhaven Turning Points in World History series presents a group of essays chosen for their accessibility. The anthology's structure also enhances this accessibility. First, an introductory essay provides a general overview of the principal events and figures involved, placing the topic in its historical context. The essays that follow explore various aspects in more detail, some targeting political trends and consequences, others social, literary, cultural, and/or technological ramifications, and still others pivotal leaders and other influential figures. To aid the reader in choosing the material of immediate interest or need, each essay is introduced by a concise summary of the contributing writer's main themes and insights.

In addition, each volume contains extensive research tools, including a collection of excerpts from primary source documents pertaining to the historical events and figures under discussion. In the anthology on the French Revolution, for example, readers can examine the works of Rousseau, Voltaire, and other writers and thinkers whose championing of human rights helped fuel the French people's growing desire for liberty; the French *Declaration of the Rights of Man and Citizen*, presented to King Louis XVI by the French National Assembly on October 2, 1789; and eyewitness accounts of the attack on the royal palace and the horrors of the Reign of Terror. To guide students interested in pursuing further research on the subject, each volume features an extensive bibliography, which for easy access has been divided into separate sections by topic. Finally, a comprehensive index allows readers to scan and locate content efficiently. Each of the anthologies in the Greenhaven Turning Points in World History series provides students with a complete, detailed, and enlightening examination of a crucial historical watershed.

Introduction

In a speech before the U.S. Congress on September 20, 2001, nine days after the terrorist attacks on the World Trade Center and the Pentagon, President George W. Bush declared a "war on terror." The terrorists, said the president, "practice a fringe form of Islamic extremism that has been rejected by Muslim scholars and the vast majority of Muslim clerics—a fringe movement that perverts the peaceful teachings of Islam." Later in the speech he added, "I . . . want to speak directly to the Muslims of the world. We respect your faith. . . . Its teachings are good and peaceful and those who commit evil in the name of Allah blaspheme the name of Allah."[1]

The practitioners of Islamic extremism Bush referred to in his speech were members of al Qaeda, a religiously inspired terrorist group led by the exiled Saudi millionaire Osama bin Laden. The men who hijacked the airplanes on September 11 were Islamic fundamentalists acting in the name of an ideology that has millions of passionate adherents all over the world today. It is difficult to say what proportion of Islamic fundamentalists approve of the tactics of Bin Laden. Probably most do not. Some of the most well-known Islamic militants, including Shaykh Fadlallah, the spiritual leader of Lebanon's Hizballah, condemned the attacks. As historian Bernard Lewis remarks, "Most Muslims are not fundamentalists, and most fundamentalists are not terrorists." Nonetheless, Lewis adds, "most present-day terrorists are Muslims and proudly identify themselves as such."[2] Regardless of the number of Islamic fundamentalists, it is clear that a significant percentage of Muslims hold beliefs antithetical to the West. Therefore it is important to understand the beliefs of the fundamentalists and the history that has led to the rise of their movement.

Islamic fundamentalism is a label Western observers apply to contemporary Islamic movements that advocate a strict observance of Islamic law and favor the establishment of Islamic states that rule according to Islamic law. As with any movement involving millions of people, there is a range of views within what is called Islamic fundamentalism. Islamic fundamentalists do not always agree about what an Islamic state would be like or how its institutions would work. In some countries Islamic fundamentalists are officially in control. States that say they are guided by Islamic law include Iran, Saudi Arabia, Sudan, and Malaysia. Prior to the overthrow of the Taliban in 2001, Afghanistan was an Islamic state.

Since they began to exert an influence on international politics in the 1970s, Islamic fundamentalists have often been in conflict with the United States—often enough to inspire the question many Americans asked in the wake of the 9/11 attacks: "Why do they hate us?" Many experts argue that hating the United States in particular or the West in general is not the main focus of Islamic fundamentalism. Observers including *New York Times* correspondent Thomas Friedman, former U.S. national security adviser Zbigniew Brzezinski, former U.S. counterterrorism chief Richard A. Clarke, and Middle Eastern political scholar Faoud Ajami have at different times reminded Americans that the terrorist acts inspired by Islamic fundamentalism are part of a "war within Islam," a war, as Ajami puts it, "for the soul of Islam."[3] Boston University professor Angela M. Codevilla writes, "anti-Western terrorism results from a war within Islam that is more serious for Muslims than for the rest of us."[4]

Some experts argue that the people Islamic fundamentalists most want to influence are other Muslims and that the governments Islamic fundamentalists most want to control are in the Middle East and South Asia. If Bin Laden's public statements can be believed, even the perpetrators of the 9/11 attacks had limited objectives, and al Qaeda will cease its attacks when Christians and Jews cease to occupy Muslim lands.

Nevertheless, the West looms large in the vision of Islamic fundamentalists. Islamic fundamentalism developed during the early twentieth century, a period when Muslims throughout the world were experiencing economic, political, and cultural domination by the West. Islamic fundamentalists blame Western interference for Islam's decline in political strength, for the fragmentation of *dar al-Islam* (the "house of Islam," that is, the territory in which Islam is the dominant religion) into many states with problematic borders, for supporting corrupt governments in the Middle East and South Asia, and for the "pollution" of Islamic culture with Hollywood glitz and American-style consumer culture. Fundamentalists reject such imported Western ideas as nationalism, socialism, feminism, and liberal democracy and instead propose a return to Islamic roots. While there is more to Islamic fundamentalism than conflict with the West, this conflict is an important part of Islamic fundamentalist thinking. The sources of Islamic fundamentalism's quarrel with the West are therefore worth exploring.

Islamic Origins and History

Islamic fundamentalists describe their beliefs and practices as a return to the roots of Islam. To understand Islamic fundamentalism and its conflict with the West, it is necessary to understand those roots and to know some basic facts about Islamic religion and history.

Muhammad, the founder of Islam, was a merchant born in the Arabian Peninsula in the late sixth century A.D. When he was forty, Muhammad underwent a profound spiritual transformation, experiencing visions in which the archangel Gabriel appeared to him and delivered messages from Allah. Muhammad recited the content of his visions to others, who became the nucleus of a fast-growing religious community centered on a belief in one God.

At the time of Muhammad's visions, Arabia was a pagan society. Mecca, Muhammad's birthplace and home, was a major trading city and the location of shrines to numerous deities who were the objects of pilgrimages and worship. The shrines' owners profited from the pilgrims who came to visit them, and Muhammad's attack on idolatry angered the most powerful people in Mecca. To escape persecution, Muhammad and his followers moved to Yathrib, a city 214 miles north of Mecca (Yathrib was later renamed Medina).

In Medina, Muhammad's movement grew. He began to call himself "the seal of the prophets," meaning that he was the last in the line of the messengers of God that included Muhammad and Jesus (whom Muhammad saw as a prophet rather than as the son of God). In 630 Muhammad and his followers attacked and conquered Mecca. They forced the leading families of the city to become monotheists, destroyed the idols, and replaced the pagan shrines with mosques.

Islamic Belief and Practice

Muhammad's recitations were written down by his followers and compiled after his death as the Koran, Islam's principal holy book. Other sayings and acts of Muhammad were also recorded in a somewhat less authoritative body of literature called the hadith. Together, the Koran and the hadith form the basis of sharia, Islamic law.

The basic creed of Islam is a set of dictates called the Five Pillars of Islam, originally described in one of the hadiths attributed to Muhammad. First, Muslims must acknowledge Allah as the only god and Muhammad as his prophet. Second, they must pray to Allah daily while facing Mecca. Third, they must fast during the daylight hours of the month of Ramadan. Fourth, they must contribute alms to the relief of the weak and the poor. Finally, if they are able, Muslims should make a pilgrimage to Mecca (called the hajj) at least once in their lifetime. The various sects that have developed within Islam over the centuries agree on these core doctrines and practices.

Islam has characteristics in common with each of the two other religions to which it is related. Like Christianity and unlike Judaism, Islam actively seeks out converts. Muslims hope that the world will one day be all Muslim, just as many Christians believe that the world's population ought to accept the divinity of Jesus. Like Judaism and unlike Christianity, Islam regulates many mundane aspects of daily life. For believers, these small acts of obedience are a kind of worship, giving a ritual quality to everyday life and imparting a sacred dimension to ordinary tasks. Like the rabbis of the Jews, the Islamic clergy (ulema) are scholars of religious law and issue rulings based on their study of Islamic religious literature. Interpreting religious law is the basis for the great political power that Islamic clerics have in an Islamic state.

Religion and State in Islam

According to Islamic thought, religion and government should be closely intertwined—much more closely, it is often said, than in Christianity. "Nowhere," writes Bernard Lewis, are the differences between Christianity and Islam more profound "than in the attitudes of these two religions . . . to the relations between government, religion, and society."[5]

The British historian Peter Mansfield attributes the Islamic belief in close relations between religion and state to the swift rise of Islam, which moved from its persecuted to its expansionist phase within the lifetime of Muhammad. He writes, "The Prophet [Muhammad], unlike Jesus, was a political leader and an organizer of genius, and in Islam there is no separation between religion and politics and no concept of a secular state."[6]

For Muslims, Islam offers the promise of a just society ruled by sharia, which Mansfield notes is "a whole system of social morality, prescribing the ways in which man should live if he is to act according to God's will. If he contravenes the sharia, his offense is against God." Unjust rulers are regarded not only as unjust but as impious. This ideal, says Mansfield, "accounts for the potent force of utopianism among Arabs—the belief that if they were to return to the ways of the Prophet and his companions the triumph of Islam in this world would be assured."[7]

Another link between religion and politics in Islam is the institution of the caliphate. Upon Muhammad's death his role as the leader of the Islamic community (the *ummah*) was assumed by a successor who was called the caliph, and this title was given to subsequent leaders of the *ummah*. Though it underwent many changes, the caliphate lasted until the twentieth century, presenting Muslims with a symbol of unity among all Muslims.

Islam's Expansion

Islam united the Arabs and inspired their conquest through jihad. Between the time of Muhammad's death in 632, the realm of Islam absorbed a vast territory that included Persia (Iran), much of the Byzantine Empire, much of North

Africa, and most of the Iberian Peninsula (modern Spain and Portugal). In 750 the Umayyads, the Arabian family that led Islam during its initial years of expansion, were supplanted as Islam's rulers by another Arabian family, the Abbasids. The Abbasid dynasty was a period of dynamic literary, religious, and scientific activity.

Christians were stunned by the rapid expansion of Islam. As Muslims conquered formerly Christian territory, millions of Christians within the newly conquered lands converted to Islam. The church itself, however, saw Islam as a heresy and often identified whoever was currently leading the Islamic armies as the Antichrist.

During the Middle Ages, Christians and Muslims viewed each other as infidels. In practice, however, Muslims were more tolerant of Christians than Christians were of Muslims. Muslims permitted Christians and Jews within the Muslim domains to practice their religion. Under Muslim law, Christians and Jews had to pay special taxes and were subjected to discriminatory legal restrictions. They were officially second-class citizens. However, over the course of centuries many Christians and Jews came to play important roles in Islamic society. Some served as merchants, sailors, physicians, interpreters, and even as advisers to Muslim leaders. In lands ruled by Christians, by contrast, Jews were persecuted and Muslims had to convert or face expulsion or death.

In the eleventh century, Christians from Europe launched a series of Crusades to recapture the holy land of Palestine from the Muslims. They conquered Jerusalem in an extremely bloody campaign that did not spare women and children. They also established a group of small Christian states in Palestine until they were defeated and expelled in the thirteenth century.

The Crusades are an important symbol of Christian and Western conquest for many Islamic fundamentalists. Some Islamic fundamentalists maintain that Christians have never given up their ambition of destroying Islam. In reality, however, the Crusades had less effect on Islam than other invasions and migrations that shook Islamic society during the

Middle Ages. For example, in the ninth century, Turkish-speaking peoples from central Asia began moving southward in large numbers. They converted to Islam, served in the Abbasid armies, and eventually assumed political control, keeping the Abbasid caliph as a figurehead. In the thirteenth century the Mongols, another group of central-Asian invaders, brutally subdued a wide swath of Muslim lands. These invaders eventually converted to Islam and were later dislodged by another group of converts, the Ottoman Turks, whose rulers assumed the title of caliph as well as sultan ("chieftain"). At their most powerful, the Ottomans were the terror of Christendom, conquering lands as far north as Hungary. The Ottomans ruled most of the Arabic-speaking Islamic lands until modern times. Other parts of *dar al-Islam* were enlarged by the military conquests of two other empires founded by Turkish peoples from central Asia: the Safavid empire of Persia and the Mogul empire in India.

The Trauma of Conquest by the West

The Crusades are a symbol of Western tyranny and expansionism in the eyes of Islamic fundamentalists today because they are viewed in the light of a later and much more thorough conquest of Muslim lands that occurred in the nineteenth century. At that time, thanks to the tremendous advantages the industrial revolution gave to European economies and military forces, a handful of European nations conquered the world, including most of the Middle East and South Asia. Western domination of *dar al-Islam* reached its height in the 1920s. Morocco, Algeria, Tunis, Syria, and Lebanon were French colonies. England either controlled or colonized Egypt, Sudan, Iraq, Palestine, and the Indian subcontinent. Russia had much earlier conquered and absorbed Islamic territory in central Asia. Of the few Islamic countries that remained independent, most, like Iran, Yemen, and Arabia, were poor and backward.

Only Turkey, which had been the core of the Ottoman Empire, managed to remake itself into an independent, centralized, secular modern state. Under the leadership of Kemal Atatürk, Turkey declared itself a republic in 1923, sending the last Ottoman sultan into exile. The following year Turkey's national assembly passed a law abolishing the caliphate. There was no longer a single ruler of all Islam even in theory.

Direct Western control of Muslim lands lasted for a relatively short period but was more traumatic than earlier conquests. While earlier conquerors had acknowledged the superiority of Arab culture and converted to Islam, the West was influenced very little by Islamic culture. The Islamic world's natural resources were exploited by the West, and Muslims became dependent on Western manufactured goods. When the Ottoman Empire broke up after World War I, the European powers carved up the Middle East among themselves. When Europeans relinquished control, many separate states were created whose borders had been drawn for the convenience of their former colonial masters. The arbitrary borders split up territories which had once been unified under the rule of the caliph, while yoking together tribal groups that were bound to come into conflict as the former colonies tried to remake themselves into modern nation-states.

Europe's period of rule over *dar al-Islam* led to another lasting grievance for Muslims. In the last days of the British Empire, Britain had helped Jewish immigrants create a Jewish homeland in Palestine, which became the modern state of Israel in 1948. The advent of a non-Muslim state in the heart of the Islamic world was an additional blow to the unity of Islam. It also undermined the prestige of the new Arab states. All the Arab states and many non-Arab Islamic states had objected to Israel's creation but could not prevent it. Despite more than one attempt, they were also unable to destroy Israel once it had been created. This inability exposed their continuing military and political weakness.

Muslim Intellectuals React to the Colonial Experience

Islamic fundamentalism was shaped by this history of Western domination and was conceived as a response to it. In 1928 a former Egyptian schoolteacher named Hasan al-

Banna founded the Muslim Brotherhood, an organization devoted to increasing the influence of Islam in Arab political life. Al-Banna, an eloquent writer and speaker, explained the fate that had befallen the Islamic world as a failure of faith. Muslims had tried to imitate the secular West, which seemed ironic since most of the West had recently been involved in the First World War, in which millions of soldiers and civilians had been killed. Al-Banna shared with many postwar Europeans and Americans a belief that Western civilization was spiritually bankrupt. "For al-Banna," notes historian Walid Mahmoud Abdelnasser, "the West was characterized by atheism, moral laxity and materialism that gave rise to destructive principles and fighting among Western peoples."[8]

Al-Banna's grievances included Western support of Zionism: Like many other Arabs, he saw the plan to settle Jews in Palestine as just another imperialist project. He also believed that the spread of many other Western ideas, including capitalism, feminism, and socialism, was dangerous for Islamic society. As Abdelnasser writes, "Hasan al-Banna accused the West of disrupting familial harmony by instigating women to revolt; impeding social peace by instigating war among classes; and undermining national unity by installing a political system in which parties monopolized gains."[9]

Al-Banna called for a return to sharia and a jihad (struggle, spiritual or military) to free Islam from Western domination. This message appealed to many Muslims. Throughout the twentieth century, chapters of al-Banna's Muslim Brotherhood multiplied throughout the Middle East, often coming into conflict with the state. Al-Banna himself was assassinated by the Egyptian government in 1949.

In India, where millions of Muslims were subjects of the British Empire, Muslim intellectuals also called for an Islamic revival. An Indian journalist named Mawlana Abul A'la Mawdudi, whose writings had influenced al-Banna, founded his own Islamist society, the Jamaat-i-Islami, in India in 1941. Mawdudi directed much of his ire at colonialism and capitalism. In common with the Communists of his time, he saw liberal democracy as a cover for the exploitation of weaker people by the ruling classes of the democratic countries. Unlike the Communists, who despised religion, Mawdudi's answer was a return to Islamic roots.

The Anti-Americanism of Sayyid Qutb

One of the writers who has greatly influenced today's Islamic extremists is Sayyid Qutb, a member of Egypt's Muslim Brotherhood who wrote in the 1950s and 1960s and was executed by the secular nationalist government of Gamal Abdel Nasser in 1966. In his best-known book, *Milestones*, Qutb offers Muslims a stark alternative between submission to Islamic fundamentalism and surrender to *jahiliyya* (pagan barbarism or the materialistic modern West).

Qutb hated America. As he wrote, "What should be done about America and the West, given their overwhelming danger to humanity . . . ? Should we not issue a sentence of death?"[10] Some writers attribute this feeling to Qutb's personal experiences in the United States, where the Egyptian ministry of education sent him to study from 1948 to 1951. American social historians describe this period in the United States as a time of buttoned-down repression, but for Qutb it was a scene of mindless sexual license and empty materialism.

Qutb's anti-Americanism was also grounded in political realities. Between the time of al-Banna and Qutb, the United States had replaced Great Britain as the Western country exercising the greatest influence in the Middle East. America's interest in the Middle East's energy resources and its competition with the Soviet Union caused the United States to become deeply involved in the politics of the region. Qutb resented America's influence as he would have resented the influence of any foreign power.

Islamic Fundamentalism Gains Power

For the first two decades after the Second World War, Islamic fundamentalism was just one of many ideologies competing for the attention of Muslims in the newly independent states of the Middle East and South Asia. Governments of countries in the Middle East and South Asia sometimes repressed Islamic fundamentalists and sometimes sought alliances with them, but Islamic fundamentalism was not viewed as the strongest force in the region's future. However, the influence of Islamic fundamentalism grew sharply after the 1967 Arab-Israeli War (the Six-Day War), when Israel defeated the combined armed forces of Syria, Egypt, and Jordan, and occupied territory in which many Arabs lived. After the war's end, Israel annexed Jerusalem, the location of some of Islam's (as well as Judaism's and Christianity's) holiest sites. This fateful action turned the Arab-Israeli conflict from a dispute about territory into a religious issue. A shock to Muslims everywhere, the Israeli victory disgraced the secular leadership of the region. Muslim intellectuals blamed the defeat on the spiritual hollowness of Arab elites, and Islamic fundamentalists began to gain a greater following.

Just as the defeat of 1967 had weakened the hand of modernizers, Islamic fundamentalists gained prestige when a charismatic Islamic cleric, the Ayatollah Ruhollah Khomeini, led an Islamic revolution in Iran in 1979, officially imposing Islamic law in a relatively rich and Westernized country. Many Iranians—most of them not Islamic fundamentalists—contributed to the overthrow of the shah of Iran's unpopular, autocratic government, which had been brought to power by the machinations of the U.S. Central Intelligence Agency in 1953. It is uncertain what proportion of the Iranian people wanted to bring about the reign of "God's government" in Iran, but after the revolution Khomeini skillfully solidified the Islamists' base of power. Millions of Americans learned of Islamic fundamentalism for the first time in 1979, when Iranian militants stormed the U.S. embassy in Tehran and took approximately seventy Americans captive with the encouragement of Khomeini. Confronting the angry, black-turbaned, bearded mullah on nightly news programs, Americans discovered that to the Iranians, the United States was the "Great Satan."

Islamic Fundamentalists at War

Islamic fundamentalism became a more militant movement during the 1980s as its true believers threw themselves into conflicts they saw as critical to the struggle to rid Islamic lands of foreign domination. Jihadists (holy warriors) fought the Soviets in Afghanistan and the Israelis in Lebanon. Invoking a novel theological justification for suicide first introduced by Khomeini, Islamic militants began using suicide attacks to get close to their targets. The targets have sometimes been enemy soldiers, but have also included civilian men, women, and children, despite the fact that Muslim law specifically prohibits the killing of noncombatants in war. The belief that a Muslim "martyred" in a suicide attack will enjoy perpetual bliss in paradise, and the honors given to suicide attackers and their families, have made suicide attackers easy to recruit.

In the 1990s militant Islamic fundamentalists continued to be involved in conflicts over territory with non-Muslims and in conflicts over ideology with Islamic governments. Following the first U.S. war with Iraq in 1991 and the planting of U.S. military bases in Saudi Arabia, the militant Islamic fundamentalist group al Qaeda began to focus its hatred on the United States. A series of attacks followed, culminating in the attacks of September 11, 2001.

A Unique Historical Experiment

Revolutionary Islamic fundamentalism has failed to bring about a better life for the people in the countries in which it has achieved power. The Islamic fundamentalist government of the Taliban in Afghanistan tortured and killed thousands of Afghans. Sudan has endured decades of civil war under an Islamic government that professes a religion alien to much of Sudan's population. The majority of the people of Iran regret the way their revolution was hijacked by Islamic fundamentalists. Iran has become a country in which people are publicly flogged, imprisoned, and executed for expressing political beliefs that oppose the ruling government. By the late 1990s the violent behavior of Islamic militants had begun to alienate many people who otherwise support the Islamic fundamentalist program of an Islamic state ruled according to traditional Islamic law.

The attacks of September 11 may have been acts of desperation and an attempt to bring a dying movement back to life by provoking a fight between the United States and the

Islamic world. Certainly the attackers succeeded in provoking a fight: Since September 11, 2001, the United States has toppled the Islamic fundamentalist regime in Afghanistan, overthrown a regime in Iraq, and seems to be poised for further interventions. It remains to be seen whether these actions will destroy Islamic fundamentalism or breathe new life into the movement.

Notes

1. George W. Bush, speech to joint session of the U.S. Congress, September 20, 2001.

2. Bernard Lewis, *The Crisis of Islam: Holy War and Unholy Terror*. New York: Modern Library, p. 137.

3. Fouad Ajami, "The War Within Islam," *Reader's Digest*, January 2005, p. 102.

4. Angela M. Codevilla, "Heresy and History," *American Spectator*, May 2004, p. 22.

5. Lewis, *The Crisis of Islam*, pp. 5–6.

6. Peter Mansfield, *A History of the Middle East*. London: Penguin, 1992, p. 13.

7. Mansfield, *A History of the Middle East*, p. 13.

8. Walid Mahmoud Abdelnasser, *The Islamic Movement in Egypt: Perceptions of International Relations 1967–81*. New York: Kegan Paul International, 1994, p. 148.

9. Abdelnasser, *The Islamic Movement in Egypt*, p. 149.

10. Quoted in Dilip Hiro, *War Without End: The Rise of Islamic Terrorism and Global Response*. New York: Routledge, 2003, pp. 66–67.

Chapter 1

The Roots of Islamic Fundamentalism

Turning | Points
IN WORLD HISTORY

Radical Islamic Thinkers Have Created a Legacy of Fundamentalism

R. Scott Appleby

The word *fundamentalist* originally designated a group of American Protestant theologians who emphasized the literal interpretation of the Bible. The term is now used to describe people as different as the Christian evangelical Pat Robertson, Iran's Ayatollah Khomeini, and some of the ultraorthodox Jews of Israel. Christian, Jewish, and Islamic fundamentalists all claim to be restoring their religions to their original purity. All wish secular law to be guided by scriptural law. All claim to interpret their holy books literally, and all interpret history as a mighty struggle leading to a final showdown between the forces of good and evil.

Islamic fundamentalists view their history as one of ancient glory followed by humiliation at the hands of European imperialists. In the eyes of Islamic fundamentalists, the nadir of their history is symbolized by the Republic of Turkey's 1924 abolishment of the caliphate, the institution that had officially ruled all Muslims in the name of Islam. In response to these perceived humiliations, radical Islamic thinkers like Sayyid Qutb began to shape the apocalyptic views accepted by many Islamic fundamentalists today. In this selection R. Scott Appleby, professor of history at the University of Notre Dame, argues that Islamic fundamentalists have distorted both Islam and history to support their worldview. Appleby is the coeditor of a five-volume study, *The Fundamentalism Project,* and author of *The Glory and the Power: The Fundamentalist Challenge to the Modern World.*

R. Scott Appleby, "History in the Fundamentalist Imagination," *Journal of American History*, vol. 89, September 2002, pp. 498–511. Copyright © 2002 by the Organization of American Historians. Reproduced by permission.

On Sunday, October 7, 2001, the Al-Jazeera television network, based in Qatar, broadcast a videotaped statement by Osama bin Laden commenting on the events of September 11. "America has been filled with horror from north to south and east to west, and thanks be to God," bin Laden exulted. "What America is tasting now is only a copy of what we have tasted," he continued. "Our Islamic nation has been tasting the same for more [than] eighty years, of humiliation and disgrace, its sons killed and their blood spilled, its sanctities desecrated."

The "Humiliation"

The period of Muslim "humiliation," that is, began with the defeat of the Ottoman Empire in World War I and the subsequent abolishment of the caliphate, in 1924, by the new secular republic of Turkey under the leadership of Mustafa Kemal Ataturk. The caliphate had been recognized by the vast majority of Muslims as the office of the successors of the Prophet Muhammad. Over the centuries, the role of the caliph varied. Under the Umayyad dynasty, established by the caliph Muawiyah I in 661, the caliphate commanded absolute religious and political power. Under the Abbasids (750–1258), its temporal role was usurped by military commanders (the sultans or emirs). In the eighteenth century the Turkish sultans of the Ottoman Empire presented themselves as caliphs—that is, as the paramount spiritual leaders and defenders of Islam. If the caliph did not wield direct political power for much of this history, his supreme spiritual authority was intended to ensure that Muslim states were governed in accordance with the Islamic law, or shari'a.

The abolishment of the caliphate, according to the reading of history favored by bin Laden and perhaps hundreds of thousands of like-minded Islamic fundamentalists, triggered the precipitous decline of Islam as a civilization-shaping force in the Arab world and beyond. Thus, the origins of Islamism (Muslim fundamentalism) are connected with the loss of a transnational and sacralized Muslim political unit. Sunni and Shiite Muslims have different historical experiences of religiously sanctioned politics; accordingly, their reactions to the fall of the Ottoman Empire and the end of the caliphate have differed. Until the ascendancy of Ayatollah Ruhollah Khomeini[1] in 1978, Shiite Muslims, who are concentrated in Iran, Iraq, and Lebanon, had suffered the loss of divinely guided political leadership since the occultation, or disappearance into hiding, of the Twelfth Imam, in 931 C.E. By contrast, for Sunni Muslims, approximately 90 percent of the Muslim world, the loss of the caliphate after World War I was devastating in light of the hitherto continuous historic presence of the caliph, the guardian of Islamic law and the Islamic state. Sunni fundamentalist leaders thereafter emerged in nations such as Egypt and India, where contact with Western political structures provided them with a model awkwardly to imitate (as in the "theo-democracy" of Maulana Sayyid Abdul Ala Maududi, discussed below) as they struggled after 1924 to provide a viable alternative to the caliphate.

In 1928, four years after the abolishment of the caliphate, the Egyptian schoolteacher Hasan al-Banna founded the first Islamic fundamentalist movement in the Sunni world, the Muslim Brotherhood (al-Ikhwan al-Muslimun). Al-Banna was appalled by "the wave of atheism and lewdness [that] engulfed Egypt" following World War I. The victorious Europeans had "imported their half-naked women into these regions, together with their liquors, their theatres, their dance halls, their amusements, their stories, their newspapers, their novels, their whims, their silly games, and their vices." Suddenly the very heart of the Islamic world was penetrated by European "schools and scientific and cultural institutes" that "cast doubt and heresy into the souls of its sons and taught them how to demean themselves, disparage their religion and their fatherland, divest themselves of their traditions and beliefs, and to regard as sacred anything Western." Most distressing to al-Banna and his followers was what they saw as the rapid moral decline of the religious establishment, including the leading sheikhs, or religious scholars, at Al-Azhar, the grand mosque and center of Islamic learning in Cairo. The clerical leaders had become compromised and corrupted by

1. leader of the fundamentalist Islamic revolution that ousted the shah of Iran

their alliance with the indigenous ruling elites who had succeeded the European colonial masters.

Even as the Ikhwan [Muslim Brotherhood] was gaining momentum in Egypt, in India Maududi was launching the prodigious career as a journalist, editor, and writer that made him the chief ideologue of Islamic fundamentalism. Modern Muslim discourse on the social, political, and economic teachings of Islam owes an enormous debt to Maududi, who coined and systematically defined terms such as "Islamic politics," "Islamic ideology," "the economic system of Islam," and "the Islamic constitution." More systematically than any other author, Maududi recast Islam as an ideological alternative to both Western liberalism and Soviet Marxism. Envisioning Islam as a comprehensive political system as well as a way of life, Maududi advocated iqamat-i-deen (the establishment of religion)—the total subordination of civil society and the state to the authority of the shari'a. Islamic law and Islamic governance should extend, Maududi taught, "from the mosque to the parliament, from the home to the school and economy; from art, architecture and science to law, state and international relations [according to scholar Mumtaz Ahmed]."

In August 1941 Maududi founded the Jamaat-i-islami, which became the major Islamist movement of Pakistan, to give institutional shape to his religiopolitical ideas. But his influence extended far beyond Pakistan and South Asia. He was a major influence on Sayyid Qutb, the ideological founder of the school of Sunni extremism to which Osama bin Laden is heir.

Despite the early virulent Islamic reactions to "Westoxication," as an Iranian intellectual [Jalal Al-e Ahmad] described the cultural colonization of Islam, the "humiliation and disgrace" visited upon "the Islamic nation" only mounted, reaching their apex with the establishment of the state of Israel in 1948 and the first of several demoralizing military defeats at the hands of the Zionists. The Arab and Muslim identities of that imagined, transnational nation clashed violently in the 1950s and 1960s following the ascent to power of Gamal Abdel Nasser in Egypt. Nasser's vision of Pan-Arab unity buttressed by state socialism captured the imagination of the

Arab Middle East. But his state-guided, state-dominated plan to build the public sector of the economy suffered from a balance of payments crisis, domestic entanglements (including

---

The Clash of Civilizations

In 1993, reflecting on the end of the Cold War, scholar Samuel P. Huntington published an influential essay suggesting that in the future the main sources of world conflict would be cultural rather than economic. In his essay, which he later developed into a book, Huntington predicts that the conflict between Western and Muslim civilizations will only increase. The following extract from his essay describes the reasons Huntington believes future conflicts will be rooted in cultural differences.

The most important conflicts of the future will occur along the cultural fault lines separating these civilizations from one another.

Why will this be the case?

First, differences among civilizations are not only real; they are basic. Civilizations are differentiated from each other by history, language, culture, tradition and, most important, religion. The people of different civilizations have different views on the relations between God and man, the individual and the group, the citizen and the state, parents and children, husband and wife, as well as differing views of the relative importance of rights and responsibilities, liberty and authority, equality and hierarchy. These differences are the product of centuries. They will not soon disappear. They are far more fundamental than differences among political ideologies and political regimes. Differences do not necessarily mean conflict, and conflict does not necessarily mean violence. Over the centuries, however, differences among civilizations have generated the most prolonged and the most violent conflicts.

Second, the world is becoming a smaller place. The interactions between peoples of different civilizations are increasing; these increasing interactions intensify civilization consciousness and awareness of differences between civilizations and commonalities within civilizations. . . .

an alleged plot by the Muslim Brotherhood), and the excessive bureaucratization and overmanagement often associated with central planning. At the same time, Nasser's political

Third, the processes of economic modernization and social change throughout the world are separating people from long-standing local identities. They also weaken the nation state as a source of identity. In much of the world religion has moved in to fill this gap, often in the form of movements that are labeled "fundamentalist." Such movements are found in Western Christianity, Judaism, Buddhism and Hinduism, as well as in Islam. . . .

Fourth, the growth of civilization-consciousness is enhanced by the dual role of the West. On the one hand, the West is at a peak of power. At the same time, however, and perhaps as a result, a return to the roots phenomenon is occurring among non-Western civilizations. . . .

Fifth, cultural characteristics and differences are less mutable and hence less easily compromised and resolved than political and economic ones. In the former Soviet Union, communists can become democrats, the rich can become poor and the poor rich, but Russians cannot become Estonians and Azeris cannot become Armenians. In class and ideological conflicts, the key question was "Which side are you on?" and people could and did choose sides and change sides. In conflicts between civilizations, the question is "What are you?" That is a given that cannot be changed. . . .

Finally, economic regionalism is increasing. The proportions of total trade that were intraregional rose between 1980 and 1989 from 51 percent to 59 percent in Europe, 33 percent to 37 percent in East Asia, and 32 percent to 36 percent in North America. The importance of regional economic blocs is likely to continue to increase in the future. On the one hand, successful economic regionalism will reinforce civilization-consciousness, On the other hand, economic regionalism may succeed only when it is rooted in a common civilization.

Samuel P. Huntington, "The Clash of Civilizations?" *Foreign Affairs*, Summer 1993.

leadership of the Arab world suffered a mortal blow when Israel won the Six Day War of 1967 and occupied the West Bank, Gaza, and the Sinai. Not least, Nasser also made the fateful choice to isolate and then outlaw the Muslim Brotherhood (which had become increasingly violent), arresting more than one thousand of its leaders and eventually executing six, including Qutb.

Sayyid Qutb's Ideas

While in prison, Qutb penned a treatise that his followers disseminated across the Sunni world *Milestones* (1960, also known as *Signposts on the Road*) became the manifesto of Sunni extremism and the justification for terrorism. In *Milestones* Qutb developed an interpretation of jihad, Islamic holy war, that would become the core doctrine of the Islamic Liberation Organization of Egypt and Jordan, the Jihad Organization and Takfir wal-Hijra of Egypt, and similar cells in Egypt, North Africa, Lebanon, Israel, Saudi Arabia, the West Bank, and the gulf states. Qutb's radical innovation was the application of the concept of jahiliyya (the pre-Islamic condition of ignorance of the guidance of God) to fellow Muslims, including Arab leaders such as Nasser, who had abandoned Islam, he charged, in favor of atheistic philosophies and ideologies. "Our whole environment, people's beliefs and ideas, habits and art, rules and laws is Jahiliyyah, even to the extent that what we consider to be Islamic culture, Islamic sources, Islamic philosophy and Islamic thought, are also constructs of Jahiliyyah!" As a result, he charged, "the true Islamic values never enter our hearts . . . our minds are never illuminated by Islamic concepts, and no group of people arises among us who are of the calibre of the first generation of Islam."

Maududi's concept of iqamat-i-deen echoes in Qutb's exhortations from prison to his fellow Muslim Brothers. Significantly for our purposes, Qutb justifies "the establishment of religion" by positing a golden age or primordial state of purity, resolve, and religious integrity, standards from which subsequent generations departed. People of the caliber of the Prophet and his companions do not arise because the vicissitudes of historical experience have eroded the social and institutional structures within which true belief flourished. True believers of the past have too often let events—the normal course of history—determine the outcome of the perennial struggle between the righteous and the unbelievers. The remedy to historical erosion? "We must return to that pure source from which those people [the earliest followers of the Prophet Muhammad] derived their guidance—the source which is free from any mixing or pollution," Qutb wrote. "From [Islam] we must also derive our concepts of life, our principles of government, politics, economics and all other aspects of life."

Qutb's dour reading of long stretches of the Muslim past informs the elements of fundamentalist ideology in *Milestones:* alarm over the perceived loss of religious integrity; refusal to compromise with outsiders; the sense of apocalyptic crisis; the envy and imitation of secular modernity juxtaposed to revulsion from its immoral excesses; and, finally, the desire to build a comprehensive religious alternative to secularism. For Qutb withdrawal from the existing compromised Islamic society was a prelude to an offensive jihad against infidels and apostates around the world. The Islamic fundamentalist movement would use the weapons and tactics of the secular world against it. [As Qutb wrote]:

> Since this movement comes into conflict with the Jahiliyyah which . . . has a practical system of life and a political and material authority behind it, the Islamic movement had to produce parallel resources. . . . This movement uses the methods of preaching and persuasion for reforming ideas and beliefs; and it uses physical power and Jihaad for abolishing the organisations and authorities of the jahili [non-Islamic] system.

Jihad is not restricted to defense of the homeland, Qutb insists. Rather, it is a command to extend the borders of Islam to the ends of the earth:

> If we insist on calling Islamic Jihaad a defensive movement, then we must change the meaning of the word "defense" and mean by it "the defense of man" against all those elements which limit his freedom. These elements take the form of be-

liefs and concepts, as well as of political systems, based on economic, racial or class distinctions. . . . When we take this broad meaning of the word "defense," we understand the true character of Islam, and that it is a universal proclamation of the freedom of man from servitude to other men, the establishment of God and His Lordship throughout the world, the end of man's arrogance and selfishness, and the implementation of the rule of the Divine Sharia'ah in human affairs.

Here Qutb broke with contemporary interpreters of Islamic law. Like fundamentalists in other religions, he invoked the doctrines of a sage who had legitimated extremism, in this case Ibn Taymiyya (1268–1328), a scholar of Islamic law who had characterized Mongols as "false Muslims" and blessed those who fought them. Qutb also retrieved the practice of ijtihad, the use of independent reasoning when no clear text was available from the Koran or the hadith (sayings) of the Prophet. Finally, he gave an extremist interpretation of a traditional precept—jihad—justifying it by recourse to "exceptionalism," the argument that the onset of crisis (here jahiliyya) requires extreme countermeasures.

In *Milestones* Qutb argued that the Prophet's prohibition against fighting was only "a temporary stage in a long journey" during the Meccan period, and he uses inflammatory language easily construed as legitimating lethal violence against Islam's numerous enemies. (It was so construed by Qutb's intellectual disciples, notably the Jihad group that assassinated President Anwar Sadat of Egypt in 1981.) Yet Qutb himself disavowed any intent to harm individuals, claiming that Islamists attack only institutions, and a sympathetic scholar [Johannes J.G. Jansen] described him as "essentially a philosopher who shunned violence."

Sayyid Qutb's Legacy

Be that as it may, Qutb's legacy includes the cadres of radical fundamentalist Muslims who created new forms of violent intolerance and religious resistance to the powers that be. Elements of his ideology have inspired fundamentalist movements and terrorist cells that grew up outside his original sphere of influence, including the Taliban, the Harkat Muja-hedeen of Pakistan, and the Armed Islamic Group (GIA) of Algeria, which has waged a terrorist campaign against the "jahili" government of Algeria since 1992. Among the terror-ist networks influenced by Qutb's notion of jihad are Al-Qaeda, which bin Laden founded in 1985. Bin Laden envi-sioned his operations as a step toward expelling the Western presence from Islamic lands, abolishing state boundaries, and creating a transnational Islamic society ruled by a restored caliphate.

Thus we return to bin Laden and his distinctive view of Western and Islamic history over the past eighty years. Like al-Banna and Qutb, bin Laden charges that mainstream Mus-lim clerics have been co-opted by dictatorial and compromis-ing rulers such as Egyptian president Hosni Mubarak or by the monarchy of Saudi Arabia, which committed the unfor-givable sin of allowing U.S. troops to be stationed near the holy cities of Mecca and Medina ("its sancties desecrated") [during and after the 1991 Gulf War following Iraq's invasion of Kuwait]. Delegitimated in many circles of the Islamic world, the state-supported religious scholars have yielded popular authority to the religiously unschooled but disgrun-tled laymen, many with educational backgrounds in engineer-ing, applied science, or business. In the late nineties, for exam-ple, the engineer bin Laden began to refer to himself as "Sheikh" Osama Bin-Muhammad Bin-laden, as he did in the fatwa he issued on February 23, 1998, announcing his legal "ruling" that every Muslim now has the individual duty to "kill the Americans and their allies—civilians and military."

Fundamentalists' Grievances

The justification for this tragic distortion of Islamic law and ethics? U.S. policy toward the Middle East and the broader Islamic world, the Islamists charge, has transparently served the narrow interests of an affluent and comfortable Ameri-can public, which consumes a grossly disproportionate per-centage of natural resources (oil-based products in particu-lar) while the mass of humanity in the countries being exploited for their oil live below the poverty level. Muslim lives and livelihoods are routinely sacrificed to support luxurious American life-styles. The United States is a great hypocrite, espousing democracy and freedom in its rhetoric while providing critical financial and military support to Israel, the Zionist interloper in the Middle East, and to anti-democratic and repressive regimes such as those of Egypt, Algeria, and Saudi Arabia, where the voice of the Muslim people is silenced.

This narrative of humiliation and disgrace at the hands of the United States is all the more compelling to its aggrieved Muslim audiences because it conforms to the dispiriting pattern of ordinary history as narrated by the fundamentalists. The plot is familiar: the virtuous true believers are overwhelmed by a treacherous, invasive, and insidious enemy whose conquest of the abode of Islam is abetted by the successful seduction of fellow Muslims who have relaxed their vigilance. Only the extreme measures and extraordinary heroism of radical religion can provide deliverance. Framing the struggles against external and internal colonization in this way fulfills the apocalyptic expectations of the most revolutionary of the fundamentalists. For they look for final deliverance, not to the world, but to God; not to quotidian political struggle against oppression and injustice, but to the self-sacrificing acts of true believers willing to risk everything to vanquish jahiliyya society once and for all.

The Islamic World's Struggle to Modernize Has Spurred the Development of Fundamentalism

Alan Richards

The Ayatollah Khomeini, leader of Iran's Islamic revolution, was correct to insist that "The revolution is about Islam, not the price of melons," arguing that Iraq's revolutionaries were driven by Islamic ideals rather than the desire to increase the material comforts of the people. However, some revolutions are led by those who are frustrated by social upheavals and fearful about their economic prospects. In this article, Alan Richards, professor of economics and environmental studies at the University of California at Santa Cruz, argues that the transition to modernity has produced fanatics and violence in many places, including Russia, China, Japan, and Germany. Richards examines the factors that he believes make the Islamic world a natural incubator for revolutionary violence, citing the low average age of the population, better educational opportunities combined with rising unemployment, increasing income inequality, urbanization, and discontent among the intellectual elites. Richards is an advisory editor of *Middle East Policy* and a frequent consultant to the U.S. government on Middle Eastern affairs. He is coauthor with John Waterbury of *A Political Economy of the Middle East.*

Today's Middle East finds itself mired in the "modernization process." The transition from a society of illiterate farmers, ruled by a literate, urban elite, into an urban, mass-educated

Alan Richards, "Socioeconomic Roots of Middle East Radicalism," *Naval War College Review*, Autumn 2002, pp. 22–37. Copyright © 2002 by the Superintendent of Documents, U.S. Naval War College. Reproduced by permission.

society with an economy based on industry and services has been deeply traumatic. Worse, such change has always and everywhere spawned grotesque violence. The modern history of both Europe and East Asia, the only places in the world where this transition has been more or less successfully accomplished, often reads like a horror novel: World Wars I and II, Stalin's Gulag, Hitler's Holocaust, Japanese fascism, the Chinese revolution, the "Great Leap Forward" and its attendant famine, and the Cultural Revolution. The American experience has also been bloody: the extermination of Native Americans, the racial violence of slavery and Jim Crow, and the more than half-million casualties of its own Civil War. Why should we expect the people of the Middle East to do better than anyone else?

Much of the violence during this transition has been perpetrated by utopian fanatics, a category that includes fascists, Nazis, Leninists, Maoists, and the followers of al-Qa'ida. Like their predecessors, today's Islamic fanatics "imagine a future" in the "restoration" of the (imagined) conditions of seventh-century Arabia. Like all fanatics, they believe that they enjoy a monopoly on truth and that those who disagree "are not merely mistaken, but wicked or mad [in the words of the political philosopher Isaiah Berlin]." They believe that there is only one goal for humanity, and to reach it they are ready to wade "through an ocean of blood to the Kingdom of Love." Fanatics have always built towers of skulls as monuments to their fantasies.

These particularly virulent fanatics are part of a larger social phenomenon, the transnational Salafi movement. This movement advocates a return to what its proponents believe to be the strict practices of the earliest Muslims. Their political ideology asserts that such a return will solve the many difficult problems facing most Muslim societies. Their slogan declares, "Islam huwwa al-hal"—"Islam [the Salafi interpretation of Islam] is the solution." Salafis include the followers of al-Qa'ida and the muwahhidiin (or "Unitarians," as they call themselves, or the Wahhabis, as others call them), partisans of the official ideology of the kingdom of Saudi Arabia. Several analysts have recently called attention to the spectrum of opinions within this movement.

Radical movements have their greatest appeal when the dislocations of the transition to modernity are most acute. Only the slaughter of World War I and its chaotic aftermath allowed the Bolsheviks to seize power in Russia. It is inconceivable that Hitler would have come to power without the Treaty of Versailles and the Great Depression. Famine, governmental collapse, and the horrors of the Japanese invasion set the stage for China and [Chinese revolutionary leader] Chairman Mao Tse-tung. The siren song of fanatics becomes most seductive when economic, political, social, and cultural crises combine and when people feel that they have been repeatedly humiliated.

The Rage of the Young

The utopian fanaticism of al-Qa'ida and other groups is nourished by the deep despair of huge numbers of young Middle Easterners, half of whom are younger than twenty. The first major social element in the noxious cocktail of religious radicalism in the region is the phenomenon of the "youth bulge."

The key demographic facts of the region are that the population is still growing rapidly but that fertility rates have declined considerably during the past decade. According to the World Bank, the population of the Middle East and North Africa is now growing at about 2.1 percent per year. At this rate, the population will double in about thirty-four years. On the other hand, population growth rates have fallen sharply in the past ten years, from 3.2 percent in the mid-1980s to 2.7 percent between 1990 and 1995. . . .

Populations will continue to grow despite falling fertility rates because fertility remains well above replacement levels and because, as a result of past population growth, many women will soon enter childbearing years ("demographic momentum"). Many countries in the region will experience a considerable rise in their population during the next fifteen years. The population may reach roughly six hundred million by 2025, some six times greater than the 1950s. Such growth poses numerous economic challenges, from food and water to jobs and housing.

Several implications follow from this demographic pattern. First, and most important, is that the majority of those in the Middle East are young—half the Arab population, 54 percent of Iranians, and 52 percent of Pakistanis are younger than twenty years old. (By contrast, only slightly more than one-quarter of the populations of developed countries—the United States, European Union, Australia, New Zealand, and Japan—are under twenty.)

The State of Education

For the first time in history, many of these youths have received some amount of education. Although the region lags behind other parts of the developing world, school enrollment and literacy have risen dramatically during the past generation. Today most Arabs and Iranians can read and write; this is not yet the case in Pakistan, where only two-fifths of adults are literate.

There is considerable variation in education among countries. More than three-quarters of the adults in Iran and Kuwait are literate, while there is between one-half to two-thirds adult literacy in Algeria, Iraq, Libya, Tunisia, Saudi Arabia, and Syria. Only about half or fewer of the adults are literate in Egypt, Morocco, Sudan, and Yemen. But even in Egypt, a laggard in this respect, virtually all children attend school. School enrollment has exploded throughout the region, though the pattern has been uneven and there is still a huge gap between girls and boys. Most boys were in school long before their sisters. In Algeria, Egypt, Jordan, Lebanon, Libya, Syria and Tunisia, nearly all children attend primary school, and roughly 60 percent of all adolescents are enrolled in secondary school. In Saudi Arabia, all boys are enrolled in primary school, but only 75 percent of girls are in school. In the least developed countries, most girls do not attend school. In Sudan and Yemen, for example, nearly all boys are enrolled in primary school, whereas only 40 percent of girls attend. In Morocco over one-third, and in Oman roughly one-fourth, of girls are not in primary school. Despite the appalling waste of human resources such undereducating of women represents, the past generation has seen an educational revolution throughout the entire region.

Certain points should be noted. First, the gap in education between girls and boys may be a factor in the current popularity of radical Islam. A rather hopeful view argues that Islamic radicalism's relentless focus on rigid gender segregation is something that only the current generation will experience. In the past, neither men nor women were educated; in the future (and the future is now, in Iran), everyone will be at least marginally educated.

Rapidly spreading education is part of the social background of what has been called the "crisis of authority" in Islam. How is it that any engineer [that is, Osama bin Laden] can issue his own fatwa[1] when in previous centuries such pronouncements were the exclusive prerogative of a small, relatively privileged elite of traditionally educated Islamic scholars (the Vama)? The widespread diffusion of education, in conjunction with the absence of hierarchical controls on religious edicts in Islam (in contrast to, say, Roman Catholicism), is creating a "religious anarchy" that provides the cultural space in which radicals can promulgate and advocate their messages.

Third, the quality of education leaves much to be desired. Education in the region stresses rote memorization, with little emphasis on analytical thinking and problem solving. Expectations have been raised, but the skills needed to meet those expectations have not been imparted. Millions of young men now have enough education to make the old, dirty jobs unsatisfying but have not acquired the skills needed to perform successfully in the modern, hypercompetitive, global economy.

More Workers than Jobs

Thanks to past birth rates, the Middle East has the most rapidly growing labor force in the world; between 1990 and 1998 it grew at 3.4 percent per year. Algeria's labor force is growing at 4.9 percent a year, Syria's at 4.8 percent, and

---

1. Islamic religious ruling; in February 1998 Bin Laden called for all good Muslims to murder all Americans as a "religious duty."

Yemen's at 5.6 percent. Compare this to the labor force growth in the European Union of 0.4 percent per year during the past decade, and the American labor force at about 0.8 percent. In other words, the labor force in the Middle East is growing four times faster than the American labor force and eight times faster than the European Union's. Although the rate of growth attributable to past population growth will decelerate in some countries, such as Tunisia, during the next ten to fifteen years, declines in fertility are always accompanied (plausibly, largely caused) by an increase in female education, which enables women to enter the labor market. It is highly unlikely that the growth of the supply of labor will decelerate within the medium term.

At the same time, the demand for labor has grown sluggishly. Simple economics tells us that given such a mismatch between the growth of demand and of supply, either wages will fall, unemployment will rise, or (most likely) some combination of both will occur, the precise mix varying with specific labor market structures. Government policies have not only reduced the rate of growth of demand for labor but also fostered inflexible labor markets. Decades of government job guarantees for graduates have induced students to seek any degree, regardless of its contribution to productivity. Governments cannot now provide the necessary jobs, and statist policies impede private-sector job creation.

Current levels of unemployment are high . . . and will probably worsen. In some countries the level of unemployment has been similar to that in the United States during the worst days of the Great Depression. Real wages have stagnated for nearly a generation, and poverty levels have either remained about the same or increased during the past decade. Unemployment and low wages primarily affect young, uneducated urbanites, whose anger is fuel for political unrest.

As usual, conflicting estimates of the "extent of poverty"—an inherently subjective concept—exist. One rather sanguine view is that of the World Bank, which holds that, compared with other regions of the developing world, the Middle East and North Africa collectively have "relatively limited" poverty. The number of poor persons—defined as those with yearly incomes of less than a "purchasing power parity" figure of $365 per year—is given at 5 percent, and the depth and severity of poverty is low. Many observers have objected to this analysis on the grounds that it set the poverty line too low relative to per capita incomes. From a political perspective, what counts is the social definition of poverty. Poverty is inevitably partly relative. Poor people in Egypt, Jordan, or Algeria do not compare themselves with the poor in Bangladesh or Madagascar; they feel "poor" relative to their fellow Egyptians, Jordanians, or Algerians. It follows that higher estimates of poverty are more politically relevant.

The Political Consequences of Poverty

What are the political consequences of poverty? It provides a fertile recruiting ground for opponents of regimes and therefore poses a challenge to governance, in at least two ways. First, some of the poor, particularly the younger ones with limited education, join violent opposition movements. Today's basic profile for a violent militant is a young man with some education who may also have recently moved to the city. Such young people are often unemployed or have jobs below their expectations. In North Africa they are colorfully known as the *hetistes*, "those who lean against the wall." Evidence from Egyptian arrest records suggests that many of those arrested for violent activities against the regime come from shantytowns surrounding large cities, usually the poorest urban areas in the country. It has been argued that the rise of Islamic radicalism in Central Asia is related to the problems of youth unemployment.

The violent opposition toward the government in Upper Egypt during the past two decades is also related to poverty. The Said (Middle and Upper Egypt) is the poorest region in the country. As elsewhere in the country, poverty has been rising there in the past ten years, thanks to the collapse of unskilled wages. Whereas real wages rose over 350 percent in real terms from 1973 to 1985 (largely due to emigration for work in the Gulf states), the decrease in regional oil production and the war with Iraq led to the return of many of these economic migrants. Such forces have brought wages down by over 50 percent for unskilled workers. As Sa'idis began moving into the cities, the problem of Islamic radicalism appeared in more visible locations—Egypt's major cities.

The creation of jobs is particularly difficult since the remedy in the long run will likely worsen the problem in the short run. The demand for labor has grown slowly because output growth has lagged and because of specific policy biases against labor-intensive, job-creating growth. Statist policies not only retard growth but raise the capital intensity—and reduce the job-creating impact—of whatever growth does occur. Changing these policies would require laying off workers in state-owned enterprises and the bureaucracy, a move that frightens many government leaders.

Not by Bread Alone

The unemployment problem is the most politically volatile economic issue facing the Middle East. It encourages many relatively educated, young, urban residents to support radical Islamic political movements. Yet we must be cautious here, for the "youth bulge" and rampant unemployment are at least as severe in sub-Saharan Africa, but we hear little of Congolese international terrorism. There are many complex cultural forces behind Islamic movements; no economic determinism is implied here. To understand how and why discontent spawned by unemployment takes a specific political and ideological form, we cannot rely alone on demography and economics. We must also look at political structures and ideological environments.

The Ayatollah Khomeini[2] is reported to have said, "The revolution is about Islam, not the price of melons." Deeper issues of identity and legitimacy are at stake. For example, it should be remembered that although unemployed, frustrated young men can turn to Islamism, they can also turn to drugs and crime, to apathy, indifference, muddling through, dogged hard work, or any number of other personal "coping" strategies. The decision to join a revolutionary move-

2. leader of the Islamic fundamentalist revolution that overthrew the shah of Iran in 1979

ment is an idiosyncratic and deeply personal one. Socioeconomic contexts may be important for understanding these movements, but they hardly provide a complete explanation for them. Nevertheless, the huge numbers of discontented young men and women are a major threat to the internal stability of the Middle East.

Youth politics always and everywhere focuses not merely on material goods but also on questions of identity, justice, and morality. Consider, for example, the politics of the American "baby boomers" of the 1960s. Impatience and Manichean thinking[3] are among the burdens of youth politics, whether in Berkeley or Cairo. Also, as criminologists point out, resort to violence is overwhelmingly a phenomenon of youth. The millions of unemployed and underemployed young men gathered in the specific political and cultural milieux of the region constitute one of the tangled roots of radicalism.

The Jungle of the Cities

The discontent of these young people is exacerbated by the fact that most of them now live in cities—cities that are crumbling. The number of Middle East urban dwellers has increased by about a hundred million in thirty-five years. Roughly half the population now live in cities, and the number is expected to rise from 135 million to over 350 million by 2025. From 1985 to 1990 the greatest growth was in secondary cities (6 percent), compared to that (3.8 percent) of the nineteen largest cities with populations of over one million in 1990. This trend continued throughout the 1990s. Public services and utilities are already overwhelmed.

Rapid urbanization erodes the government's legitimacy in at least two ways. First, it strains the infrastructure and budget. The government's perceived inability to provide housing, sewerage, potable water, and garbage collection raises doubts about its fundamental purpose. Second, the process of migration to the cities is always disorienting. Whether in Ayacucho [home of Peru's violent Shining Path, Communist extremists] or Asyut [in Egypt], the mixture of rural-urban

3. viewing life as a struggle between absolute good and absolute evil

migration with discontented provincial intellectuals proves to be highly toxic (if not yet fatal) to existing governments. The newly arrived migrants provide fertile fishing ground for Islamic militants, particularly when the migrant cannot find work and the (allegedly) decadent mores of the cities shock his sensibilities. . . .

Some may object that (as far as one can tell) most of those responsible for the crimes of 11 September were privileged and educated. This, however, is entirely to be expected. [The British writer] George Orwell once quipped that "revolutionaries can always pronounce their aitches." Revolutionaries are often, even typically, from relatively privileged backgrounds. [Bolshevik revolutionary leader Vladimir] Lenin was no muzhik, and [Chinese revolutionary leader] Mao Tse-tung was the son of a rich peasant; yet the political and economic conditions of Russia and China when they were young profoundly shaped their opinions and ideals. People who knew Mohammed Atta (one of the 11 September hijackers) in Germany heard him speak of the "fat cats" running Egypt. It is no surprise that the "shock troops" of a revolutionary movement are educated and privileged. It would be quite ahistorical, however, to argue that their existence—or their appeal—is independent of the social conditions of their societies. Monocausal explanations of complex historical phenomena are always foolish.

It is also worth remembering that radicalism reaches far wider than al-Qa'ida. Movements in Algeria, Egypt, Palestine, Pakistan, Yemen, Central Asia, and Southeast Asia include many diverse actors.

A Historical Analogy

The fanatics of al-Qa'ida display a close resemblance to the nihilists and other terror-prone, would-be revolutionaries of nineteenth-century Russia, as described by the Hungarian writer Tibor Szamuely: "The Russian intelligentsia was a social stratum composed of those politically aroused, vociferous, and radical members of the educated classes who felt totally estranged from society. . . . The alienation of the intelligentsia from society was to a great extent inherent in the country's rudimentary social structure. . . . [Unlike the West, Russia had no interest groups capable of giving strength, support, and substance to the intellectuals' protest. . . . The Russian intelligentsia had neither a place nor a stake in the existing order of things.". . .

Further similarities emerge. For example, in nineteenth-century Russia, as in the past generation of the Muslim world, there was a dramatic expansion of universities, whose doors opened for the time to less privileged young men, often from rural backgrounds [according to Szamuely]." [After the Crimean War,] there was a marked shift in the social composition of the student body in the universities. . . . [I]t came to be made up more and more of so-called *raznochintsy*, 'people of diverse rank': sons of clergymen, peasants, petty officials, army officers, artisans, and tradesmen who had become divorced by virtue of their education or inclination from their fathers' social station and could no longer fit into the official estate system. In a manner that Szamuely finds "very understandable," instead of feeling gratitude for the opportunity for upper mobility the "student-*raznochinets* brought with him a deep sense of the injustices of Russian life . . . [that] rapidly turned into hatred of the existing order." Szamuely also notes that the intolerant utopianism of the student revolutionaries was a mirror-image of the violence of the tsarist state. Here too there are important parallels in many Muslim countries.

The Failure of Governments

The incompetence and authoritarianism of many Middle East and Muslim governments represent vital sources of the phenomenon of Islamic radicalism. These governments are overwhelmingly unelected, unaccountable, and corrupt. They provide no legitimate outlets for the discontentment of youth. Unsurprisingly, the young despise them. The old ideologies of these governments, largely varieties of nationalism, are perceived as failures. They have delivered neither material goods nor a sense of dignity at home or abroad. The half-century-long failure of Arab states to resolve the Palestinian situation and the inability of Pakistan to ease the lot of

Kashmiri Muslims[4] have contributed to the evident corrosion of the regimes' legitimacy. Nationalism has not disappeared; it has been assimilated into the Islamists' discourse. . . .

Outsiders can do very little to promote institutional change, as the United States learned to its dismay in Russia and elsewhere. The deep cultural crisis of contemporary Islam's confrontation with modernity can be resolved only by Muslims.

4. inhabitants of Kashmir, a Muslim majority province ruled by India

Islamic Organizations Have Played a Pivotal Role in Promoting Fundamentalism

John L. Esposito

Islamic fundamentalism had been developing for many years before it attracted the world's attention with the 1979 Iranian revolution. As John L. Esposito observes in the next selection, it has existed as a coherent ideology since the 1920s, when two influential thinkers, an Egyptian schoolteacher named Hasan al-Banna and an Indian journalist named Mawlana Abul Ala Mawdudi, began to formulate the ideas that inspire today's radical Islamic activists. Hasan al-Banna founded the Muslim Brotherhood in Egypt in 1928, and Mawlana Mawdudi established the Jamaat-i-Islami (Islamic Society) in India in 1941. Both movements espoused a restoration of Islamic power and rule, and both blamed Westernization for the problems Muslim societies faced. The Muslim Brotherhood and the Jamaat recruited followers from many sectors of society, including students, workers, and young professionals. Their ideology and organizational example have had a profound influence on current Islamic activism. John L. Esposito has had a distinguished academic career as a professor of diplomacy, religion, and Middle Eastern affairs. His books include *Unholy War: Terror in the Name of Islam* and *The Islamic Threat: Myth or Reality?*

Modern Islamic organizations have been the driving force behind the dynamic spread of the Islamic resurgence. They have also been the focal point or embodiment of the Islamic threat in the eyes of Western governments as well as many governments in the Muslim world. For some, Islamic movements represent an authentic alternative to corrupt, exhausted, and ineffectual regimes. For many others, they are a destabilizing force—demagogues who will employ any tactic to gain power. The violence and terrorism perpetrated by groups with names like the Party of God, Holy War, Army of God, and Salvation from Hell conjure up images of religious fanatics with a thirst for vengeance and a penchant for violence who will stop at little. The assassination of Anwar Sadat [Egypt's president between 1970–1981], the taking of hostages in Lebanon, and the hijacking of planes embody a "Sacred Rage"[1] that has become all too familiar. Yet again the reality is far more complex than its popular image. The majority of Islamic organizations would claim that, where permitted, they work within the political system and seek change from below through a gradual process of reform. Many Islamic organizations today espouse political liberalization and democratization. Their members participate in elections and serve in legislatures and cabinets.

Given the pivotal role that Islamic movements have played and continue to play both in the politics of the Muslim world and in the plans, calculations, and responses of Western governments, understanding their nature, goals, and activities becomes critical in assessing Islamic movements and the Islamic threat.

While Islamic revivalism and Islamic movements are integral to Islamic history and in some sense may be seen as part of a recurrent revivalist cycle in history, most movements today differ from those of earlier centuries in that they are modern, not traditional, in their leadership, ideology, and organization. If we speak of fundamentalism as a return to the foundations of Islam, the Quran, and the example of the Prophet in order to renew the community, then these movements are neofundamentalist or neorevivalist, for they look to the sources of Islam not simply to replicate the past but to respond to a new age.

In trying to understand the origins and nature of modern

---

1. from Robin Wright's 1985 book *Sacred Rage: The Wrath of Militant Islam*

Islamic movements, two organizations in particular dominate the landscape of the Muslim world in the twentieth century. Contemporary Islamic activism is particularly indebted to the ideology and organizational example of the Muslim Brotherhood and the Jamaat-i-Islami (Islamic Society or Group). Their founders and ideologues, Hassan al-Banna and Sayyid Qutb of the Brotherhood and Mawlana Abul Ala Mawdudi of the Jamaat, have had an incalculable impact on the development of Islamic movements throughout the Muslim world. They are indeed the trailblazers or architects of contemporary Islamic revivalism, men whose ideas and methods have been studied and emulated from the Sudan to Indonesia.

Hassan al-Banna (1906–49), a schoolteacher and former disciple of the Islamic modernist Rashid Rida, established the Muslim Brotherhood (Ikhwan al-Muslimin) in Egypt in 1928, while Mawlana Abul Ala Mawdudi (1903–79), a journalist, organized the Jamaat-i-Islami in India in 1941. Both movements arose and initially grew in the thirties and forties at a time when their communities were in crisis. Both blamed European imperialism and a Westernized Muslim leadership for many of the current problems.

In Egypt the Brotherhood's critique of Western imperialism and the ills of Egyptian society in time found a receptive audience among the religiously inclined as well as the more Western, secular-oriented elites. Initial faith in liberal nationalism had been shaken by the defeat of the Arabs in Palestine, the creation of the state of Israel with British and American support, Egypt's continued inability to shake off British occupation, and massive unemployment, poverty, and corruption. Muslim Brothers greatly enhanced their credentials as patriotic sons of Egypt and Arab nationalists in their significant participation in the 1948 Palestine war and again in the 1951 Suez crisis [when Egyptians and the British fought for control of the Suez Canal].

In South Asia Mawlana Mawdudi had witnessed the collapse of the Ottoman empire and the failure of the Caliphate Movement to save that empire from being dismembered by Britain and France for its support of Germany during World

War I. Growing Hindu assertiveness in the Indian Freedom (Independence) Movement in South Asia contributed to Mawdudi's perception of the continued deterioration of Muslim power and the threat to Islam and the Muslim community. Mawdudi blamed European colonialism and the emergence of modern nationalism, a foreign and Western ideology which divided rather than united peoples, replacing the universal or Pan-Islamic ideal and solidarity with a more tenuous and divisive identity based upon language, tribe, or ethnicity.

Similar Responses to Western Domination

Hassan al-Banna and Mawlana Mawdudi, who were contemporaries, were pious, educated men with traditional Islamic backgrounds and knowledge of modern Western thought. Both saw their societies as being dependent on the West, politically weak, and culturally adrift. Each in his early years had been an anticolonial nationalist who turned to religious revivalism to restore the Muslim community at home and universally. These founders and ideologues of their organizations drew on the example and concerns both of eighteenth-century Islamic revivalist movements like the Wahhabi of Saudi Arabia and nineteenth- and twentieth-century Islamic modernist predecessors for their critique of Muslim society, their revivalist and reformist worldview emphasis on organization, and their sociopolitical activism. They did not simply retreat to the past but instead provided Islamic responses, ideological and organizational, to modern society. Hassan al-Banna and Mawlana Mawdudi appropriated and reapplied the vision and logic of the revivalist tradition in Islam to the sociohistorical conditions of twentieth-century Muslim society. In a very real sense they modernized Islam by providing a modern interpretation or reformulation of Islam to revitalize the community religiously and sociopolitically. However, they did this not by purifying Islam of cultural accretions or un-Islamic beliefs and values or by restoring early practices of the community, however authentic. They self-consciously reapplied Islamic sources and beliefs, reinterpreting them to address modern realities. Yet they distinguished their method from that of Islamic modernism, which they equated with the

Westernization of Islam. If Islamic modernists legitimated the adoption of Western ideas and institutions by maintaining their compatibility with Islam, al-Banna and Mawdudi sought to produce a new synthesis which began with Islamic sources and found either Islamic equivalents or Islamic sources for notions of government accountability, legal change, popular participation, and educational reform.

Hassan al-Banna and Mawlana Mawdudi shared a common anti-imperialist view of the West, which they believed was not only a political and economic but also a cultural threat to Muslim societies. Westernization threatened the very identity, independence, and way of life of Muslims. Indeed, they regarded the religiocultural penetration of the West (education, law, customs, values) as far more pernicious in the long run than political intervention, since it threatened the very identity and survival of the Muslim community. Imitation of or dependence on the West was to be avoided at all cost. The Brotherhood and the Jamaat proclaimed Islam as a self-sufficient, all-encompassing way of life, an ideological alternative to Western capitalism and Marxism. They joined thought to action, creating organizations that engaged in political and social activism.

Though hostile to Westernization, they were not against modernization. Both Hassan al-Banna and Mawlana Mawdudi engaged in modern organization and institution building, provided educational and social welfare services, and used modern technology and mass communications to spread their message and to mobilize popular support. Their message itself, though rooted in Islamic revelation and sources, was clearly written for a twentieth-century audience. It addressed the problems of modernity, analyzing the relationship of Islam to nationalism, democracy, capitalism, Marxism, modern banking, education, law, women and work, Zionism, and international relations. Mawdudi far more than al-Banna wrote extensively and systematically, attempting to demonstrate the comprehensive relevance of Islam to all aspects of life. The range of his topics reflected his holistic vision: Islam and the state, economics, education, revolution, women.

Principles of Islamic Fundamentalism

Despite differences, al-Banna's and Mawdudi's reinterpretations of Islamic history and tradition produced a common ideological worldview which has inspired and guided many modern Islamically oriented sociomoral reform movements. This worldview not only governed their organizations but also informed Islamic movements that sprang up throughout the Muslim world in subsequent decades.

Among the primary principles of al-Banna's and Mawdudi's ideological worldview were the following:

1. Islam constitutes an all-embracing ideology for individual and corporate life, for state and society.

2. The Quran, God's revelation, and the example (Sunnah) of the Prophet Muhammad are the foundations of Muslim life.

3. Islamic law (the Sharia, the "path" of God), based upon the Quran and the Prophet's model behavior, is the sacred blueprint for Muslim life.

4. Faithfulness to the Muslim's vocation to reestablish God's sovereignty through implementation of God's law will bring success, power, and wealth to the Islamic community (*ummah*) in this life as well as eternal reward in the next.

5. The weakness and subservience of Muslim societies must be due to the faithlessness of Muslims, who have strayed from God's divinely revealed path and instead followed the secular, materialistic ideologies and values of the West or of the East—capitalism or Marxism.

6. Restoration of Muslim pride, power, and rule (the past glory of Islamic empires and civilization) requires a return to Islam, the reimplementation of God's law and guidance for state and society.

7. Science and technology must be harnessed and used within an Islamically oriented and guided context in order to avoid the Westernization and secularization of Muslim society.

Both the Brotherhood and the Jamaat saw but two choices, darkness or light, Satan or God, ignorance (that which is un-

Islamic) or Islam. At the heart of the message of the Brotherhood and the Jamaat was the conviction that Islam provided a divinely revealed and prescribed third alternative to Western capitalism and Soviet Marxism.

Scripture and tradition were appealed to and reinterpreted by the founders of these modern religious societies. The inspiration and continuity of the past were coupled with a response to the demands of modernity. This combination of past and present are demonstrated not only by their reinterpretation of Islam but also by their organization and activities. Organizationally, the Brotherhood and the Jamaat followed the example of the Prophet Muhammad (also emulated by seventeenth- and eighteenth-century revivalist movements) in gathering together believers committed to establishing societies governed by God's law. They were to be a vanguard, a righteous community within the broader community—the dynamic nucleus for true Islamic reformation or revolution, returning society to the straight path of Islam.

Recruiting a Generation of Leaders

Both organizations recruited followers from mosques, schools, and universities: students, workers, merchants, and young professionals. They were primarily urban, based among the lower middle and middle classes, with whom they were especially successful. The goal was to produce a new generation of modern-educated but Islamically oriented leaders prepared to take their place in every sector of society. However, while al-Banna worked to develop a broad-based populist movement, Mawdudi's Jamaat was more of an elite religious organization whose primary goal was to train leaders who would come to power. An Islamic revolution was ultimately necessary to introduce an Islamic state and society. However, this Islamic revolution was to be first and foremost a social rather than a violent political one. The establishment of an Islamic state first required the Islamization of society through a gradual process of social change. Both organizations espoused an "Islamic alternative" to conservative religious leaders and modern, secular, Western-oriented elites. The *ulama* were generally regarded as passé, a religious class whose fossilized Islam and cooption by governments were major causes of the backwardness of the Islamic community. Modernists were seen as having traded away the very soul of Muslim society out of blind admiration for the West.

Though these organizations were quick to denounce the evils of imperialism and the cultural threat of the West, both the Brotherhood and the Jamaat nevertheless realized that the Muslim predicament was first and foremost a Muslim problem, caused by Muslims who had failed to be sufficiently Islamically observant. Its rectification was the primary task of Muslims. Rebuilding the community and redressing the balance of power between Islam and the West must begin with a call or invitation (*dawa*) to all Muslims to return to and reappropriate their faith in its fullness—to be born again in the straight path of God. Both the Brotherhood and the Jamaat reemphasized and interpreted the concept of *dawa*. The call to Islam has two aspects: an invitation to non-Muslims to convert to Islam, and the calling of those who were born Muslim to be better Muslims. Both organizations focused on the latter, the transformation (Islamization) of the individual and society. The reversal of the fortunes of Islam and of the Muslim community was to be accomplished through a social revolution. Religious commitment, modern learning and technology, and activism were combined as the Brotherhood and the Jamaat disseminated their interpretation of Islam through schools, publications, preaching, social services, and student organizations.

Neorevivalism and the West

Like secular and Islamic modernists, al-Banna and Mawdudi acknowledged the weakness of Muslim societies, the need for change, and the value of science and technology. However, they criticized both secular and Islamic modernists for excessive dependence on the West, the cause of the continued impotence of Muslim societies. On the one hand, secularists separated religion from society and took the West as the model for development: "Until recently, writers, intellectuals, scholars and governments glorified the principles of European civilization . . . adopted Western style and manner." Despite their anticolonial politics, secular Muslim leaders were in effect regarded as indigenous Western cultural colonizers. On the other hand, Islamic modernists were also criticized: in their zeal to demonstrate the compatibility of Islam with modernity, they employed or relied upon Western values, producing a Westernized Islam.

> All these people in their misinformed and misguided zeal to serve what they hold to be the cause of Islam, are always at great pains to prove that Islam contains within itself the elements of all types of contemporary social and Political thought and action. . . . [T]his attitude emerges from an inferiority complex, from the belief that we as Muslims can earn no honour or respect unless we are able to show our religion resembles modern creeds and is in agreement with most of the contemporary ideologies. [Mawdudi]

In contrast to Islamic modernists, these neorevivalists were more sweeping in their indictment of the West and their assertion of the total self-sufficiency of Islam. They maintained that Muslims should not look to Western capitalism or communism (white or red imperialism) but solely to Islam, the divinely revealed foundation of state and society. The Brotherhood charged that faith in the West was misplaced. Western democracy had not merely failed to check but contributed to authoritarianism (the manipulation of the masses by modern elites), economic exploitation, corruption, and social injustice. Western secularism and materialism undermined religion and morality, society and the family. The inherent fallacy of Western secularism, separation of religion and the state, would be responsible for the West's moral decline and ultimate downfall. Finally, the Brotherhood maintained that, despite Arab subservience to the West, the West had betrayed the Arabs in its support for the Israeli occupation of Palestine: "The Palestine question became the starting-point for attacks on the United States . . . [and resulted in] the full identification of Zionism with crusading Western imperialism [according to historian Richard Mitchell]." In contrast to Islamic modernists, the goal of the Brotherhood and the Jamaat was not to render

Islam compatible with Western culture, but to create a more indigenously rooted, authentic Islamic state and society through a process of renewal or Islamization based upon "a return to the principles of Islam . . . [and] the reconciliation of modern life with these principles, as a prelude to a final Islamization (of society)" [as Hasan al-Banna wrote].

Denunciation of the West did not mean wholesale rejection of modernization. Both al-Banna and Mawdudi distinguished between Westernization and modernization, between Western values and modern ideas and institutions. Thus the best of science and technology as well as political ideals could be appropriated, though selectively and carefully, if separated from Western values contrary to Islam and informed instead by Islamic values. In the final analysis, the renaissance or reformation of Islam would not come from reason and secularism but revelation. As Mawdudi noted:

> We aspire for Islamic renaissance on the basis of the Quran. To us the Quranic spirit and Islamic tenets are immutable; but the application of this spirit in the realm of practical life must always vary with the change of conditions and increase of knowledge. . . . Our way is quite different both from the Muslim scholar of recent past and modern Europeanized stock. On the one hand we have to imbibe exactly the Quranic spirit and identify our outlook with the Islamic tenets while, on the other, we have to assess thoroughly the developments in the field of knowledge and changes in conditions of life that have been brought during the last eight hundred years; and third, we have to arrange these ideas and laws of life on genuine Islamic lines so that Islam should once again become a dynamic force; the leader of the world rather than its follower.

Mawdudi's attitude toward democracy provides an excellent example of his method. Since Islam's worldview was God-centered rather than human-centered, a parliamentary democracy based upon popular sovereignty rather than divine sovereignty was unacceptable. Mawdudi rejected democracy—that is, Western democracy, which in the name of majority rule permitted practices such as alcohol consumption and sexual promiscuity that were contrary to God's law. However, parliamentary political participation or consultative assemblies subordinated to Islamic law, God's law, were permissible. Here both al-Banna and Mawdudi reinterpreted and utilized the Islamic concept of consultation (*shura*) to provide Islamic justification. Mawdudi preferred to speak of the Islamic system as a "theodemocracy," as distinct from a theocracy or clerical state, in which the popular will was subordinated to and limited by God's law. Mawdudi did not shrink from those who ridiculed him for "religious authoritarianism." Indeed, Mawdudi did not envision submission to God's absolute authority as a deprivation of man's liberty, but rather as a condition of it. Thus he had no problem characterizing an Islamic government or theodemocracy as "Islamic totalitarianism."

The Arab-Israeli Conflict Has Triggered a Revival of Islamic Fundamentalism

Mir Zohair Husain

In 1948 Israel was created as a Jewish state against the will of all the Arab countries in the Middle East, most of which have remained officially at war with Israel ever since. For over half a century, both secular and Islamic Middle Eastern countries have suffered humiliating defeats at Israel's hands. The worst of these occurred in 1967, when Israel defeated the combined forces of Egypt, Syria, Jordan, and Lebanon and occupied East Jerusalem and other Arab territories. As Mir Zohair Husain argues in the next selection, Muslims throughout the Middle East and around the world have become extremely frustrated with their inability to defeat Israel, and this frustration has fueled the growing movement for Islamic fundamentalism. Husain describes the major military and diplomatic defeats the Arab world has suffered that have motivated Islamic fundamentalists, including the Arab-Israeli War of 1948–1949, the 1956 Suez War, the 1967 Arab-Israeli War, and the 1973 Arab-Israeli War. Husain is associate professor of political science at the University of South Alabama. He is the author of *Global Islamic Politics*.

The Arab-Israeli conflict has contributed to the global revival of political Islam in two ways. The Palestinian people's inability since 1948 to wrest any substantive concessions from the Israeli government through peaceful negotiations, and the failure of the secular PLO [Palestine Liberation Organization] leadership after decades of struggle to deliver on their promise of Palestinian autonomy, have disenchanted Palestinian Muslims specifically and all Muslims generally. Furthermore, the military ineffectiveness of secular Arab regimes in wars with Israel has frustrated and alienated many Muslims. Consequently, the people of the Muslim world are turning increasingly to Islam as the answer to this muddled, bewildering, and long-festering conflict.

The Plight of the Palestinians

No question, the truest victims of this dispute are the Palestinians—a people homeless, stateless, and friendless. They have been ill-served by incompetent and unscrupulous leaders and have been exploited and persecuted by colonial and neocolonial powers. The leaders of Muslim countries have paid mere lip-service to their dream of a Palestinian homeland. Moreover, their most basic human needs for food, clothing, shelter, and jobs have gone largely unmet.

In 1948, as the state of Israel took its first breath, thousands of Palestinians were terrorized and driven from their homes by overzealous Zionists. Others maintain that these Palestinians fled on the urging of neighboring Arab governments, who initially rejected Israel's right to exist and considered the Jewish state a foreign neocolonial cancer in the heart of the Arab world.

Despite these conflicting accounts of the initial Palestinian diaspora, it is indisputable that many thousands of Jewish refugees were emigrating to Israel from around the world while 700,000 Palestinians were becoming refugees, living in squalor in Egypt's Gaza Strip, Jordan's West Bank, Syria, and Lebanon. As the Jews returned to Zion, the Palestinians lost their state and home. The Arab-Israeli wars of 1967 and 1973 contributed to the Palestinian exodus, and to swelling refugee camps. Likewise, many Palestinians were victimized in the Jordanian Civil War of 1970 and in two Israeli invasions of Lebanon in 1978 and 1982. Although these conflicts targeted the Palestine Liberation Organization (PLO), many innocent Palestinians suffered. For example, following the PLO evacuation of Beirut in 1982, two thousand Palestinians, most old men, women, and children, were slaughtered in the Sabra and Shatila refugee camps in Lebanon. The attackers, who acted with Israeli army complicity, were members of the paramilitary wing of the Christian Phalangists—a tightly organized rightist political party committed to preserving the Maronite Catholic control of Lebanon.

The 1.2 million Palestinians who remained in what had been Palestine and was now under Israeli jurisdiction were hardly any better off. Through a systematic policy of discrimination and persecution, the powerless Palestinians in Israel were relegated to second-class Israeli citizenship or became little more than refugees in the occupied West Bank and Gaza Strip. A dramatic increase in numbers in the Israeli government's settlement policy in those territories uprooted thousands of Palestinians to make way for newly arriving Zionists.

The predicament of the Palestinians in the last fifty years has been psychologically devastating. They have been stripped not only of the land of their fathers, but of their very identity. While they have focused primarily on the Israelis in their struggle to establish a Palestinian state, whether adjacent to or in the place of Israel, their enemies are not always Zionists.

Serious and sometimes explosive tension underlies the relationship between Palestinians and other Arabs. While Egypt, Syria, and Jordan have warred with Israel ostensibly in the name of the Palestinian plight, Palestinians recognize that Egypt fights only for Egypt, Syria fights only for Syria, and Jordan fights only for Jordan. National interests motivate the actions of the Arab states neighboring Israel. . . .

Thus, the alienation of the Palestinians is complete; their identity, uncertain. They cannot identify themselves according to a homeland. They have none. Yet they consider themselves once and future Palestinians. Their current situation is best characterized as being in limbo with their identity in flux. In fact, many Palestinians refer to their struggle as not merely an independence movement, but an unfolding revolution. Given this chronic and unresolved crisis of identity, the Palestinians are susceptible to Islamic revivalism, and Islam as a source of identity and security. . . .

Muslims all over the world are understandably exasperated with their leaders for having failed to defeat the Israelis, either militarily or diplomatically, in the last five decades. Politically active Fundamentalist and Traditionalist groups are today successfully attacking the status quo and mobilizing the masses by promising to defeat and destroy Israel. The Muslim people tired of their dictatorial regimes— mainly governed by Muslim Pragmatists and Modernists— are heeding the call of the Fundamentalists and Traditionalists. Thus, the Arab-Palestinian-Israeli conflict, unresolved after fifty years, is not only contributing to the Islamic revival, but is radicalizing it.

The First Arab-Israeli War: 1948–1949

In November of 1947, the United Nations General Assembly adopted Resolution 181, which called for the partition of Palestine into two sovereign states, one Jewish and one Arab. The Palestinian Arabs and the Arab League rejected the resolution, and conflict between Palestinian and Jewish settlers in the region grew more pronounced. The British, who for decades had administered Palestine, evacuated their forces on May 15, 1948, unable to further referee the conflict. Immediately, Jewish settlers proclaimed the establishment of the state of Israel. Concurrently, five Arab armies, in the name of the Arab League, invaded Palestine to eradicate the new Jewish state. However, the Arab advantage in numbers and strategic positioning were squandered by their gross ineptitude and consistent failure to mount a joint offensive. Thus, the Israelis won the war by December of 1948.

The results of the first Arab-Israeli war were profound. First, the land allocated to the Palestinians by U.N. Resolution 181 had been either conquered by the Israelis or divided between Egypt and Transjordan. No Palestinian state, with three foreign powers occupying it, could come into being. Arab-Palestinian tension was rooted in this development. Arab defense of Palestinian rights had degenerated into a land grab— Transjordan took the West Bank, Egypt the Gaza Strip. The Palestinians grew increasingly aware that they could count only on themselves. Second, the Palestinian refugee problem became acute. Banished from their homes in Israel, the Palestinians were now truly homeless and stateless. And third, the victory of tiny Israel against numerically superior Arab forces was both surprising and embarrassing to the Muslim world. The people accused their civilian governments of incompetence and corruption. Consequently, incapable of defending either the Palestinians or themselves, these corrupt governments were toppled by military coups and populist leaders.

The failure of Arab regimes to defeat Israel and the consequent internal upheaval was particularly significant in Egypt. Different groups coalesced in common opposition to the discredited government of King Farouk. In this atmosphere of despair, Egypt's Gamal Abdel Nasser, leader of the Free Officers Movement, overthrew Farouk's regime in 1952. Nasser rose to power concomitantly with an ideology of Arab socialism, pan-Arabism (pan-Arab nationism), and anti-Zionism, becoming president himself in 1954. . . .

The 1956 Suez War

On July 26, 1956, Nasser nationalized the strategically vital Suez Canal, a decision that prompted British, French, and Israeli forces to stage a military strike against Egypt. Although the Israelis performed well, the Anglo-French operation floundered. Immediately, the United States forced the British and the French to abandon their efforts, and likewise persuaded the Israelis to evacuate the Sinai Peninsula and the Gaza Strip.

The results of the brief Suez War were threefold. First, Israel proved, yet again, it was militarily powerful. Second, the Egyptians agreed to the demilitarization of the Sinai and the stationing of U.N. forces in the Gaza Strip. Third, the war was a major political victory for Nasser. By standing up to the West and to Israel, Nasser now enjoyed unequaled stature throughout the Muslim world. He became the idol of the masses. The popularity of his ideologies of pan-Arabism and Arab socialism became enshrined in "Nasserism."

Nevertheless, the voices of Islamic revivalist discontent could still be heard within Egypt. As Nasser undertook the socialist transformation of his country, and improved relations with the Soviet Union, the Egyptian religious establishment feared their country was drifting toward atheistic communism. To defend his policies from the attacks of the Traditionalist *ulama* [Muslim religious community], Nasser co-opted clerics (with such offers as money or jobs for relatives). When this failed, he intimidated them. Thus, Nasser persuaded a number of the *ulama* either to endorse his foreign and domestic policies, or to abstain from criticizing them.

The *Ikhwan* [the Muslim Brotherhood, a radical Islamist organization], meanwhile, was unsatisfied. In August 1965, fearing a resurgence of the Fundamentalist organization, Nasser spread a story of a second *Ikhwan*-sponsored plot to assassinate him. Again, Nasser's security forces hunted down, arrested, and imprisoned *Ikhwan* leaders and activists. This, however, was hardly the end of the Fundamentalist revivalism in general, or the *Ikhwan* in particular. Events in 1967 would favor the reemergence of Islamic revivalism, and would discredit Nasser's ideologies of pan-Arabism and Arab socialism. In fact, Nasser himself made the transition from secularist to pragmatist.

The 1967 Arab-Israeli War

For ten years following his spectacular performance in the 1956 Suez Crisis, Nasser decided to avoid direct military confrontation with Israel while he strengthened the Egyptian military and gloried in his position of preeminence among Arab leaders. Nevertheless, by 1967 events overtook the charismatic Egyptian president, resulting in a war that humiliated his military and tarnished his glory.

Unable to resist either challenges to his reputation or Soviet reports of a fictitious Israeli attack plan against Syria, Nasser took steps that would test the legitimacy of his regime and of his ideology and that would provoke the Israeli leadership. Nasser sent U.N. forces packing, remilitarized the Sinai Peninsula, and proclaimed a blockade, which he never enforced, of the strategically important Strait of Tiran. Initially, these steps restored Nasser's standing as the leader of Arab nationalism. However, Nasser's decisions would soon embarrass and humble him.

Considering Nasser's actions as equivalent to a declaration of war, Israel launched a preemptive air attack against Egypt and Syria that destroyed the Arab air forces on the ground. Israel then took the Sinai Peninsula from Egypt, the West Bank and East Jerusalem from Jordan, and the Golan Heights from Syria. The Arab response, where it occurred, was inconsequential. Within six days, Israel had crippled the military capability of Egypt, Syria, and Jordan; had conquered large segments of Arab land, which could be used as a bargaining chip in future peace negotiations; and had seized the holy city of Jerusalem. Having achieved its objectives fully, Israel accepted a U.N.-brokered cease-fire.

In Egypt and throughout the Muslim world, the psychological injury inflicted by the Israelis was enormous. A period of intense self-examination descended upon Muslims. Nasser, his secular socialist ideologies discredited by the overwhelming defeat, turned to Islamic themes and ritual observances to heal the wounds and relieve the trauma plaguing the Egyptian people. Nasser, famed for his erstwhile secular orientation, turned Pragmatist. He stopped using socialist rhetoric and resorted to an Islamic idiom to rationalize the astounding Arab defeat on the battlefield. Nasser maintained that defeat had been God's will and, therefore, not preventable by any precaution or preparation. He stressed Islamic virtues, like patience and perseverance in the face of adversity. The government even encouraged Islamic activities to help the nation cope with its failure and shame. For instance, on June 19, 1967, Nasser personally participated in the festivities marking the Prophet Muhammad's birthday. This event was heavily covered by the Egyptian media, which prior to the 1967 war had been discouraged from covering such religious events. Moreover, as Nasser continued to emphasize Islam, he fired his secular socialist advisors or encouraged them to resign; he introduced economic liberalization; and he made fraternal overtures to the wealthy, traditional, pro-Western, monarchical regimes of the Persian Gulf whom he had scathingly denounced and even subverted in the previous decade (1957–1967). Meanwhile, numerous Islamic institutions, *masjids*, and the *ulama*, which had been tightly controlled by the government, were allowed to function with relative freedom in the prevailing environment of shock, humiliation, and sadness. Even restrictions on the Fundamentalist *Ikhwan* were relaxed, and many of its members were released from jails.

Muslim Fundamentalists quickly took advantage of their newfound freedom and of the emotional religious atmosphere to offer a simple explanation for the Arab world's shattering defeat: Egypt and other countries had strayed from the "straight path" of Islam that had brought progress and glory in the past. By importing and embracing alien Western ideologies like nationalism and socialism, the Muslim world suffered chronic divisiveness, greater poverty, lack of freedom, and a weaker belief in Islam.

The *Ikhwan al-Muslimun* went further and declared that Arab defeat in the 1967 war was an effective condemnation of the secular policies characteristic of present regimes that ignored or violated the principles of the *Shariah* [Islamic law]; a sign of God's revenge for the oppression Muslims had endured under Nasser's dictatorial regime; and God's punishment for Nasser's alliance with the atheistic Soviet state. The *Ikhwan*, in essence, attributed defeat to a lack of faith and stated, "Israel is a religious state, based upon the tenets of Judaism. The Egyptians, who had depended upon a secular ideology, could not hope to withstand the power of religious faith." The *Ikhwan* believed firmly that the imported Western ideologies of socialism, nationalism, and secularism—enshrined in Nasserism—had been defeated, and the only cure for the Muslim world's ills lay in Islamic fundamentalism. Only the staunch practice of Islam would renew Egyptian dignity and courage, or would inspire Egyptians to give their lives as martyrs in a martial *jihad* against Israel. Thus, revivalism gained favor, as had Nasserism before it, on the promise to vanquish Israel.

Arson at *Al-Aqsa* Mosque and Nasser's Death

After the 1967 Israeli occupation of Jerusalem's eastern section, frustration and anger steadily built throughout the Muslim world. This frustration was aggravated by the Israeli government's attempts to Judaize the city after 1967 by expropriating Arab lands, demolishing Arab homes, expelling eminent political and intellectual leaders of the Arab community, and requiring Arab schools to teach a history that destorted Arab claims to Palestine.

On August 21, 1969, a deranged Australian Zionist set fire to the *Al-Aqsa* mosque in East Jerusalem, and the Muslim world rose up in protest. The arsonist's sacrilege seemed to many Muslims all too symptomatic of Israeli abuses upon East Jerusalem.

Two days following the fire, Nasser penned a letter rife with Islamic imagery and symbolism to his defense minister.

> We shall return to Jerusalem and Jerusalem will be returned to us . . . we shall not lay down our arms until God grants His soldiers the victory and until His right is dominant, His house respected and true peace is restored to the city of peace.

Meanwhile, there was a vigorous discussion in the media and a proliferation of literature examining the centrality of Jerusalem for Islam. Later, in 1970, the fifth conference of *Al-Azhar*'s Academy of Islamic Research devoted a substantial part of its proceedings to a discussion of the Islamic nature of Jerusalem and Palestine. In essence, in Egypt and throughout much of the Muslim world, the arson and desecration of the *Al-Aqsa* mosque reinforced the revivalist trend already pronounced since the 1967 war. Likewise, it reminded revivalists that Israel stood between the *umma* and sacred Jerusalem. Israel, therefore, remained a significant enemy.

The death of Nasser in 1970 increased the Egyptian regime's reliance on the politics of Islam and thus directly contributed to Islamic revivalism. Nasser's successor, Anwar Sadat, heightened political Islam by fully lifting the ban of the political activities of the *Ikhwan al-Muslimun*. Sadat's motives were simple. Unleashing the *Ikhwan* effectively neutralized the influence of the socialists who sought to topple the Sadat government. . . .

The 1973 Arab-Israeli War

While the defeat inflicted on the Arabs by Israel in 1967 led to a period of intense self-evaluation and laid the groundwork for the Islamic revival in several Arab nations, the Arab-Israeli War of October 1973 added great impetus to the incipient revival. Although the 1973 war was fought to a military stalemate, and the Arabs regained none of the lands lost to them in 1967, the conflict began with a successful Arab invasion of Israel's fortified military positions. There were three consequences of this initial success. First, throughout the Muslim world the Arab effort was perceived as a limited victory. Second, the widely held myths of Arab disunity and military inferiority were dashed. And third, the myth of Israeli invincibility was similarly discredited.

An important feature of the 1973 war was the Arab emphasis on religious symbolism, an emphasis indicative of the influential role played by religion in Egyptian society following the 1967 war. For example, the 1973 war was launched by Sadat during Islam's holy month of Ramadan. The operational code name for the crossing of the Suez Canal by Egyptian forces was "Badr," a reminder of the first Islamic victory under Prophet Muhammad over the *kafirs* in A.D. 623. Moreover, the battle cry in the 1973 Ramadan War was *"Allahu Akbar"* (God is most Great). The battle cry of the Arabs in the Six Day War of June 1967 had been the less-than-inspiring "Land, Sea and Sky," which implied protecting the territory of the Arab world—a secular nationalist idea, rather than a religious one. The 1967 battle cry also implied faith in military equipment and the tactics of military engagement, rather than in God. Many Muslims throughout the world attribute the 1973 Arab victory to God and His modern-day, holy warriors. Thus, Islamic revivalists could later point out that trust in Islam is the surest way to defeat the Israelis.

Madrassas Have Contributed to the Spread of Islamic Fundamentalism

Aijazz Ahmed

Madrassas are religious schools in the Middle East and South Asia that are reputed to foster harsh varieties of Islamic fundamentalism as well as fierce anti-American sentiments. The Taliban members who brought totalitarian Islamic rule to the war-weary country of Afghanistan in the 1990s were the product of Pakistani madrassas. In this selection, reporter Aijazz Ahmed describes the madrassas in Pakistan. He states that the majority of the students in Pakistan's twenty-five thousand madrassas are poor and that some must beg for food to survive. The madrassas offer them one of the few opportunities for people in the underclass of Pakistani society. The curriculum at these schools focuses on Arabic literature and grammar, Koranic teachings, and Islamic jurisprudence. Students rarely learn subjects such as computer science or chemistry that would help them compete in the modern world. Defenders of the schools deny that they are training grounds for terrorists; nevertheless, Ahmed notes that these religious schools are supported and influenced by fundamentalist Islamic organizations such as Jamaat-i-Islami and that the students tend to blindly follow the teachings of Islamic fundamentalism. Aijazz Ahmed is a reporter for *Asia Times Online*.

I lost my sight for a while as I entered the dark, cold room, but as my eyes adjusted, I made out the figure of a small boy sitting on the rough floor, deep in concentration with a Koran, the Muslim holy book, in his hands.

Fareed, only in the ninth year of his life, was totally oblivious to my presence and to his surroundings, so intent was he on memorizing the Koran, hunched up at the religious school or *madrassa* in Rawalpindi (the sister city of the capital [of Pakistan] Islamabad) of Tajweed-ul-Quraan. Fareed was enrolled at the seminary by his orthodox father, Ubaid Ullah, where he joined almost 500 other children with the aim to secure a place in heaven, where he believes that he will be able to play with black-eyed heavenly nymphs.

Fareed has nothing to do with terrorism or politics, and he has only a vague knowledge of the catastrophe of September 11, and what happened in Afghanistan subsequently. He is at the *madrassa* for one reason only, and that is to memorize the 77,934 words of the Koran by heart so that he can recite it in full—a recitation in Arabic that takes about 10 hours. Muslims believe that a person who memorizes the Koran will secure a seat in heaven for his parents and the next seven generations.

Another student at the *madrassa*, Yunis, on the other hand, cuts a very different figure. Although his goal of learning the Koran is the same as Fareed's, he is politically charged, with a vision of the dismemberment of both Israel and the United States, which he sees as symbols of terrorism and injustice around the globe and the number one enemy of Islam and the Muslim *ummah* (community).

Both Fareed and Yunis come from the suppressed poor underclass of Pakistani society, where opportunities are few, and they, along with orphans, make up the majority of the students at the country's *madrassas* as Pakistan has few other institutions to take care of the homeless and the underprivileged. Interestingly though . . . an increasing number of children from wealthy urban families are being enrolled in the seminaries.

Students at the *madrassas*, since the subjects that they learn are sacred and derived from god, are not allowed to sit on benches or at desks to study. Humiliation is their fate, and as such they must sit on the floor. Life at the school is hard, with few diversions from study, such as sport. All of the students live in hostels attached to the schools, but invariably these have poor facilities, not to mention the luxury of beds or heating. Fareed, for instance, shares a small room with eight colleagues.

"I am here to learn and memorize the Koran," whispers Fareed in a low, frightened tone. "I am here to make the dream of my father a reality, and of mine as well. I want to become a religious scholar and secure a good birth in heaven for me and my whole family. No matter what treatment me and my colleagues meet here, God will balance everything in heaven," says the youngster.

Twenty-five Thousand Religious Schools

The growth of seminaries in Pakistan has been phenomenal, almost 300 percent faster than regular government and private schools. Before partition in 1947, there were 2,500 registered religious schools on the Indian subcontinent (which now consists of Pakistan, India and Bangladesh).

Today, there are more than 10,000 registered religious schools in Punjab province alone, while in the whole of Pakistan there are more than 25,000, catering to more than 1.6 million children. In addition, a further 25,000 to 40,000 non-registered schools provide lessons on the Koran to an almost equal number students.

The Western world widely depicts the students at the *madrassas* as terrorists in the making. Talat Masood, a researcher and a retired lieutenant general in the Pakistani army, comments, "The people in the *madrassas* are neither demons nor heroes . . . they have insecurities, pain, hopes and frustrations. There is a very professional, unbiased and balanced approach towards *madrassa* education, which contrasts radically with the Western depiction of Muslim religious education in such institutions," he says, adding, "They are human beings just like us."

Kamil Khan, a student at a large *madrassa*, adds, "We are not terrorists, nor are we supporters of Osama bin Laden or anyone else. But if you [the West] continue treating us in this way, indeed, some of us could join hands with them. It is the injustice and one-sided policy of the United States and the Jewish state of Israel that has forced people to raise guns."

Funding and Control of the *Madrassas*

The *madrassas* receive their funding from several sources. Wealthy Muslims are bound by religion to spend a fixed portion of their wealth for the betterment of the poor, while such Muslim countries as Saudi Arabia, Iran, Sudan and Libya provide funds, in addition to charitable organizations. The students also beg for bread and butter in the evenings for themselves and their other colleagues.

A few students pay fees, but the amount is nominal. "That is why we have to collect *chanda* [donations] and food from the common man," said Mufti Jamil of Islamabad. Religious schools have a wide and strong backing from some political parties, notably the Jamaat-e-Islami Pakistan, all factions of the Jamiat-ul-Ulma-e-Pakistan, (almost five, with the biggest one being that of chief Taliban supporters Maulana Fazlur Rehman and Maulana Sami-ul-Haq), two rival factions of the Tehrik-e-Jaffria Pakistan, other Shi'ite groups, the Sipah-e-Sahaba Pakistan and its splinters, and other religious political, semi-political and non-political organizations and non-Pakistani Muslim (Arab) NGOs [nongovernmental organizations].

The Jamaat-e-Islami Pakistan, the Jamiat-ul-Ulma-e-Pakistan and Shi'ite groups are the major stakeholders in the *madrassas*. They control almost 60 percent of the total *madrassa* population, and indirectly influence the students according to their political and strategic interests. But no political party is directly or officially involved in running the *madrassas*, rather they control them through five federations (*wifaqs*).

These are constituted according to various Islamic schools of thought, or sects, such as the Deobandi (originating from India); the followers of Imam Abu Hanfia (a moderate Muslim scholar in the early centuries of Islam); Ahl-e-Hadith (in which people blindly follow the sayings of the Prophet); Bralvi (another school of thought on the subcontinent) Shi'ites; and the Jamaat-e-Islami.

Despite its intention to bring the *madrassas* under tighter control, the government has yet to achieve anything concrete. An ordinance banning *madrassas* from admitting foreign students, from receiving foreign funding and limiting their operations has fallen by the wayside as, under the constitution, it did not receive approval from parliament within the mandatory period of six months.

A committee formed by the government . . . to modernize the *madrassas* has not even met once against fierce opposition to any government meddling in their internal affairs, especially with regard to curriculum. Government sources now concede that now Prime Minister Zafarullah Khan Jamali will not risk raising the issue again, at least not in the near future.

Even within Pakistan, the *madrassas* are viewed from different spectrums. In the traditional Muslim mindset, they are seen as doing good as they propagate Islam, while for others the schools are seen as spreading ignorance, intolerance and illiteracy in an already backward Pakistani society.

Religious Schools with a Changing Political Function

Madrassas were introduced about 300 years ago on the Indian subcontinent by then Muslim monarchs and rulers to produce a bureaucracy capable of running the day-to-day affairs of state, especially in terms of financial and legal issues, according to the wishes and pleasure of the king. Later, the seminaries took on the responsibility of producing a Muslim leadership to lead the liberation movement against the British rulers on the subcontinent.

Professor Dr Manzoor [Ahmed], a renowned scholar, writer and researcher, comments that nowadays many *madrassas* have taken an unfortunate direction. "The new role of the *madrassas* and [the influence] of religious elements has added nothing but hatred against non-Muslims and different sects of Islam. Although some major schools produced better results and play their role for religious harmony, many inject the poison of extremism, sectarianism and ignorance and have become a source of increasing ignorance and religious intolerance in Pakistani society."

He points out that the curriculum of the *madrassas* is not competitive in today's world, as the schools do not teach advanced physics, chemistry, biology, computer science or information technology; rather the subjects were set 300 years back. The standard curriculum of the seminaries includes logic, Arabic literature, Arabic grammar, understanding the Koranic teachings, interpretation of the Koran, *hadith* (sayings of the Prophet) and Islamic jurisprudence.

The *madrassas* issue degrees up to master's level which are recognized by the country's University Grants Commission. These master's students, with extra study, can eventually become muftis capable of issuing *fatwas* on issues relating to religion or religious provisions in day-to-day affairs. Many ordinary graduates join other religious schools as teachers, or start their own *madrassas*. In . . . national elections, the government recognized degrees issued by the *madrassas*. For the first time, all candidates had to have at least a degree to be eligible to stand for the parliamentary polls.

Maulana Sharif, the principal of an Islamic seminary attached to a government-controlled mosque in Islamabad, differs with Manzoor. "We [*madrassas*] are doing well; it is we who are keeping the Islamic values and traditions intact for hundreds of years. If the religious schools had not been there, the religion of Islam and the society of so-called Muslims would have faced irreparable losses at the hands of liberals and Western agents. Islam essentially encourages pursuit of knowledge and provides a great opportunity at the individual level and the society level, and scope for debate and dialogue while agreeing on the basic faith," he said.

Renowned poet, scholar and researcher, Said Iftikhar Arif, says that Islam is not a religion of terrorism; rather it prohibits terrorism and extremism in any shape. "We, the Muslims of the subcontinent and in particular Pakistan, are guardians of a great heritage of beautiful, loving, tolerant Islam propagated mainly by the mystics or the sufis, because of which Islam evolved into an inclusive faith." Each federation of the relative sects translates the subjects taught at the *madrassas* according to their faith and sect. Mufti Bashir, head of the biggest *madrassa* in Rawalpindi, explains, "All subjects that we teach have come from God, we only make students understand these subjects."

"We open the minds of the students, Islam encourages knowledge and debate, our education system makes students a guard of Islamic values, we are not striving to make them experts of modern science and technology," says Maulana Sharif in response to a query as to why subjects such as economics and modern science are not taught in the *madrassas*.

Comments Maulana Sami-ul-Haq, the man who taught many of the former Taliban cabinet in Afghanistan, "Advancement and competence in modern education is not our job or duty, it is the duty of modernists and our critics who support the Western educational system. We have not failed, we are still competent enough to interpret Islam and resolve issues related to Islam, but it is a failure of cultured secularists in modern day education that Pakistan is a backward society.

"Since we are keeping the Islamic faith and values, that is why the United States targets Muslims and our *madrassas*," he adds. "Yes, we are not rich enough and we have limited resources, indeed, the practice of begging for food by students damages their personalities, but still they are better Muslims," he says.

Learning About Jihad

Adds a student, Bihar Ali, "We don't get military training, nor are we offered guns, but certainly we have been taught jihad, which is a basic duty of Islam." Although the word jihad has ominous overtones in the West, it merely means to struggle for Islam. One can wage a jihad against poverty or illiteracy. Only in its extreme form does it refer to war.

"Jihad is not terrorism; rather it is a struggle against terrorism to eliminate injustice and cruelty from the earth," says Maulana Sharif. "Since we teach jihad, so the West is afraid of us. If our students are or were busy in jihad in Afghanistan or Kashmir, it is the failure of the country's Interior Ministry and that of the Pakistani army, who abandoned their basic duty to protect and safeguard Pakistan and Muslims," Maulana Sherif asserts.

Religious leaders and teachers at the *madrassas* also deny involvement in crossing borders into Indian-administered Kashmir. "We are not involved in infiltration as propagated by India, and if somebody from the *madrassa* is doing it; it is again a failure of Pakistan's Interior Ministry and the Indian forces," says Maulana Sharif.

Awal Khan, a student of higher classes at Fazlur Rehman's *madrassa*, gives his view. "No religious schools are involved in sectarianism; rather it was a gift of US Afghan policy. For its interests, the US administration encouraged jihad and jihadi groups for a proxy war against Russia, and now these groups are powerful and uncontrollable. Only the US and the previous Pakistani government of General Zia ul-Haq are responsible." Maulana Sharif says, "Such contradictions and inter-relationships exist in all societies, within families, at social and cultural levels, in politics, and even within strict institutions like *madrassas*. We are not responsible for increasing religious intolerance; again, the governments of Pakistan and the unjust policies of the Western world and America are responsible.

"The strict vigilance of the religious schools and their activities makes it next to impossible for them to provide terrorist training and support any kind in this regard," said Maulana Sharif. "Intelligence agents can easily make their way at least five times a day into any *madrassa* in the country, but even then some supporters of terrorism or extremists may lurk in some *madrassas* in far flung areas," he added.

"It is the duty of the government to check this infiltration if it prevails, we give admission to all Muslim students, whether Pakistani or not, and again the government must ensure visas and proper documents for people to enter Pakistan," observed Mufti Azam (a man who can issue decrees on Islamic affairs), Maula Hasham Zai of the famous Jamia Banori Town, Karachi.

Counters Interior Minister Faisal Saleh Hayat, "By and large, *madrassas* are doing well and they are providing safe and constructive education to children. We don't allow illegal students from other Islamic countries to study in *madrassas*. We are keeping a strict vigilance and observing practice in this regard," he added. . . .

Records show that *madrassa* students are not widely a part of the jihad in Kashmir. To name a few, Ghulam Abbas, Arif

Hussain, Usman Atique, Mudassir Rashid, Mehmood Riaz, Abul Asim, Mohammad Sabir Shahid Mehmood Shafqat, Abdul Sattar, Faisal Mahmood, Sadaqat, Naweed and Niaz all died in Indian-administered Kashmir in different skirmishes with Indian security forces, and they were all from the regular Pakistani education system, mostly Christian missionary schools, such as Saint Patrick's Karachi, La Salle Multan, Atchison Lahore, Cathedral Lahore and Saint Patrick's Quetta, or government high schools and colleges.

They embraced death due to the influence of the Islamic groups and political parties such as the Jamaat Islami, the Lashkar Tayab, the Mujahideen Albaddar, the Jamiat Ulma-e-Islam and other groups that have student organizations. Certainly *madrassa* students went in their thousands to the jihad in Afghanistan, but mainly from the Pashtu-speaking areas to fight against the Northern Alliance, along with the Taliban. The US saw Islam as an important force against the Soviets, and with its backing, the *madrassas* became the training ground for the fighters who defeated the Soviets in Afghanistan in 1989 after nearly a decade of war.

Nevertheless, many *madrassa* students have violent personalities due to long harsh treatment by their teachers. They are politically charged and attached blindly to their respective interpretations of their faith and ideology. They seldom have the capability to analyze developments taking place around them. Although they are not a formal part of any pan-Islamic movement or Muslim Brotherhood campaign, and they are not being trained by bin Laden or anyone else against a superpower for jihad, they have a love bond with Islam and the Islamic *ummah*, and this can trigger the violent man inside them as they have blind faith and rigid standards.

Certainly, then, they are catalysts for jihad because of the influence and education they receive in the *madrassas*.

Chapter 2

Islamic Fundamentalism Achieves State Power

Turning | Points
IN WORLD HISTORY

Saudi Arabia: The World's Oldest Islamic Fundamentalist State

Joseph Nevo

Saudi Arabia is a theocratic state in which the royal family of the House of Saud controls some of Islam's holiest sites and the Middle East's richest oil reserves. The practice of Islam shapes every aspect of life for citizens in Saudi Arabia, whose constitution is the Koran. As Joseph Nevo explains in this selection, the Al Saud family achieved political legitimacy by forging an alliance in the 1700s with the spiritually influential Wahhab family, who formulated the puritanical Islamic creed known as Wahhabism. The Saudi-Wahhabi state ruled according to the strict religious principles of Wahhabism, suppressing all other forms of Islamic rites.

Nevo notes that in the modern era a conflict between state and religion has developed. In an attempt to modernize and improve their relations with other nations, the rulers have altered some of their policies. As a result, the ulema, or religious leaders, who formerly had proselytized for an uncompromising faith, began to serve as state agents justifying secular reforms. Some of the Muslim fundamentalist citizens in Saudi Arabia have thus become critical of some of the state religious leaders, whom they see as too lax. In the 1980s and 1990s Islamic militants from Saudi Arabia's upper class attacked what they saw as their rulers' corruption. The Saudi response—buying off the opposition and exiling them—has funneled money into the treasuries of Islamic extremists around the world. Nevo, a history professor at Tel Aviv University, is the author of *King Abdulla and Palestine: A Territorial Ambition* and coauthor with Ilan Pappe of *Jordan in the Middle East 1948–1988: The Making of a Pivotal State.*

Saudi Arabia is the most theocratic state in the contemporary Sunni Muslim world. By definition, a non-Muslim cannot be a Saudi citizen. The idea of religious pluralism has neither meaning nor support in many segments of the population, and religious norms and practices are encouraged, promoted and even enforced by the state. The Saudi constitution is the Quran, and the shari'a is the source of its laws. Even the Basic Law of Government (*al-nizam al-asasi li'l hukm*), issued in 1992, stressed their supremacy. Moreover, in order to underline that there is no other, mundane source of legislation, the use of terms such as *qanun* (law) and *musharr'i* (legislator) are practically forbidden as they imply Western-style statutory enactment. They are substituted by *nizam* (regulation) and *marsum* (decree), which are supposed to complement the shari'a, not to take its place. . . .

Religion Is a Source of National Unity

While nationalism, usually associated with modernization and secularization, preaches the love of society and state and promotes loyalty to them, in Saudi Arabia religious faith and loyalty to the ruling family are still predominant components of the collective identity. . . .

Islamic issues account for more than a third of the reading material in the textbooks of the Saudi public schools. About a third of the elementary schools' curriculum is religious studies and together with Arabic they make up more than half the curriculum. Similarly, a third of Saudi Arabia's university students major in Islamic studies. The state defines the main goal of its educational system as to promote Islamic values and 'to aim the students in the true Islamic direction'. The entire raison d'etre for the introduction of modern education into Saudi Arabia is that 'Islam teaches us that the pursuit of knowledge is a religious duty for every Muslim' [according to Saudi law]. Moreover, even cabinet ministers with a 'secular' educational background, who head mundane departments such as Industry, Electricity, or Planning, to phrase the rationale of their policies in religious terms. The objectives of the second five-year plan of 1975–80, for example, included 'maintaining the religious and moral values of Islam over the developing human resources [sic]'. The Saudi regime has also introduced and promoted national symbols such as an anthem and a flag . . . but they too are dominated by Islamic motifs and reflect a religious Weltanschauung [worldview], as well as loyalty to the ruling dynasty.

The House of Saud achieved substantial power owing to a bond with a religious harbinger. The supreme position the dynasty has enjoyed in the Arabian Peninsula for two and a half centuries arises from the facility and acumen with which members of the Al Saud family utilize religion as a unifying instrument and as a source of political legitimacy for their rule. . . .

Wahhabism

The Wahhabi doctrine (derived from the Hanbali school of Sunni Islam) was first preached in Najd in central Arabia in the 1740s by a native Muslim scholar, Muhammad Ibn Abel al-Wahhab. The school he founded was later named after him. He called for the reinstatement of exactly the same religious, social and political customs that had been practised by the prophet Muhammad and his followers, namely adherence to the Quran and the sunna as the only sources for religious conduct, and the rejection of any new element or concept introduced into Islam thereafter; those were branded as *bid'a*. The most important Wahhabi tenet was *tawhid*, the oneness of God. Not only is God omnipotent, he is the one and only who is such. No person or object possesses divine traits, so no one and nothing can or should mediate between a human being and God. The use of such an intermediary was considered *shirk* (polytheism, idolatry).

These were not merely theoretical theological rulings. They had considerable impact on daily life, because the cult of holy places (i.e., objects mediating between man and God) was common and widespread then in central Arabia. Muhammad Ibn Abd al-Wahhab's call for the destruction of such places shook the prevailing religious and social order in Najd. Leaders of the local sedentary communities regarded him as a menace to peace and stability as well as a threat to their own authority. He was expelled from several places and his life was threatened.

Eventually the Amir of Dir'iyya (a small town just northwest of Riyadh), Muhammad Ibn Saud, took him under his patronage, becoming one of his first and most obedient disciples. The cooperation between Muhammad Ibn Abd al-Wahhab and Muhammad Ibn Saud yielded two interrelated occurrences: the establishment of the Al Saud dynasty as the political masters of most of the Arabian Peninsula and the simultaneous spread of Wahhabism and its installation as the predominant Islamic school in those same territories.

That bond between umara and ulama (statesmen and divines) marks the modern inception of the use of religion as an instrument for both consolidating a collective identity and legitimizing the ruling family. It served the interests of the two parties, in the spirit of the political writing of Ibn Taymiyya. This scholar, whose most stringent interpretation of the teachings of Ibn Hanbal (founder of the most orthodox of the four Islamic schools) was adopted by Muhammad Ibn Abd al-Wahhab, held that religion and state are indissolubly linked. Without the coercive power of the state, religion is in danger, and on the other hand, without the shari'a the state becomes a tyrannical organization.

Alliance of Book and Sword

Muhammad Ibn Saud realized that the alliance with the preacher indeed gave him a clear advantage over his peers; these were the chieftains of small towns in Najd, whose sources of support—like his own until he met Ibn Abd al-Wahhab—consisted of tribal loyalty, traditional leadership, military and political strength and a territorial base. The insertion of the religious component (in the new, dynamic, version) not only facilitated continuous military victories over neighbouring tribes and nearby settlements, it created a sort of a nascent Najdi territorialism. Cooperation between the

Book and the Sword helped to unify the whole area and transformed the authority of dozens of local rulers into a comprehensive supra-local and supra-tribal structure. Under Wahhabi-Saudi rule appeared first indications (particularly among the sedentary population) of loyalty to the 'state' or to the ruler, which enjoyed a certain consensus. It had not, as always before, to be constantly kept alive by military victories or to be enforced by coercion, and it even survived occasional

Wahhabism and the Saudi Kingdom

Wahhabism, the Islamic sect whose doctrines are taught in Saudi-financed madrassas and mosques throughout the world, rejects the practices of other Muslims as non-Islamic.

Sunni Islam, the majority Islamic faith, is a religion of laws, of legal schools and jurisprudence. For Sunnis, God has made law for humanity to live. There are four great schools of the religious law in Sunni Islam. One of these schools is named for Ibn Hanbal (A.D. 780–855), who believed that the law should be seen in a very "boiled down," literalist way that leaves little room for interpretation, adaptation or concessions to modernity.

The Hanbali school of law would probably have died out, discarded by believers as too extreme for "real life," except for an 18th-century scholar named Muhammad Abd al-Wahhab, who lived in what is now Saudi Arabia. Abd al-Wahhab embraced Ibn Hanbal's ideas and convinced a desert chieftain named Ibn Sa'ud to accept his version of Hanbalism as the official faith of what eventually became Saudi Arabia. This faith, popularly known as Wahhabism, rejected the right of all other Muslims to believe and practice Islam in their own ways. It particularly condemned Sufi brotherhoods for their attempts to experience God personally rather than through the rigid observance of Islamic law.

Wahhabism continues to condemn all other Muslims. It cites the Quran's description of war made against unbelievers in the first centuries of Islam to justify, indeed to demand, unceasing war to the death against other less observant Muslims and

defeats. The same alliance also prevailed in the second Saudi state of the nineteenth century and in the current kingdom of Saudi Arabia.

Less than two generations after the first meeting of the Imam and the Sheikh cooperation between Muhammad Ibn Saud and Muhammad Ibn Abd al-Wahhab gave rise to an empire that embraced the entire peninsula. All forms of Islamic rites (and of course non-Islamic, mainly pagan) were

especially against non-Muslim unbelievers. This war against the "infidels" is the jihad, a moral obligation of every true Muslim. The Wahhabis, however, insist on an understanding of jihad that other Muslims have long since left behind. For the great majority of "the faithful," jihad has long been divided into the "Greater Jihad" and the "Lesser Jihad." The lesser jihad is the jihad of war, death and blood. The greater jihad is the inner struggle of every pious Muslim to bring himself closer to God through self-denial, charity and a moral life. This was not, and is not, the Wahhabi way. For them, the unbeliever, including non-Wahhabi Muslims, must accept their view of orthodox religious practice or suffer the consequences.

The early followers of this sect, generally condemned in their day as heretics by other Sunni, did their best to spread their rule by force across the Arabian Peninsula until in the late 18th century the Ottoman Turkish governor of Egypt sent his army into the area and utterly crushed them. From that time until the creation of modern Saudi Arabia at the beginning of the 20th century, Wahhabism was a little-known offshoot of Islam. At that time, Abd al-Aziz al-Sa'ud, the first king of Saudi Arabia, unified the Arabian peninsula by force. By 1925, this process was largely completed. In the new Saudi state, Wahhabism was the official faith and the only one sanctioned by the state. To this day no Christian, Jewish or other religious establishment is allowed in the kingdom.

Patrick Lang, "Wahhabism and Jihad: A Challenge to Religious Tolerance," *America*, March 10, 2003.

violently suppressed and replaced by Wahhabi tenets. The Saudi domain was actually a Wahhabi state. Not only was Wahhabism willingly or forcibly professed by all its subjects, the state was administered according to the strictest religious principles, just as the early Muslim community under the Prophet Muhammad was ordered. Spoils of war were divided precisely along the guidelines set by the Prophet, which also determined the duties and the taxes imposed on the people. Even the institutions established by Muhammad Ibn Saud and his successors bore the names of the similar ones created in the seventh century. The most conspicuous of these was Bayt al-Mal (the treasury).

Making of Today's Saudi Arabia

Twenty years after the first Saudi-Wahhabi state was destroyed by a powerful foreign invader (Muhammad Ali of Egypt in the early nineteenth century), it was again revived. This resurrection was possible owing to the tremendous will for political survival of Muhammad Ibn Saud's descendants and to the vigour of religious fervour. Wahhabism still existed as a factor that allied the Najdi population with the Saudi dynasty. Just before the turn of the nineteenth century the second Saudi-Wahhabi state fell again, this time at the hands of a neighbouring Amir, a former vassal of the Saudis and a practising Wahhabi himself. The path of Ibn Rashid, ruler of Jabal Shamar, to take Riyadh was eased by internal strife within the Al Saud family and court intrigues that ignited a civil war. The formation of the third and present Saudi state, at the beginning of the twentieth century, and its trials and tribulations on the way to its crystallization as a nation-state have been accompanied by a continuing religio-political partnership.

Religion continued to serve as an instrument of expansion and control. The still prevailing power of Wahhabism precipitated the remarkable achievements of King Abd al-Aziz, founder of the third Saudi state (the Kingdom of Saudi Arabia since 1932), during the first half of the twentieth century. Nevertheless, the king's endeavours for modernization and nation building brought to the surface an imminent conflict between state and religion. The technical innovations he introduced, such as motor vehicles and communications, essential for consolidating his authority and implementing his political aims, were prescribed by religion as *bid'a*. Abd al Aziz had to mobilize his ulama to legalize them. These religious leaders who formerly had been responsible for encouraging and strengthening the Islamic faith in the spirit of the uncompromising Wahhabism, were now required to function as state agents and to check manifestations of religious radicalism. They had to explain and justify secular reforms and changes, against which they used to preach constantly in Islamic terms. No wonder that some zealous Muslims, whose religious ardour until then had been fostered by the same ulama, questioned their religious authority and defied their rulings. A rift between Muslim fundamentalists on the one hand and the institutionalized religion and the state on the other, was inevitable.

Islamist Challenges to Saudi State

In the late 1920s this rift indeed turned into a violent conflict between the 'state' and the *ikhwan*. The latter were Bedouin encouraged by Abd al-Aziz to settle and engage in sedentary agriculture, and who also constituted a trained military body at his service at all times. Since those nomads had been persuaded to change their way of life by religious propagandists, their settlements soon turned into bastions of Islamic zeal and fundamentalism. They became more ardent and zealous Muslims than their master and became a source of embarrassment for him. They opposed Ibn Saud's policy of improving relations with the neighbouring Arab states (whose inhabitants they considered infidels), and worked against his modernization campaign (which, they charged, contradicted true Islamic values). Some of them vied with the authority of the Saudi dynasty and jeopardized its rule; the king was compelled to confront them militarily, and duly crushed their opposition.

This pattern, of Muslim zealots challenging the monarchy and its religious establishment, later repeated itself on several occasions. In September 1965 a small group led by Prince Khalid Ibn Mus'ad Ibn Abd al-Aziz attacked the newly erected television studio in Riyadh. In November 1979 a larger group of religious zealots led by Juhayman al-Utaybi captured the Grand Mosque in Mecca and held it for a few weeks. In both cases similar allegations against the House of Saud and its ulama were made, accusing them of deviation from the truly Islamic path. Al-Utaybi was said to preach for the revival of the *ikhwan* movement and not a few among his group were offspring of the original *ikhwan*. Their grievances were subsequently taken up by various Islamic opposition factions and individuals, in the 1980s and the 1990s, who then consisted of many young middle-class urbanites. These protesters were more numerous, more sophisticated, better educated, better organized and of different socioeconomic origin and background than their predecessors of 1979. Occasionally they were joined and even led by members of the state's ulama, who, despite being on the government payroll, feared that Western culture and technology would threaten the traditional Saudi-Wahhabi way of life. Their public protest in 1991 and in 1992 (which included demands not only for religious reforms but also for social justice, equality before the law, and an end to government corruption) cost many their freedom and some even their lives. Yet in addition to persecuting these oppositionists, the regime endeavoured to refute their accusations. Saudi scholars took pains to show that the kingdom was ruled according to the strictest Islamic principles, which included public participation and social justice.

Wahhabism as State Religion

Wahhabism, as the historical setting indicates, has not been just a fundamental militant reform movement characterized by merciless imposition of its doctrines by enthusiastic disciples upon the general population. It has also been a state religion, namely, Islam has been applied to defend the state and its resources and to safeguard its interests, as well as those of the ruling dynasty.

Wahhabism enjoyed this protected and convenient status of a state religion almost from its inception, from the time when it came under the patronage and custody of a political power. From the outset the history of Wahhabism has been interrelated with the House of Saud, that is, with political authority. The dual characteristics of Wahhabism as a militant reform movement and as a state religion suggest an inherent contradiction. The latter is more conformist and institutionalized, is inclined to accept and support the existing order, and is obviously less militant.

As long as the 'state' was an amorphous, dynamic and expansionist entity, with frequently changing boundaries and internal structure, this contradiction could be ignored, or at least kept low-key. It became a real problem when the dynamic phase of state building, as well as its territorial expansion, came to a close. The efforts at fusing the various regions into a single state intensified in the late 1940s and the early 1950s. The acuteness of the problem was then exacerbated by two major events: (a) the copious influx of oil royalties and the ensuing technological changes, which challenged the peculiar nature of Saudi society and accelerated its exposure to what was considered an undesirable alien influence; (b) the death, in 1953, of King Abd al-Aziz, founder and builder of the third Saudi state, who practically moulded the country during his reign which lasted more than half a century. His eldest surviving son and successor, Saud, did not fill the personal and political vacuum left by the death of his father, especially since the latter was a very charismatic figure.

Every Saudi ruler since Abd al-Aziz (until now all of them his sons) pursued his father's policy of making Islamic ideology central to his reign. As it has been impossible, under the conditions prevailing in Saudi Arabia, to rectify the aforementioned contradiction, the aspect of state religion has gradually become the more dominant component of modern Wahhabism, while the other aspect, its militancy, has been somewhat undermined and discouraged. This tendency has been deliberately fostered by the ruling dynasty. On the one hand it has been intended to curb any dangerous growth of the dynamic, missionary attribute of Wahhabism that might jeopardize the building of a Saudi state. Simultaneously, the regime has sought to institutionalize the religious faith and to create a religious establishment that would legitimize the modernization policy, whose secular nature, as indicated, was censured by Islamic zealots. The rebellion of the *ikhwan* and its repression by Ibn Saud is a telling instance of both aspects of that policy.

In recent decades, then, the royal family has made relentless efforts to cultivate Wahhabism both as a state religion and as an essential attribute of Saudi national identity. The latter aspect is meant to substitute the declining and anachronistic militant nature of Wahhabism. The regime is well aware that a by-product of such a policy is the imminent emergence of fundamentalistic groups, inside and outside the Saudi establishment, who regard state religion as too lax and endeavour to reinstate the original, puritan spirit of Wahhabism.

Iran's Islamic Revolution

Gilles Kepel

In 1979 Islamic fundamentalists overthrew the U.S.-backed shah of Iran and created a theocratic state. Led by a charismatic Shiite cleric, the Ayatollah Khomeini, the Iranian revolution was backed by both secular and religious opponents of the shah's regime. In this essay Gilles Kepel describes the way Khomeini used alliances with secular opponents of the shah to impose an Islamic rule that only a minority of the Iranian people desired. Khomeini's skillful manipulation and subsequent betrayal of his former allies helped him to keep firmly in control of the state until his death in 1989. The Iranian revolution caused the rulers of other Muslim countries to give more power to cleric leaders in hope of avoiding the shah's fate, Kepel argues. As a result, the clerics gained greater authority over the morals and standards imposed upon Muslim citizens. Kepel is a widely published writer on modern Islam. His recent books include *Allah in the West: Islamic Movements in America and Europe*, *Jihad: The Trail of Political Islam*, and *Bad Moon Rising: A Chronicle of the Middle East Today*.

The year 1979 will be remembered in history for the victory of the Iranian revolution and the proclamation of the Islamic Republic. Of all events in the contemporary Muslim world, this one has been the most scrutinized and analyzed by those who would unearth the causes of a tidal wave that nobody predicted, not even the protagonists themselves. . . .

Iran had enjoyed great prosperity in the years prior to the revolution, largely due to the high price of oil, of which it was the world's second largest exporter after Saudi Arabia. The shah prided himself on possessing one of the world's most powerful armies and having access to highly sophisticated American military equipment, which he used to police the Gulf and block Soviet expansion to the Indian Ocean. But the maintenance and handling of this military hardware required large numbers of American personnel, whose presence on Iranian soil provoked the fury of Ayatollah Khomeini. In 1964 he openly accused the shah of abdicating national sovereignty. The result was a fifteen-year exile, during which the ayatollah developed his political theology for the future Islamic Republic of Iran and from which he returned victorious in February 1979, carried aloft by the triumphant revolution.

What accounts for this dramatic turnabout? A primary factor was political unrest within Iran's student radicals, middle classes, and urban poor. Beneath the brilliant surface of modernization that the shah had projected and promoted, Iranian society was developing serious flaws. The monarchy and Savak (secret police) had muzzled debate on the regime's policies; the imperial system that had encouraged the growth of an educated urban middle class, through a system of schools substantially superior to those of Iran's neighbors, denied that class any semblance of political voice. At best, its members could become functionaries and managers in the imperial administration. The absence of free speech and a free press inhibited the development of a democratic culture in Iran. Liberal and socialist intellectuals preserved the legacy of the National Front led by Mohammed Mossadegh, the prime minister whose nationalist government was toppled by a CIA-backed coup that brought the shah to power, but in the early 1970s this clique had little or no influence in Iran, despite the aura of its leaders.

The vacuum created by the absence of democratic institutions provided a space for radical sentiment to grow. It began among Iran's students, who by 1977 numbered close to 175,000. Of these, 67,000 were studying abroad, mostly in the United States. Student radicalism in Iran drew on two main ideological sources: Marxism in its various forms, and a movement within Islam that came to be called socialist Shiism. . . .

Marxists Join with Islamists

A few young Marxists began projecting all the messianic expectations of communists and Third World peoples onto revolutionary Shiism. Ali Shariati was the most outspoken representative of this movement; his fame and influence among Shiites had no equivalent in the Sunni Muslim world. Socialist Shiites viewed the seventh-century death of Imam Hussein (the original "oppressed" one—*mazloum*) at the hands of the Sunni Umayyad Caliph as the analog of the Iranian people's modern oppression by the shah. The movement found its most militant expression in the guerrilla tactics of the People's Mujahedeen, whose acts of violence were comparable to those of the fedayeen. The mujahedeen's activities won the sympathy of the regime's opponents, but the group failed to enlist recruits beyond its core constituency of students. The educated, secular middle class as yet saw no reason to involve itself in so violent and radical a struggle. In purely practical terms the movement presented no immediate danger to the empire, which brutally repressed it nevertheless.

Rapid modernization, fueled by petro-dollars, destabilized two other important Iranian social groups: the traditional devout middle class associated with the bazaar, and the masses of young immigrants from the countryside, who had been drawn to town by the promise of prosperity, only to end up in the packed slums of Tehran. . . .

Culturally, both the devout middle class and the urban working class were alienated from the secular, modernist ideology favored by the regime. They viewed the world and their place in it through the filter of Shiism as preached by their clergy. In the bazaars, traditional life was spatially structured around the mosques and *imamzadehs*—tombs of saints much venerated by Shiites in their devotions. In the anarchic, jerrybuilt slums on the outskirts of the city, the primary source of order was Shiite places of worship, where citizens gathered to listen to their turbaned clerics teach the Koran and the deeds of the great imams. Here, religious leaders not only indoctrinated the masses but also functioned as agents of social stabilization and containment. They blessed the profits of the bazaaris, redistributed their alms, and educated the children while fathers and elder brothers went into the city center, seeking work and wages.

Yet the relationship between the imperial power and these religious networks was strained. The mullahs, ridiculed as "black" reactionaries because of their dark robes, saw the numbers of their traditional madrassas cut by the state, which sought to replace them with modern, government-controlled schools—policy that drew fury from the exiled Khomeini. The Shiite clergy was hierarchical and organized under the authority of ayatollahs, the most respected of whom were "sources of imitation" (*marja-e taqlid*). As recipients of the zakat (alms), they were independent, both financially and politically, from the state authorities, to which they paid only lip service (*ketman*). Their situation contrasted sharply with that of Sunni ulemas in other countries, with whom the state usually maintained close relations—rewarding them with political offices, paying their salaries, and in return receiving their blessing. During the reign of Muhammad Reza Pahlavi, the Iranian clergy added to the Shiites' traditional distaste for the regime a much more specific hostility provoked by the shah's open mistrust of the mullahs. Thus, in the mid-1970s, Iran's bazaars and slums contained a readily identifiable devout middle class and an impoverished younger generation, both of whom were culturally estranged from the ideology of a state that essentially ignored their existence. At the same time, they were strongly structured by the Shiite clergy, in whose hierarchy the state had no reliable representation. Quite the opposite was the case in most Sunni-dominated countries. . . .

Growing Discontent with the Shah

Despite Iran's growing social discontent and the political frustration it engendered, the imperial system functioned without serious difficulty until 1975, when a 12.2 percent drop in oil prices created major economic and social stresses. The regime reacted by launching a large-scale anti-speculation campaign that hit the bazaar very hard; its best-known merchants were thrown into prison and publicly humiliated. From that moment on, the merchants bitterly opposed the shah, and their guilds (*asnaf*) became conduits for the mobilization of men and means to bring him down. At the same time, the new measures against speculation upset the modern bourgeoisie by obliging companies to sell a part of their capital to their employees, without winning much credit from the workers themselves.

As the shah's isolation grew, the support of his principal ally, the United States, was weakened by the election of Jimmy Carter to the White House in November 1976. The brutal tactics of the Savak became a target of the new American president's human rights policy, and Carter himself applied pressure on the shah to liberalize Iranian civil society. Naturally enough, the secular middle class took this criticism as a signal that the United States had withdrawn its unconditional support for the Pahlavis. The year 1977 saw a spate of meetings and demonstrations by the liberal opposition, which for the first time in many years was not repressed by the regime. . . .

The "moment of enthusiasm" that transformed agitation against the shah into an Islamist revolution was triggered by a purely fortuitous event. This was the publication by a Tehran newspaper of an insulting attack on Khomeini in January 1978. The ayatollah was in exile at the time, living at Najaf in Iraq; but the entire opposition, including the secular middle class and those pious Muslims who opposed the doctrine of velayat-e faqih, rose up in his defense. Khomeini then unleashed his own partisans: on his instruction, the bazaar closed down completely, and a number of people were killed during a series of demonstrations in the holy city of Qum. A celebration on the fortieth day after these deaths led to another wave of bloody demonstrations in Tabriz, the metropolis of Iranian Azerbaijan. Thus began a spiral of provocation, repression, and polarization that rose steadily until the shah was forced to depart. Through their religious rhetoric, Khomeini and his disciples orchestrated these demonstrations, bringing into the streets, shoulder to shoulder, students from the madrassas and impoverished urban youths to be shot down as martyrs by the police, while the bazaar guilds raised funds for the victims' families.

Khomeini Disguises His Intentions

As the movement became more radical, Khomeini was able to mobilize the entire network of mosques in Iran, where the majority of mullahs who had hitherto withheld endorsement of his doctrines now fell into line behind him. This clerical network was supported by over 20,000 properties and buildings throughout Iran, where people gathered to talk and receive orders. The system had no equivalent among the secular opposition or among the Shiite socialists, who had done their best to rid themselves of clerical influence. Now they found themselves having to obey the ayatollahs, who controlled the lion's share of the resources available to support the revolution.

In the meantime, Khomeini adjusted his political rhetoric in order to appeal to an audience beyond his immediate circle of followers. In 1978 he made no mention of the doctrine of theocracy, which was bitterly contested among the clergy and would have scared away the secular-minded middle class had it known of it and understood its possible consequences. On the other hand, he made abundant reference to the "disinherited" (*mustadafeen*), so vague a term in Khomeini's parlance that it encompassed just about everyone in Iran except the shah and the imperial court. He borrowed the word from Shariati and had never used it before the 1970s. After Shariati's death in exile in June 1977, the term had become a rallying cry of the Shiite socialist students, who maintained a strong distrust of the clergy. In making use of this vocabulary, Khomeini (who had always refused to condemn Shariati while he was alive, despite the demands of other clerics) won the approval of substantial numbers of younger Islamist intellectuals. Bearded young engineers, doctors, technicians, and lawyers, whose counterparts in Egypt had clashed head-on with the ulemas of Al Azhar in the last months of [Egyptian president Anwar] Sadat's regime, now fell into line behind Khomeini. Thus, when he left Iraq in October 1978 for his final period of exile at Neauphle-le-Château on the outskirts of Paris, Khomeini was able to carry with him several figures from this group, notably the future short-lived president of the Islamic Republic, Bani Sadr.

In November 1978 Karim Sanjabi, one of the leaders of the

liberal National Front, made a pilgrimage to Neauphle to join Khomeini, while the head of the Tudeh Communist party officially recognized the ayatollah as his guide. At this time Khomeini announced that the goal of the revolution was to establish "an Islamic Republic which would protect the independence and democracy of Iran." Here he employed a term —democracy—that he would denounce as "alien to Islam" only a few months later, during the debate over what the new republic should be called. The general submission to Islamist cultural hegemony reached its climax during the most spectacular demonstrations against the shah, on December 10 and 11, 1978, corresponding to the ninth and tenth days of the Muslim month of Muharram, when Shiites commemorate the martyrdom of Imam Hussein. On these days Khomeini ordered hundreds of thousands of people to defy the shah's curfew by shouting "Allah Akhbar" from every terrace and rooftop in Tehran. It was a powerful demonstration of the Islamist cultural grip on the revolution. One month and five days later, the shah was driven out of Iran forever.

This Islamist victory was made possible by Khomeini's extraordinary ability to unify the various components, religious and secular, of a movement whose single point of departure was hatred of the shah and his government. Khomeini allowed each group to invest the movement with its own particular political dreams, which were not dispelled until the purges began in the aftermath of victory. The fusion of the revolutionary clerics with the young Islamist intellectuals mobilized the bazaaris and ordinary working people to unite in the common expectation of an Islamic Republic and the implementation of the sharia—without calling attention to the very different aspirations projected upon this nation by their respective class interests. This alliance also caught the imagination of the secular urban middle class. Incapable of asserting a cultural identity of their own, they felt obliged to go along with the dominant Islamist philosophy so that any benefits of revolution would not pass them by.

Upon his return to Tehran on February 1, 1979, Khomeini had to take account of the contradictory expectations of the immense host that had come together to welcome him home. His response was to set about eliminating all of his secular allies and establishing a theocracy. . . .

Eliminating Former Allies

Khomeini's defeat of the secular middle class and liberals was accomplished both judicially and politically within a few months. Following the referendum approving the Islamic Republic in March—enshrining Islamism in the nation's very name—an Assembly of Experts was elected in August. This assembly, which was dominated by the ulemas and the PIR (Party of the Islamic Revolution) now devised a new constitution. This contained articles establishing the velayat-e faqih and gave absolute power to the Guide, in the person of Khomeini. Objections to this theocracy were raised by the liberals, the Kurdish (Sunni) minority, one of the leftist parties, and a few clerics, who called it a restoration of dictatorship. Confronted by this coalition of his opponents, and on the pretext of protesting the shah's admission to the United States for treatment of the cancer that would kill him shortly afterward, 500 "students in the line of the imam" (Khomeini), led by a PIR official, stormed the American Embassy on November 4, 1979.

The U.S. diplomats inside were taken hostage and held until January 1981, following Ronald Reagan's defeat of Jimmy Carter for the presidency. Having no authority whatsoever to free the hostages, [provisional government head Mehdi] Bazargan resigned, setting a political seal on the crushing defeat that the secular middle class had already suffered in the streets. Shortly afterward, Ayatollah Shariat-Madari, the leader of those ulemas who had opposed Khomeini's theocracy, was placed under house arrest. He remained incarcerated until his death in 1986. . . .

War Turns Opponents into Martyrs

When [Iraq's dictator] Saddam Hussein's army invaded Iran on September 22, 1980, it handed Khomeini a perfect opportunity to mobilize this remaining sector of the population one last time, in such a way as to exhaust it politically and expend its energy in a paroxysm of martyrdom. At the front, the regiments of ill-trained young Iranian volunteers (*bassidjis*) were cannon fodder for the Iraqis. Hundreds of thousands of the most active and motivated militants gave their lives to defend their fatherland and its revolution, while millions more of their countrymen were pinned down for years in the trenches. Thus the soldiers of Year II of the Islamic Republic entirely vanished from the domestic political scene, and with them went any possibility that the impoverished urban working class might find some way of advancing its specific interests. . . .

The appalling butchery of the eight-year war against Iraq gave the younger generation of poor Iranians an incentive to return to the former [Shiite] tradition of martyrdom, pushing the ritual of self-flagellation to the point of self-immolation—the ultimate sacrifice. No longer at issue was the transformation of the world, for the revolution had clearly failed to satisfy that expectation; rather, the young men developed a new desire—a longing for death—as a response to the failure of Iran's revolutionary utopia and the pressures of war with Iraq. The Shiite death wish took on massive dimensions with the sacrifice of the bassidjis at the front. The volunteers wrote letters and last testaments to their families, asserting their longing for death in the crudest, most detailed vocabulary of Shiite martyrology. What these tragic documents describe in religious terms is no less than the political suicide of the young urban poor of Iran in the 1980s.

Khomeini's regime celebrated the martyrdom of the nation's young by cloaking itself in the legitimacy their sacrifice conferred. To this day, hyper-realist murals can still be seen in Iranian cities, displaying portraits of war martyrs whose names drip with blood. . . .

The Ripple Effect of the Iranian Revolution

At first, the Islamic Revolution in Iran was able to draw on deep reserves of sympathy among opponents of authoritarian regimes throughout the Muslim world. Before purges, executions, and atrocities tarnished its image, the revolution demonstrated that a movement springing from a broad spectrum of society could bring down a powerful government, even one closely connected to the United States. This victory was enough to make world leaders who had hitherto paid little heed to Islam begin to take its revolutionary potential much more seriously. Through Khomeini, the example of the Iranian revolution convinced many observers that Islam had supplanted nationalism as the principal factor in the political, social, and cultural identity of certain countries.

Regimes in Muslim countries viewed the shah's fate as an object lesson, and many of them became ostentatiously religious, in the hope of avoiding what had befallen the Persian monarch, who had never bothered to hide his contempt for the "men in black." Governments sought to head off social movements that, by annexing the vocabulary of Islam, threatened to unite everyone with an ax to grind and bring down the established power. The ulemas, having been steadily harassed during the nationalist period, now found themselves fawned upon by princes eager for the Islamic legitimacy their blessing could confer. In return, the clerics demanded greater control over culture and morals, avenging themselves on their secularist intellectual rivals—whose influence they diminished through the intimidation and censorship governments were suddenly willing to brandish on their behalf. Through the ulemas, Muslim elites sought accommodation with the devout bourgeoisie, whose approval or neutrality sanctioned the repression of the more radical Islamist intellectuals at work among the young urban poor. The partnership was an uneasy one, with each side looking for advantage and seeking to impose its own conditions. In general, the ulemas came out on top, as representatives of proper standards and values within society and within the Islamic movement itself. The losers were the bearded engineers, computer scientists, and physicians who had spearheaded the Sunni radical groups throughout the 1970s and had held the sheiks in low esteem.

The Muslim world as such had been under Saudi religious domination since the creation of the Islamic conference in 1969 and the triumph of petro-Islam in the war of October 1973. But after 1979 the new masters in Iran considered themselves the true standard-bearers of Islam, despite their minority status as Shiites.

Islamic Militants Seize Power in Sudan

Judith Miller

In 1989 the National Islamic Front, a branch of Sudan's Muslim Brotherhood, took control of Sudan in a military coup, imposing a harsh brand of Islamic law on a country with a large non-Muslim minority. As *New York Times* correspondent Judith Miller describes in this account based on several visits to the country, the coup was the culmination of a long drift toward Islamic fundamentalism begun in the 1970s by military ruler Gaafar al-Nimeiri. Miller notes that in Sudan, the imposed religion has certainly not united people but has increased divisions between them, adding to a tragic history of slavery and government instability. It has also increased the bitterness of a prolonged civil war. In 1998 the National Islamic Front was renamed the National Congress Party and still controls the country. Miller reported from Sudan on separate occasions in the 1970s, 1980s, and 1990s. Her books on Middle East politics and terrorism include *God Has Ninety-nine Names: Reporting from a Militant Middle East* and *Germs: Biological Weapons and America's Secret War.*

In 1976 many Sudanese still expected their country to become, as its then ruler Gen. Gaafar al-Nimeiri promised, the "breadbasket of the Arab world." His vision did not seem as preposterous then as it does today. Nearly $800 million a year—more than half of the Sudan's national budget—was pouring in from the Gulf, Japan, Europe, and the United States. Sudan had 200 million barrels of proven, recoverable oil reserves, much of it in the south and, because of the war, yet to be exploited. Nimeiri was building an ambitious irrigation system along the Nile, known as the Jonglei Canal Project, intended to carry life-giving Nile waters to the potentially fertile desert. The British-inspired Gezira Scheme —more than 2 million acres farmed by almost 100,000 tenant farmers—produced three-quarters of the country's lucrative cotton crop, which accounted for more than half of Sudan's export earnings. A UN study estimated that by 1990 as many as 40 million acres of land could be under cultivation.

President Nimeiri had made peace with the rebellious south in 1972, ending a seventeen-year-long civil war in which at least 500,000 Sudanese had died. The Addis Ababa accords granted southerners considerable autonomy, the right to continue using English along with Arabic, a more equitable share in resources, and most critically, religious freedom, exactly what the southern rebels, who later were known as the Sudan People's Liberation Army (SPLA), had demanded as the price of peace. Sudan, the largest country in Africa, one-third the size of the continental United States, was too large and too diverse to be governed centrally. Southerners were almost one-third of the population. Only about half of the Sudanese were Arab Muslims; Sudan was divided among more than five hundred tribes who spoke more than a hundred languages. Christians and pagans in the south would never choose to be ruled by northern Muslims in the name of Islam.

Nimeiri's Rule

When I first met him in 1973, I was impressed with Nimeiri, a Muslim Arab who came from a family that was devoted to the Mahdi[1] and his descendants. Though mercurial and corrupt, Nimeiri was a shrewd conciliator, a patriot, and flexible enough to shift alliances and political course if circumstance warranted it, as they often did in Sudan. Coming to power in a 1969 military coup as an admirer of Egypt's Gamal Abdel Nasser and radical Arab nationalism, Nimeiri eventually tried to crush all his major opponents: the Ansar, the strongest neo-Mahdist Islamic movement in the Sudan, headed then, as

---

1. Muhammad Ahmed (1845–1885), a remote descendant of the Prophet Muhammad

now, by Sadiq al-Mahdi, the Mahdi's great-grandson; the Khatmiya, the second-largest Muslim tribal grouping; Hassan Turabi's then insignificant Muslim Brotherhood; and the more influential Sudanese Communist Party. After the Communists nearly ousted Nimeiri in 1971, Nimeiri concluded he had more to fear from his once-leftist allies than from the Islamic parties. So in what would become a recurring theme in Sudanese politics, he embraced Islam, purged his government of leftists, and offered senior posts to men with Sufi and traditional Islamic backgrounds. Courting Sufi leaders by giving them money to build more mosques and religious centers, Nimeiri himself began conducting Friday prayers at mosques in different towns and villages.

Nimeiri, alas, lacked charisma. Flabby, black-skinned, and tainted in the eyes of many of his racist northern countrymen by his facial scars—inflicted by tribal healers to protect children against the Nile's innumerable eye diseases—he was a poor orator. Unable to attract Sudanese support away from traditional rival political and religious groups, particularly Sadiq al-Mahdi's Ansar, Nimeiri switched tactics in 1977 and did what President Sadat of Egypt was unwilling or unable to do: In addition to his own embrace of Islam, he made a deal with other Islamists—with the Ansar and Turabi's Muslim Brotherhood—to stay in power. Sadiq al-Mahdi ended his overt opposition to Nimeiri's regime. His brother-in-law Turabi not only broke with the opposition but joined Nimeiri's government. In 1979 his loyalty was rewarded: Turabi was named attorney general. Nimeiri increasingly emphasized his own "Islamic" orientation and, more significantly, let Turabi open an Islamic bank, a decision that would have far-reaching consequences for Sudan in less than a decade.

Turabi and Sadiq al-Mahdi continually pressed Nimeiri to make Sudanese law conform with sharia, the Islamic holy law. But Nimeiri resisted imposing Islam on his heterogeneous country, for southern leaders had repeatedly warned him that doing so would mean relegating Christian Sudanese to *dhimmi*, a "protected" minority community, and denying Sudanese pagans, who are not even "Peoples of the

Book," any rights at all. The south would have little choice but to resume the ruinous civil war.

But the longer Nimeiri ruled, the more eccentric and autocratic—and apparently devout—he became. Soon he was speaking more and more openly about the need for an "Islamic" lifestyle in his country. In 1980, a year after the Islamic revolution in Iran, he published a book, *Al-Nahj al-Islami Limadha?* (*Why the Islamic Path?*), in which he praised Islam as the best way to achieve Sudanese unity. While the ghostwritten book stopped short of endorsing the imposition of Islamic law, Nimeiri's apparent effort to capitalize on growing Islamic fervor in Sudan and bolster his popularity in the Arab Muslim north worried southerners. At about that time, Nimeiri issued a directive to government ministries—"Sober Leadership," it was called—that warned officials against drinking in public or engaging in un-Islamic conduct. In the early 1980s he ordered senior army officers to take Islamic indoctrination classes three times a week at a center where Turabi, his former nemesis and now senior foreign affairs adviser, lectured. Among Turabi's students were several young officers who would later oust Nimeiri, including President Omar Hassan al-Bashir, Sudan's current Islamic ruler.

Imposing Sharia

Even supposedly well-connected diplomats had difficulty explaining Nimeiri's stunning decision in 1983 to impose sharia, the so-called September laws. Nimeiri's Islamic legal code surprised even Turabi, who was then heading a committee charged with revising Sudan's laws to ensure their consistency with sharia. Sadiq al-Mahdi and other Muslim leaders denounced Nimeiri's new penal code as too harsh. But Turabi embraced it, and until Nimeiri imprisoned him less than three months before his overthrow in 1985, Turabi, who had admitted to having fainted when he saw his first Islamic amputation, defended the new laws and their severe corporal punishments. Such punishments, he told me at the time, did not "shock" the Sudanese. "In Zaire and elsewhere in Africa," he said coolly, "thieves are often crucified or beaten to death. So Africans are used to amputations and flogging."

The civil war that Nimeiri had ended resumed. And the war, in turn, led to economic stagnation that further weakened Nimeiri's hold on power.

Former advisers and aides have long speculated about why Nimeiri imposed an Islamic code, with its gruesome penalties, such as amputating the hands of thieves, in a country where hunger was so prevalent. Nimeiri told me that a "revelation" had come to him in a dream. Some former advisers argued that faced with a deteriorating economy, Nimeiri was trying to bolster his plummeting popularity through an alliance with a political faction that he thought needed him more than he needed them—Turabi's Muslim Brotherhood. Turabi, for his part, always insisted that his inclusion in Nimeiri's government was mere "window dressing," a ploy by the sly Nimeiri that never translated into real power for him or the Brotherhood. Still others thought that Nimeiri, sensing that Islam was on the rise after the Arabs' humiliating 1967 defeat by Israel, Iran's 1979 revolution, and the assassination of Egypt's Sadat by radical Islamists in 1981, was trying to position himself in the forefront of what he considered a winning trend. Besides, becoming more Islamic would mean even more aid from wealthy Saudi Arabia and the conservative Gulf. But desolate, isolated Sudan was hardly a likely leader of the region's Islamic revival. And virtually all of Nimeiri's opponents had better Islamic credentials than his. Some wise analysts argued that Nimeiri had simply lost touch with political reality after ruling for so long. . . .

A Coup Raises Hopes of a Freer Society

In the first week of April 1985 thousands of Sudanese, led by trade unionists and students, who had a long and proud tradition of political activism, rioted to protest food shortages and rising prices. Nimeiri was visiting President Reagan at the White House at the time. On April 6, 1985, the defense minister, Gen. Abdel Rahman Mohammed Hassan Siwar el-Dahab, considered Nimeiri's close friend, seized power in a bloodless coup, citing "the worsening situation in the country." Thousands of people thronged the streets singing in celebration of Nimeiri's ouster. . . .

The bloodless coup of 1985 had released an intense, long-suppressed yearning for political freedom that I shall never forget. While Nimeiri tolerated no political parties except his own, some thirty-five parties had emerged since his ouster the week before. Hardly an evening passed without a political rally. The previous evening, [*Sunday Times* reporter David] Blundy and I had joined some ten thousand people—Many trucked in from villages and towns hours away from Khartoum—at an N.I.F. [National Islamic Front] rally where Hassan Turabi, the Brotherhood leader just released from jail, had urged the faithful to "fight for a real Islamic revolution," a

---

Islamic Extremism in the Horn of Africa

Revolutionary movements thrive on disorder. In the Horn of Africa, poverty, war, and political instability verging on chaos provide fertile ground for a determined Islamic fundamentalist movement.

While the endemic conflicts in the Horn [of Africa] are attributable to a wide range of causes, radical Islamic movements are intimately involved in some of the region's turmoil.

A quick inventory underscores the point. Sudan has been home to a fundamentalist Islamic regime since 1989; for a number of years in the 1990s it even hosted Osama bin Laden and his Al Qaeda organization. The Sudanese government's insistence on imposing Sharia law on its southern, non-Muslim populations has been one of the factors fueling the long-running civil war there. In Ethiopia, where about half of the population is Muslim, the government has been waging a decade-long battle against Islamist insurgencies. Those insurgency groups enjoy support from external Islamic backers waging jihad on what they consider an oppressive Christian regime. Eritrea, the population of which is split evenly between Muslims and Christians (Orthodox), has to date managed to keep religious politics relatively depoliticized, but Eritreans are expressing growing concern over "identity politics" issues voiced by its mainly coastal Muslim population. . . .

Kenya's Muslim population—comprising 25–30 percent of the total population—has for the most part kept its political ac-

government "that will not beg," a regime that was "neither East nor West." "Islam is the solution!" the mob chanted as Turabi spoke. But there were many other voices and points of view. The euphoria contrasted sharply with M.O.B.'s [Islamic intellectual Muhammed Omar Beshir, called M.O.B. by reporters] somber mood. . . .

The Sudan was in economic misery. Four million Sudanese and a million refugees had been affected by drought and famine. Government debt was soaring; Sudan's pathetic infrastructure continued to collapse, particularly the links between the north and south that had been attacked by the

---

tivity within the parameters of legal party politics, but it includes radical elements sympathizing with or actively supporting *al-Ittihad* (Islamist) cells. Kenya was also the site of the 1998 terrorist attack on the U.S. embassy by non-Kenyan Islamic Extremists. Because large sections of its border areas and many of the teeming slums of Nairobi are essentially beyond the control of Kenyan police, Kenya remains a convenient haven for Islamic radicals and weapons smugglers.

Finally, there is Somalia, a country that has endured over a decade of civil war, recurring famine and complete state collapse. Despite—or perhaps because of—the fact that it is the only country in the Horn of Africa which is almost entirely Muslim, Somalia has not historically been home to the same level of radical Islamic political activity as has been the case in neighboring, religiously divided states. But over the course of the past decade, Islamic political activity has dramatically increased in Somalia. Sharia courts have sprung up throughout the country; *al-Ittihad* groups have temporarily seized control of several ports and towns; *al-Ittihad* cells exercise influence within the political and commercial elite; and in a few instances, evidence suggests that Somali *al-Ittihad* cells as well as secular factions have hosted and facilitated the operations of radical non-Somali Islamists such as Bin Laden's Al Qaeda.

Ken Menkhaus, "Political Islam in Somalia," *Middle East Policy*, March 2002.

rebels. Much of the middle class had emigrated. Would they return? Were development and democracy conceivable without them?

But there were even deeper reasons for concern, Beshir said. Modern Arab and African history were strewn with examples of military officers who had seized power and then refused to relinquish it. Even if the new military junta turned power over to civilians, would they govern more wisely and justly than the previous regime? Why would modern Sudanese history make one optimistic? . . .

Whereas most Sudanese Muslims probably thought that sharia should be the law of the land, Christians and pagans in the south opposed Islamic law, and who could blame them? M.O.B. was right: Establishing peace and equality between the Arab north and the non-Muslim south would be dreadfully difficult. Personal rivalries and ethnic and sectarian tensions were deep and historic. The two leading parties were both religiously based and had roughly equal support in the country. Thus, the fringe parties—the Communists and the Muslim Brotherhood—were decisive in any coalition government, an inherently unstable situation. The north was deeply racist toward the "infidels," the nonpeople of the south whom, less than a century ago, Muslim Arab slave traders had bought and sold. Many northerners still considered this the natural order of things, though it was unfashionable to say so. "We were the slavers; they were the slaves," Beshir had reminded us—a bitter legacy, as the protracted civil war had shown.

Given the Sudan's dilapidated infrastructure, rampant corruption, and devastated economy, a new democratic government composed of the same petty old men with their endless quarrels would probably not succeed. Beshir's mood had not improved a week later when we went to the sprawling, dusty university to say good-bye. "The traditional civilian leaders won't dare abolish sharia, and there can be no peace with the south without that," M.O.B. predicted. "I'm sorry to say this, but there will be another coup, probably in about three years. That was in 1985."

He was wrong by less than a year. . . .

Sudan Under the National Islamic Front

I had vowed never to return to "Islamic Sudan" after spending time in Khartoum in 1992, three years after Turabi's National Islamic Front had seized power. What I had seen during that trip had shocked and depressed me. But I had agreed to return once more to interview Turabi, now militant Sunni Islam's chief theorist, for *Foreign Affairs*, the foreign policy journal read by American and foreign members of the policy elite. I had really come back to see whether this Islamic paradise was on the brink of being overthrown, as my dissident Sudanese friends had told me. . . .

Turabi's modern, self-styled Islamic government had seized power in June 1989 in what seemed a standard military coup d'état. The democratic but ineffective government of Sadiq al-Mahdi, the Mahdi's great-grandson, was ensured legitimacy, respect, and political influence by his illustrious name alone. But Sadiq had been a disastrous prime minister. His indecisiveness, particularly his unwillingness to do what was needed to end the protracted civil war, had further impoverished Sudan and exasperated even his staunchest supporters.

Initially, few had known what to make of Lieutenant General Bashir and the junior officers who had arrested their commanders and seized power. After seven years of democratic chaos, the relieved Sudanese hoped that the new military junta would, as it had promised, end the debilitating civil war and save their country.

Within months, however, it became clear that Sudan was not ruled by the traditional Egyptian-tutored military alone but also by a clique of militant Islamists who had infiltrated the government, only a few of whom had risen through the armed forces. These quiet men behind the coup—Sudan's real rulers, as it would turn out—were activists in the National Islamic Front, the Muslim Brotherhood group long dominated by Turabi, who was, I recalled, also the deposed prime minister Sadiq al-Mahdi's brother-in-law.

Turabi, fluent—and persuasive—in at least four languages, had served in almost every one of Sudan's democratic governments and military regimes when he wasn't imprisoned by one of those same governments. Though he was jailed briefly after the 1989 coup, he soon emerged as the leading behind-the-scenes counselor to the young and inexperienced "Niffers" [National Islamic Front members]. . . .

In March 1991 the regime had introduced its own version of sharia that broadened the code to cover more offenses than were included by either Nimeiri or Sadiq al-Mahdi. This time, the penal code, the centerpiece of the new ostensibly Islamic order, reflected Turabi's literal interpretation of Islam's injunctions. Apostasy, defined as "every Muslim who propagates the renunciation of the creed of Islam, or publicly declares his renouncement thereof, by an expressed statement or conclusive act," meant death if the apostate did not "repent." An armed robber could be killed and then crucified if the robbery involved murder or rape; a thief could lose a right hand and a left foot. A married female adulterer was to be stoned to death; a Muslim who drank alcohol received up to forty lashes; a suicide attempt was punishable by a year in prison and/or a fine; an abortion that was not required to save the mother's life or was not the result of rape could result in up to three years in jail and/or a fine; a homosexual was subject to a hundred lashes and imprisonment of up to five years. "Gross indecency," which was defined as "any act contrary to another person's modesty," brought forty lashes, the same as the penalty for someone who wore an "indecent or immoral uniform which caused annoyance to public feelings.". . .

Turabi, whom the Reagan administration and Saudi Arabia had warmly supported for his staunch anticommunism, particularly in Afghanistan, was given a visa to the United States in 1992 even after Khartoum supported Iraq in the Gulf war and over the strong protests of human-rights and Sudanese exile groups. Sudan was not added to the State Department's list of countries that sponsor or aid terrorism until the summer of 1993, and only after five Sudanese nationals were indicted in New York in connection with the latter phase of the World Trade Center bombing plots—the scheme to blow up the United Nations and New York bridges and public buildings. . . .

[During my 1994 interview with him,] Turabi denied any

connection with the plots to bomb the World Trade Center and other public buildings and landmarks in New York, though there was substantial evidence of Sudanese complicity with the Islamic radicals involved in the conspiracy. Sheikh Omar Abdel Rahman, the Egyptian cleric who had inspired and blessed some of the operations, had spent several weeks in Sudan at Turabi's invitation shortly before his arrival in New York. Five of the eleven people convicted for their involvement in the planned attacks, moreover, were Sudanese nationals. Two members of Sudan's mission to the United Nations had developed extensive contacts with these compatriots, American investigators had told me. And Sudan's entire mission to the United Nations had been named as "unindicted coconspirators" in the plot to blow up New York bridges and monuments.

"I never met Omar Abdel Rahman here," Turabi asserted. "He never met one important person in this country. He wanted to go to Yemen, and there was no direct flight. So he came and stayed here for seven whole days!"

"Your government has behaved very badly," [Turabi] declared. "Five months ago, your ambassador came here, to this office, to read me a piece of paper," he said. I made a quick calculation. That would have been soon after Sudan was placed on the terrorist list in 1993. "He said to me: 'If you do anything to prejudice American interests anywhere in the world, anything, we'll take military measures against you that will destroy your economy entirely.' The paper had no heading, no signature. He read it without hearing anything from me. It was tantamount to war, an awful thing!" Turabi exploded. "I told him this was stupid of your government. Because if you threaten the Sudanese, they won't be frightened. They will be provoked, and they will react!"

"And if you bring Americans here, they will love you as in Vietnam. We would enjoy it! This is what I told your ambassador," he recounted. "So I know the American government is anti-Islamic." By now the smile was gone.

Many Sudanese now believed that their government had degraded Islam, Gassan Bedri, the dean and son of the founder of Afad University, a private college in Omdurman, told me.

"Islam, to them, has become merely a slogan," he said. Restaurants, roads, and buses have been given Islamic names, but only their names had changed. The economy was still ailing; roads were still unpaved; buses were still overcrowded. "They must brainwash the young," he said, "because their Islam is increasingly at odds with the people's Islam."

I recalled the frustration of Turabi's true spiritual and political predecessors—the Mahdi and *Kalifa* Abdullahi—over their inability to change Sudanese character. Charles Neufeld, a German merchant who had been enslaved in the Mahdiya for a decade, noted, for example, that Sudanese had never approved of the stonings of confessed women adulterers, though such punishment was mandated by the Koran. The government, he wrote, was unable to persuade those in attendance to throw stones with the sufficient force to stun or kill a sinner.

Increasingly, the modern-day Islamic regime was confronting that same Sudanese culture. Sudanese women might be forced to wear a head scarf under their *thobes*, but the N.I.F. would probably not "persuade" them to abandon *thobes* altogether. Public life may have become as arid as the desert surrounding Khartoum, but in private Sudanese tried to live normal lives, to celebrate the festivals they had always cherished. The Mahdiya had not changed Sudanese character, much less human nature. But many more Sudanese would suffer white Turabi's regime tried.

It was fashionable now to say that Turabi's government was dramatically different from those that had preceded it since independence. But was it really? Nimeiri, when he grew desperate enough, had imposed a crude Islamic penal code and vowed to build an Islamic state in Sudan. His ostensibly democratic successor, Sadiq al-Mahdi, had resisted abrogating sharia and had never tired of telling anyone who would listen that Sudan was an Islamic society. Like Turabi, he had dismissed Salman Rushdie[2] as a "silly man" who had

2. Rushdie is an Indian-born novelist and essayist. In 1989 Ayatollah Khomeini of Iran issued a fatwa promising Rushdie's execution for his criticism of Islam. Rushdie lived in hiding until 1997. As of 2005, Iran still has a fatwa out against him.

written a book "offensive" to Islam. The main difference between them was that the fastidious Sadiq, with his English porcelain, had believed in Islamic "democracy" and did not feel that people should be killed for apostasy that "undermined" an Islamic state.

Most Sudanse governments, to a greater or less degree, had reflected the spirit of Sudan's first Islamic regime: the nineteenth-century Mahdiya. Unlike Egypt, whose independence was secured by secular Arab nationalists, national liberation in Sudan was still connected in the country's consciousness with the Mahdi and hence with Islam. It would be difficult for Sudan to escape its twin legacy of slavery and militant Islam no matter who governed. This, in turn, had grave implications for Sudanese efforts to build a "secular," democratic state and to the end the civil strife between the Arabized north and Africanized south. . . .

I could only hope that one day the Sudanese would rise up, that they would pour into the streets, as they had in 1964 and 1985, to rid their country of these vile rulers. But the regime was prepared to kill thousands, and even if the Sudanese somehow managed to oust this "Islamic" police state, then what? Would the country not succumb to the same pathology that had debilitated it for so long? I could not help thinking about what Father Ohrwalder wrote after he had escaped from captivity in the Mahdiya almost a century ago. "The old days of rejoicing have vanished, all is anguish and fear, no man's life and property are secure; everyone has perforce to break the laws, which are most of them quite impractical, and at the same time, are in constant fear of spies, who are everywhere. There is no security, justice, or liberty; and happiness and content are unknown," the priest lamented. "The Sudan lies open in its desolation and nakedness. In the name of the Sudan people, whose misery I have seen, and in the name of all civilized nations," he wrote, how long would the civilized world "watch unmoved the outrages of the *kalifa* and the destruction of the Sudan people?"

This time, however, neither Britain nor anyone else would come save Sudan. Only the Sudanese could do so, and the price might be terrible—the outcome dubious.

Afghanistan Becomes an Islamic Dictatorship

Angelo Rasanayagam

Afghanistan became a major front in the Cold War be-tween the Soviet Union and the United States in the 1970s and 1980s, when the Soviets moved in troops to prop up Afghanistan's unpopular Marxist government. Mujahideen (Arab religious warriors) from all over the Middle East flocked to Afghanistan to fight the Communists. The U.S. Central Intelligence Agency worked with Pakistan's intel-ligence agencies to channel funds to the "Afghan freedom fighters" (as the Reagan administration called them). The Soviets finally withdrew from Afghanistan in 1989. The long war left Afghanistan in chaos, ripe for takeover in 1996 by the Taliban, the harshest Islamic regime yet known. As Angelo Rasanayagam describes in this selection, the Taliban worked hard to impose their extreme version of Islamic law on Afghanistan but did little to build up the necessary institutions of a state. They did not try to make their government representative of its citizens or respon-sive to practical needs. Instead, they gave great attention to regulating the length of beards and ensuring the chastity of women while leaving desperate problems like food and health services to international aid organizations. The Tal-iban were driven from power in 2001 after the United States went to war against Afghanistan as part of its global war against terrorism. Rasanayagam was chief of mission for the United Nations in Iran and a number of other countries before becoming director of the UN High Com-mission for Refugees office in Peshawar, Pakistan.

Angelo Rasanayagam, *Afghanistan: A Modern History*. London: I.B. Tauris & Co. Ltd. 2003. Copyright © 2003 by Angelo Rasanayagam. Reproduced by permission of the publisher.

The leader of the Taliban, Mullah Mohammad Omar, was born in 1959 into a family of poor landless peasants belonging to the Hotak clan of the Ghilzai Pashtuns. The family had no status, tribally or socially. As a young man of 21, Omar had to fend for his fatherless family and, needing a job, moved to the village of Singesar in the Maiwand district of Kandahar province [in Afghanistan], where he became the village mullah and opened a madrasa [religious school]. Between 1989 and 1992, after the Soviet withdrawal, he joined the fighting ranks of the Khalis faction of the Hizbi-i-Islami against the Najibullah regime. He lost an eye in combat. The installation of a mujahideen [holy warrior] government in Kabul had not brought peace, and groups of madrasa students and disillusioned mujahideen gathered round Omar to discuss what they could do to end the depredations of the Kandahari warlords. Their concerns were immediate. In early 1994 Omar enlisted the help of 30 madrasa students to free two teenage girls who had been abducted and raped by a warlord. He also intervened, or so the story goes, when two warlords fought over a young boy they wanted as a catamite. The victims were rescued and summary justice meted out to the perpetrators. Omar's reputation spread, and other appeals for his intervention began to pour in. The rest is history.

Wrapped in the Cloak of the Prophet

The Taliban militants chose Omar as their leader for his piety and not for any special qualities, charismatic or other. In March 1996, in anticipation of the projected Taliban attack on Kabul to topple the Rabbani government, some 1200 ulema and mullahs from around the country gathered in a shura in Kandahar and nominated Omar as Amir al-Muminin (Commander of the Believers), a military title first assumed by the second Islamic caliph [traditionally, the leader of Islam, successor to Mohammed], Omar, in Medina. Mullah Omar wrapped the Cloak of the Prophet around him to give him Islamic legitimacy as amir of Afghanistan. No Afghan ruler had adopted the Islamic title since Dost Mohammad in 1834; the use of the Prophet's cloak, preserved in Kandahar, was even more symbolic. The council that nominated him was not the traditional Afghan loya jirga but the Arab shura, an Islamic council convened to achieve community consensus (*ijma*).

The method of selection was a throwback to the shura convened by the third of the first four 'Rightly Guided Caliphs', 'Uthman, to elect his successor. The legitimacy that this act conferred was Islamic, thereby making it both religious and political. As [Western expert on political Islam] Olivier Roy says, 'one need only skim the literature of the ulemas, or the Islamists, or listen to the sermons in the mosques, to admit that there is an Islamic political imagination dominated by a single paradigm: that of the first community of believers at the time of the Prophet and of the first four caliphs.'

In Afghanistan the ulema directly and collectively assumed power, electing Mullah Omar, who was neither charismatic nor a dynamic tribal leader, as their amir. Although of undeniably Deobandi inspiration, they applied a 'legal system' based exclusively on their particular interpretation of the shari'a that incorporated elements of the Pashtun tribal code, the Pashtunwali. But when the two were in conflict or in contradiction, the primacy of the shari'a [religious law] was reaffirmed, as in Mullah Omar's 1998 decree restoring certain property rights of women that the code violated. Despite their anti-Shi'a stance and bloodily repressive actions against the [Shi'ite religious sect] Hazaras, which is Deobandi and Wahhabi in inspiration, the Taliban formed an alliance subsequently with the Hazara Shi'ite religious hierarchy led by Shaykh Akbari. This alliance was founded on their common relationship to the categories of the ulema and would be incomprehensible in a narrowly tribal or ethnically oriented system.

The Taliban in Power

The shura left unanswered the question of how the Taliban would govern Afghanistan, nor did it lay out any plans for the country's economic and social development. Ruling structures did, however, emerge after the ousting of the Rabbani government in September 1996. These consisted of a ten-member Supreme Shura in Kandahar presided over by Omar and two committees that reported to him and took directives from him—a military shura and a Kabul shura. The Kabul shura was in fact a sort of cabinet with each of its 14 members assuming nominal ministerial functions.

Although members of the Kabul shura, the 'ministers', were more pragmatic and flexible—as in their dealings with the United Nations and NGOs [nongovernmental organizations]—their 'decisions' were often overruled by Mullah Omar and his dogmatic Kandahar shura. There was thus a confusing dichotomy of power that did not make life easy for those who had to deal with them. The Taliban had a unified but not a monolithic power structure.

When the mujahideen entered Kabul in April 1992, there still remained a government infrastructure of ministries and municipalities functioning chiefly at the lower administrative levels. This infrastructure collapsed after the arrival in 1996 of the Taliban in the city, which they considered a nest of corruption. Their subsequent pruning of the government bureaucracy was part of their explicit policy of rooting out corruption. The Taliban replaced all senior Hazara, Tajik and Uzbek bureaucrats [that is, members of three clan groups] with inexperienced Pashtuns so that ministries effectively ceased to function. Their exclusion of women from employment also meant that schools ceased to operate, the majority of teachers being women. Their gender policies likewise sorely affected the health services.

There were no native Kabulis in the Kabul shura that dealt with the day-to-day problems of government. It referred important decisions to the Supreme Shura in Kandahar, which was dominated by Mullah Omar's original friends and colleagues, mainly Durrani Pashtuns. They were called 'the Kandaharis'. Although the core membership appeared permanent, provincial governors, military commanders, tribal elders and ulema took part in the Kandahar shura when important questions were debated or when strategy was being planned. It was thus in practice a loose and amorphous body.

Senior Taliban officials in Kabul, Herat and Mazar, such as the governors, mayors and police chiefs, were invariably Kandahari Pashtuns who did not speak Dari, the lingua franca of these cities, or did not speak it well. There were some non-Kandaharis among the provincial governors, but they were all from outside the region they administered, and were prevented from building up a local power-base by Omar, who shifted them around, or sent them as commanders to the battle fronts. Their power was even further reduced by the lack of funds at their disposal to carry out any serious economic rehabilitation or development. Thus political power was centralized at the level of the Kandaharis under Omar, to whom all revenues were also remitted. He reportedly made payments in cash, for such items as the salaries of administrators and military officers, from tin trunks kept under his bed.

Mullah Omar also headed the military shura which had a chief of general staff and chiefs of staff for the army and air force. But there was no clearly discernible hierarchical structure of officers and commanders. The Taliban movement began and largely remained a military organization, composed initially of madrasa student volunteers and defectors from the mujahideen and warlord militias, and later enlarged by conscription. Individual Pashtun commanders from specific Pashtun regions were responsible for recruiting men, paying them and looking after their needs in the field, acquiring the resources to do so—money, food, fuel, transport, weapons and ammunition—from the military shura. The majority of Taliban fighters were not paid salaries and it was their commander who was responsible for paying his men an adequate sum of money when they returned to their families on leave. Those who were paid regular salaries were those from the former communist armed forces, such as those commanded by Najibullah's defence minister, General Tanai, who defected to Pakistan after his failed coup in 1990 and was later mobilized by the ISI [Pakistan's Inter-Services Intelligence agency] to assist the Taliban in their drive to power. These Pashtun mercenaries—tank drivers, gunners, pilots and mechanics—perhaps made all the difference in making the Taliban an effective fighting machine. . . .

After their occupation of Herat and Kabul, the Taliban closed all schools for girls, forbade female employment (which meant in effect that boys' schools could also not function as the majority of their teachers were women), confined women to their homes, imposed the *burqa*—a tight head covering that allowed only the eyes to be seen—on women venturing outside their homes, and prohibited male doctors from attending to their women patients in the few functioning hospitals and clinics. These injunctions were carried out by an ever-vigilant religious police on the Saudi Arabian model called the Ministry for the Promotion of Virtue and the Suppression of Vice. It was perhaps the only well-manned and well-funded institution to function under the Taliban.

Taliban strictures came to a head in 1998: new edicts, inspired by their own bizarre version of the shari'a, were issued, stipulating the exact lengths of beard to be mandatorily worn by adult males, prescribing a list of Muslim names to be given to newborn children, abolishing the celebration of the traditional spring festival of Nawroz (considered an un-Islamic relic of ancient pagan rites), enforcing the previous ban on all music and dancing and the possession of music tapes and video cassettes, and the flying of kites. But it was the gender issue that raised the greatest international outcry. In Kabul the Taliban shut down the few makeshift schools for girls organized in private homes by volunteer female teachers; the religious police forced women off the streets and insisted that householders blacken their windows to render their women invisible from the street.

The Taliban vs. Aid Workers

Taliban hardliners also seemed intent on forcing UN agencies and NGOs that employed large numbers of educated Afghan women in their programmes to leave the country by provoking a number of incidents that tested their patience to the limit. In February 1998 the UN halted all its aid operations in Kandahar and pulled out its staff after the Taliban had beaten up some of them. In June the Taliban barred all women from attending general hospitals, and ordered all Muslim female expatriate staff visiting or working in the country to be chaperoned by a male blood relative (*mehram*) —an impossible demand to meet, as agencies had increased the number of female aid-workers to satisfy previous Taliban pressures and to gain access to Afghan women needing help. The Taliban then insisted that all NGOs working in Kabul move out of their offices and relocate to a single disused and decrepit building, the former Kabul Polytechnic. Twenty out of 30 NGOs voted to pull out of the country if the Taliban demand was not retracted, but the Taliban insisted that the issue was not negotiable. The European Union (EU), a major funding source for NGOs, suspended all humanitarian aid to areas under Taliban control. Lakhdar Brahimi [the U.N. special envoy to Afghanistan] went public regarding the UN's frustrations by saying that the Taliban was 'an organization that hands out edicts that prevent us from doing our job'. But the Taliban did not relent. On 20 July they closed down all NGO offices by force, and an exodus of foreign staff began. On the same day the bodies of two staff members from the UNHCR and WFP [World Food Program] who had previously been kidnapped were found in Jalalabad, but no explanations for their deaths were offered by the Taliban.

No one questions the need for humanitarian assistance in Afghanistan—a country that has long been near the bottom of the world's list in terms of human development. Over 20 years of war, during which over a million people are estimated to have died and 700,000 women been made widows, added new records to the grim list: the number of refugees and internally displaced people, the increasingly large numbers dependent on food support, the proportion of physically and mentally disabled people, the widespread lethal presence of land mines and unexploded ordnance, the collapse of industrial activities and of the opportunities for gainful employment outside a precarious indigenous agriculture. The UNDP dropped Afghanistan from its rankings in the 1997 edition of its *UN Development Report* when the gathering of relevant data became unmanageable.

Three successive years of drought made the situation infinitely worse. According to the UN some 3.8 million people were close to famine conditions. A three member USAID technical team that surveyed affected areas of western and northern Afghanistan in June 2001 confirmed the possibility of starvation unless urgent measures were taken. At the time, the WFP was feeding 3 million Afghans a day, in the cities, in camps for internally displaced persons and in rural areas, with food mainly donated by the United States. Were the efforts of the UN system and of the NGOs to be disrupted for any reason, there would have been a colossal humanitarian disaster. . . .

A Disinterest in State Building

Curiously enough, in the five years after they occupied Kabul, the heart and symbol of past state authority, the Taliban did not appear to have given any priority to state-building, nor to the development of the economic and social infrastructure that is essential for the functioning of a viable state and for the welfare of its citizens. According to [journalist] Ahmed Rashid: 'the limited reconstruction which the Taliban has undertaken is entirely limited to improving the efficiency of smuggling and drugs trafficking, such as repairing roads, setting up petrol pumps, and inviting US businessmen to set up a mobile telephone network which will qualitatively speed up the movement of drugs and illicit trade'.

In fact traders found a new social status in Afghanistan. Kandahar, the Taliban 'capital' from where the reclusive Mullah Omar issued his decrees, is located on a principal axis of trade and developed into a busy commercial centre, with trading networks established between Pakistan and Central Asia, and with the United Arab Emirates where large numbers of Afghans and Pakistanis lived. This was all part of a decentralized laissez-faire economy that was in keeping with the centuries-old traditions of Islam, where the right to hold private property is held sacred, and trading is considered a legitimate source of wealth. . . .

Pakistan . . . had prematurely recognized the Taliban as the government of Afghanistan during their temporary occupation of Mazar-i-Sharif in September 1997, persuading Saudi Arabia and the United Arab Emirates to follow suit. In October 1999, with 90 per cent of the country and 27 of its 31 provinces under its virtual control, the Taliban laid formal claim to the Afghan seat at the United Nations. Their bid was not only rebuffed, but the UN's Security Council voted that same month to impose economic sanctions, including a ban on international flights to and from Afghanistan. The sanctions were to take effect in 30 days if the Taliban did not extradite, for trial in a US court, the Saudi businessman, Osama bin Laden.

The Taliban and Osama bin Laden

Bin Laden, or at least members of a terrorist network traceable to him known as al-Qaeda, had been implicated in the simultaneous bombings of the US embassies in Dar es Salaam, Tanzania, and Nairobi, Kenya, on 7 August 1998. The suicide bombings had killed 235 people including 13 Americans, and injured 5500 others. The majority of the victims were African civilians. The US retaliated on 28 August by firing 67 cruise missiles from aircraft carriers in the Indian Ocean at bin Laden's alleged terrorist bases in Zhawar in Paktia province. Bin Laden himself had drawn attention to his anti-American crusade in a 28 May interview given to an ABC News reporter, John Miller, describing a so-called *fatwa* [Islamic religious ruling] he had issued calling for the killing of Americans: 'We do not differentiate between those dressed in military uniforms and civilians; they are all targets in the fatwa.' But the retaliatory (and ineffective) missile attacks in Afghanistan, and on a pharmaceutical factory in Khartoum, Sudan, made bin Laden an instant hero of many in the Muslim world.

The United States took the lead in keeping the bin Laden issue at the top of the agenda in their efforts to combat international terrorism. Bin Laden was again implicated in the suicide bombing attack on the USS *Cole* in the harbour of Aden, Yemen, in September 1999, and headed the FBI's list of most wanted men. An initial reward of US$5 million offered for his capture was raised to $10 million. On 19 December 2000 the UN Security Council imposed new sanctions on Afghanistan, expanding the list to include the closure of terrorist training camps, the freezing of Taliban assets abroad, and an embargo on the import of arms and of the chemicals required for the production of heroin. The Taliban response was to reject the sanctions, and their leader, Mullah Omar, was provoked to state unequivocally: 'We will never hand Osama over to anyone and [will] protect him with our blood at any cost.'

While the Taliban pursued their diplomatic campaign for recognition of their regime as the government of Afghanistan, their refusal to remove one of the chief obstacles to international recognition—the extradition of bin Laden—was a contradiction which could be explained only by their espousal of a pan-Islamist ideology that pursued its own inner logic, and was remarkably consistent in practice.

Mullah Omar was neither a head of state nor a head of government. He was proclaimed 'Commander of the Believers' by an assembly of ulema and he covered himself symbolically with the Cloak of the Prophet. He was amir of an Islamic emirate that was more religious than statist in its connotations, and Kandahar, not Kabul, was the 'capital' of Taliban Afghanistan. Theirs was a 'theocratic' regime, legitimized by religion and not by a nationalist ideology nor by tribal genealogies, which had no equivalent in the contemporary Muslim world. . . .

However perverse the Taliban ideology, which made mainstream Muslims flinch, it was applied to their actions with a consistency bordering on the irrational. To the Taliban the monumental Buddhas of the Bamyan Valley that had awed travellers and visitors for centuries were only symbols of idolatry, susceptible to worship—contemptible vestiges of the pre-Islamic past. Their wanton destruction in February 2001 was carried out despite worldwide appeals at the highest levels, by leading religious authorities in the Muslim world such as the Rector of Al-Ashar, or even by their ideological mentor, Maulana Samiul Haq of the leading Deobandi theological school near Peshawar. To the Taliban, the Bamyan statues (and the pre-Islamic tombs, shrines and priceless images in the Kabul museum that were also destroyed) were symbols of the non-Muslim 'Other', like the Hindu merchants of Kabul's bazaars who were required to wear shameful badges of identity (such as the Jews of medieval Europe or, as people recalled with a shudder, the Jews who went to their slaughter in Nazi death camps).

Taliban fanaticism and intolerance went against the grain of traditional Afghan attitudes influenced by Sufism, the mystical side of Islam that is tolerant of diversity. The arrest in August 2001 of eight Western humanitarian workers who had been accused of Christian proselytism was also a result of their peculiar mind-set, their pseudo-religious paranoia. As some observers had noted at the time, and revelations since September 11 have now confirmed, the fanatical intolerance that drove the Taliban to actions that were uncharacteristic from an Afghan point of view were actually signs of the increased ideological hold on the simple Mullah Omar of the radical Wahhabi militant, Osama bin Laden, and his foreign al-Qaeda entourage that had their headquarters in Afghanistan.

With regard to their policies towards women, when time-honoured tribal practices of the Pashtuns were seen to be in contradiction with the shari'a, the primacy of the shari'a was upheld under threat of punishment, as in Mullah Omar's seven-point decree in the autumn of 1998 with regard to women's rights in matters of inheritance and marriage. The sixth point declared notably that a woman's marriage was her personal affair, and that no one in the family, including her father or a brother, had the right to interfere. . . .

In Afghanistan the Taliban showed themselves unwilling, or unable, to build the institutions of a state, or to assume any responsibilities for the social and economic welfare of their fellow countrymen. These tasks they left to the international community of UN agencies and NGOs funded by foreign donors. However, far from encouraging them in their humanitarian endeavours, or assisting them, they kept creating difficulties for them. Their priorities lay elsewhere: fighting their opponents and engaging in a militant but woolly-minded pan-Islamic campaign inspired by dangerous foreign terrorist groups that could create only mischief for their neighbours.

Islamic Fundamentalism in Pakistan

Samina Yasmeen

Pakistan was created in 1947 when the British colonial possession of India was divided into India, a predominantly Hindu country, and Pakistan, a predominantly Muslim country. Since Pakistan's founding there has been a struggle among those who favor a secular government, those who seek a liberal Islamic government, and those who desire a fundamentalist Islamic government. In addition, as Samina Yasmeen explains in this article, Pakistanis have had to endure widespread government corruption and frequent military coups. Yasmeen notes that over the years, Pakistan's various governments have nurtured radical Islamic organizations, which they have then found difficult to control. In the late 1990s Pakistan was virtually the only ally of Afghanistan's fundamentalist Islamic Taliban government. After the terrorist attacks of September 11, 2001, however, Pakistan became a U.S. ally in the war on terror, and the military government of General Pervez Musharraf began to seek a "middle way" of governing that avoids either extreme of secular modernism or Islamic orthodoxy. Yasmeen is a senior lecturer in international politics in the Department of Political Science at the University of Western Australia, Perth.

Pakistan is a classic example of a state which has experienced shifts along the spectrum of liberal and orthodox Islamic views. It also stands out for the role played by the state in sponsoring Islamic orthodoxy and then finding itself a hostage to the societal forces thus unleashed. . . . To some extent the origin of this conflict resides in the independence struggle for Pakistan. The leaders of the Muslim League used Islam to mobilise support among the masses for carving out an independent state for Muslims from British India. The idea, while originating in central India, was used to garner support for such a state comprising East Bengal, North West Frontier Province (NWFP), the Punjab, Sindh and Baluchistan.

Pakistan Was Not Envisioned as a Theocracy

Despite the use of Islam as a unifying force, however, the founders of Pakistan did not envision a theocratic Islamic state. On the contrary, they either did not address the issue of the nature of the state that was to be created for Muslims of British India, or favoured a liberal Islamic state. This was evident in the approach adopted by Mohammad Ali Jinnah, the founder of Pakistan, around the time of the partition of India in August 1947. He avoided identifying the place of Islam in the proposed state for Muslims. When religion was mentioned, he clearly expressed his opposition to turning Pakistan into a 'theocratic state ruled by priests with a divine mission'. Equally significantly, in his inaugural address to Pakistan's Constituent Assembly on 11 August 1947, he presented a vision of state for Muslims which was liberal and moderate enough to accommodate cultural and religious differences. 'You will find', he said, 'that in the course of time Hindus would cease to be Hindus and Muslims would cease to be Muslims, not in the religious sense, because that is the personal faith of each individual, but in the political sense as citizens of the State. . . .

Islamists and Liberals Vie for Control

Religious groups in Pakistan, however, opposed the liberal Islamic notions of a state. Interestingly, they had initially opposed the creation of Pakistan on religious grounds. They argued that nationalism and state sovereignty were Western ideas that ran counter to the notion of the *umma* [religious community] in Islam. Muslims were seen as part of a global community of believers who could not be bound by or restricted to artificially created state boundaries. So opposed were they to the creation of Pakistan that some of them declared Jinnah to be a *kafir* (non-believer). Once Pakistan was created, some of these religious scholars, notably Mawlana Abul Kalam Azad, adhered to their opposition and chose India as their home. Others, including Mawlana Mawdudi of Jamaat-i Islami opted for Pakistan. The choice was accompanied by a shift in the views on Pakistan. Instead of adhering to the idea of a global *umma*, Mawdudi and other scholars including Mawlana Shabbir Ahmed Othmani of Jamiat Ulama-i Islam, came to emphasise that Pakistan was created as an Islamic state and not merely a state for Muslims. The emphasis on the theocratic nature of the state prompted them to demand that the primacy of divine will be acknowledged in the construction of the new political order. The orthodox interpretations of the Qur'an and prophetic traditions were to be the source of law in the new state and not some liberal notions of humans determining the constitution of Pakistan.

In this struggle for opposing notions of the Pakistani state, liberals/modernists held sway for a major part of the country's formative years. They acknowledged the ideas presented by the ulema [Islamic clergy] and even incorporated into the constitution but stopped short of changing the liberal Islamic nature of the state. The ulema assisted them in this process by generally not agreeing among themselves. The First Constituent Assembly, for instance, adopted the 'Objectives Resolution' on 12 March 1948 which affirmed that Pakistan would be an Islamic state, and that its laws would be drafted on the basis of Qur'an and sunna. To facilitate this process it also established the Basic Principles Committee (BPC) which was supported by a board of Talimat-i Islamia (Islamic Teachings) under the chairmanship of Mawlana Nadvi. But the first BPC report ignored the advice given by the board while drafting its suggestions on how to ensure that Islam formed the basis of the polity. The attitude caused an uproar among ulema who tried to jointly enunciate the principles of an Islamic state. In response to this reaction, the second BPC report issued in December 1952 accorded a special status to ulema in ensuring that no proposed legislation ran counter to

Islamic principles. However, when Pakistan's first constitution was adopted in 1956, no mechanism was provided for that purpose. Instead, the constitution restricted itself to declaring Pakistan an Islamic Republic, emphasising the role of Islam, and requiring the President to set up an organisation of Islamic research. Specifically, no legal procedure was established to ensure that laws repugnant to Islam could not be enacted.

This process of acknowledging but not allowing the orthodox ulema to determine the place of Islam in Pakistan continued as the military gained strength and ultimately took over power in 1958. As a successor to the British Indian army, and by virtue of being trained and equipped by the United States during the early days of the Cold War, the military stood for liberal/modernist ideas. Instead of subscribing to orthodox Islamic ideas, it favoured the idea of realising Pakistan's true potential as an Asian state. . . .

Islamic Parties Gain Power

The state policies, however, coexisted with an imperceptible shift in societal attitudes towards Islam. The shift was caused by a number of factors. Paramount was the traumatic experience of the Indo-Pakistan War of 1971 which resulted in the secession of East Pakistan as Bangladesh and the imprisonment of more than 90,000 Pakistani prisoners of war by India. As in the case of Egypt following the Arab-Israeli war of 1967, the war with India caused a reassessment in Pakistan of the place accorded to Islam in the country. People wondered if the defeat had been caused by them veering away from the 'true' path of Islam. The process was paralleled by the rise of an educated middle class after the developmental policies of the 1960s. At the same time mass migration of an unskilled labour force to the Middle East enabled a new group of Pakistanis to experience fast, upward social mobility. As in other Muslim states, these new entrants into the middle class felt unsure and insecure in a system where the elite predominantly subscribed to Western and liberal Islamic ideas. The situation provided a fertile ground for Islamic parties, including the Jamaat-i Islami and the Jamiat

Ulama-i Islam which presented themselves as the inter-preters of 'real' Islam. They also targeted educational institutions, including colleges and universities, where student wings of the Islamic parties emerged as major contenders for power. The tide slowly began to shift away from the emphasis on the pre-eminence of the human will and towards accepting the significance of divine will. By 1977, enough change had taken place for the opposition parties to join together and campaign for the elections on the grounds of introducing *Nizami-e-Mustafa* (a system of government based on the traditions of the Prophet Muhammad) in Pakistan.

The [government of Ali Bhutto (1971–1977)] remained impervious to these changes until after the 1977 elections which were heavily rigged. Faced with the backlash from the opposition, the Pakistan National Alliance (PNA), he resorted to the selective use of Islam for retaining power. In the interest of regime maintenance, he responded favourably to the suggestions by the CII [Council of Islamic Ideology] to ban gambling and horse-racing, alcohol, and night clubs. He also declared Friday to be a weekly holiday. The PNA refused to accept these changes and demanded his removal. The resulting tension and civil unrest finally created the justification for the military regime to intervene in July 1977 and take over power.

The Military Regime and State-Sponsored Islam

The military's intervention ushered Pakistan into an era of state-sponsored Islam. General [Muhammad Zia-ul-Haq, leader of the 1977 military coup] had initially expressed the intention of holding fresh elections within ninety days. Soon he shelved these plans and chose to rule Pakistan indefinitely. To legitimise this shift and ensure the process of regime maintenance, he resorted to a revised interpretation of Islam's place in Pakistani society and politics. In marked contrast to the previous regimes, Zia shifted to the divine will end of the spectrum. Repeating the arguments presented by orthodox ulema over the last three decades, he argued that 'as a soldier of Islam' he was determined to realise Pakistan's true identity as an Islamic state. This was to be done by implementing Islamic teachings enshrined in the Qur'an and sunna under the guidance of religious leaders. Such an approach led to a de facto alliance between the military and Islamic parties, particularly the Jamaat-i Islami under Mawlana Mawdudi's leadership.

Building upon the ideas of Mawdudi, General Zia took a number of steps aimed at truly Islamising Pakistan. A number of institutions were set up for the purpose and the process was guided by the CII. Although the 1973 Constitution had been held in abeyance, the council was allowed to function, and its area of operation widened. It was entrusted with the task of making recommendations and advising the government on the Islamic nature of proposed or already promulgated laws. It was also to engage in the process of 'Islamising' the constitution. . . .

The process of institutionalisation also extended downwards into society. Religious schools (dini madaris), became the main beneficiaries of this process. Madaris (sing. madrasa) had traditionally coexisted with formal educational institutions in Pakistan. Zulfiqar Ali Bhutto had attempted to streamline them and also formally recognise their qualifications. But the number of these madaris, with their focus on religious education, had remained limited. The Zia regime changed the pattern by providing support to those enrolled in the madaris and, hence, encouraging the proliferation of such institutions. . . .

The Cold War Protects Pakistan from Western Criticism

Religious minorities became the other major target of the symbolic Islamisation in Pakistan. As 3.3 per cent of the country's total population, Christians, Hindus, Ahmadis, Sikhs and other religious groups were given rights as equal citizens in the 1973 Constitution. Soon after coming to power, General Zia-ul-Haq ended this equality. In September 1978 he introduced an amendment to the electoral system which was later embodied in the 1973 Constitution (Articles 51 and 106). By virtue of this amendment, separate electorates were created for non-Muslims in National and provincial assemblies which became operational in 1985. Not only could non-Muslims not vote for Muslim candidates, but they also had to elect their own representatives from across the country and/or the provinces. The psychological space available to non-Muslims was also reduced by an amendment to the Pakistan Penal Code (295–C) which made blasphemy punishable by death. While blasphemy had always been a criminal act, by making even insinuation a criminal act, the law opened the doors to those who did not want non-Muslims to practise their religion freely. At the same time, Ahmadis, who were declared non-Muslim by the Parliament in 1974, were barred from calling their places of worship 'mosques', reciting *Azaan*, and directly or indirectly passing themselves as Muslims or referring to their religion as Islam.

These discriminatory acts would have normally drawn criticism from western liberal societies. But regional developments created conditions in which General Zia's agenda for introducing orthodox interpretations of Islam was supported by western liberal democracies. The Soviet invasion of Afghanistan in December 1979 caused the United States to identify Pakistan as the front-line state that could help roll the Soviets back. In return for economic and military assistance, General Zia accepted this role and opened up Pakistani territory for training camps where people could be prepared for Jihad. Dini madaris played a major role in this process. They emerged as the centres where the language of jihad was communicated to those enrolled with the ultimate aim of using them in the war against the Soviet Union. The process necessitated a working relationship between the US Central Intelligence Agency (CIA) and Pakistan's Inter-Services Intelligence agency (ISI). The ISI became the main conduit for weapons and funds to those engaged in jihad in Afghanistan. It also developed an interest in retaining and further promoting the cause of jihad as a means of strengthening its own position within Pakistani governmental structures. . . .

Promoting Jihad in Afghanistan and Kashmir

The return to democracy after General Zia's sudden death in August 1988 did not mark the end of the primacy of orthodox Islam in Pakistan. To a great extent this stemmed from the political structure General Zia had established during his eleven years of rule. As a quid pro quo for return to nominal democracy in 1985, he had secured an amendment to the 1973 constitution and altered the balance of power between the president and the prime minister. Upon his death, therefore, a troika emerged in which the military remained the balancer. It became apparent that any elected prime minister would remain in power for the term of the pleasure of the president and/or the Chief of the Army Staff (COAS). This, in turn, added a strong element of uncertainty among the two dominant political parties: the Pakistan Muslim League (PML) led by Nawaz Sharif and the PPP led by Benazir Bhutto. Unsure of how long they would remain in power, both the parties and their respective leaders focused on retaining the goodwill of other parliamentarians and the military. They also engaged in rampant corruption with the view to recouping the amount they had already spent in the elections. Cumulatively, these practices created a situation in which the democratically elected governments could not last, on average, for more than two and a half years. . . .

The eleven years of state-sponsored Islam had created groups within government circles with a vested interest in perpetuating orthodoxy. The military, for instance, had metamorphosed from being a secular and professional organisation to one which included elements that believed in and supported the policies initiated by General Zia. His death did not weaken their views. On the contrary, they built upon the orthodoxy introduced during the military regime and introduced the notion of religiously based strategic depth. Believing that they had succeeded in pushing the Soviets out of Afghanistan, they opted for pursuing a similar policy vis-à-vis the Indian part of Kashmir. The unfinished agenda of the partition, they maintained, could also be finished in Kashmir by waging a jihad. By installing a pro-Islamabad Islamic regime in Afghanistan, the argument evolved, Pakistan could also acquire a strategic depth that would deny the Indians any significant gains in a war. The logic necessitated the continuation of an active role by the

ISI as the promoter of the concept of jihad, as well as the supplier of weapons to those willing to operate in the Indian part of Kashmir. This, in turn, contributed to a proliferation in the number and variety of Islamic groups in Pakistan. . . .

The links between elements in the state and non-state Islamists were further strengthened after the rise of the [radical Islamic] Taliban in Afghanistan. That the Taliban were educated in the language of jihad in madrasa was evidence for others that 'real Islam' could prevail. As the Taliban proceeded to implement an extremely rigid version of Islam in Afghanistan, the Islamists in Pakistan came to develop their own history of regional struggles. The criticism in international circles was seen as evidence for the validity of true Islamic ideas and was placed in a historical context: like the first Islamic state in Medina, a number of those subscribing to orthodox Islamic ideas argued, the Taliban were also facing opposition and oppression from non-believers. But the oppression was to be short-lived with a pre-destined victory for Taliban. The 'success' of the Taliban was seen as proof that similar ideas could prosper in Pakistan as well. . . .

Return to Military Rule and Liberal Islam

On 12 October 1999, the military once again seized power in Pakistan. General Pervez Musharraf presented a vision of a united, prosperous and secure Pakistan as the agenda for the regime which was 'forced to intervene' in politics. By emphasising the comprehensive, and not fractional, nature of security, he clearly established his liberal outlook. Combined with his identification of Kamal Atatürk [the secular-minded founder of modern] Turkey as his role model, this articulation of a security concept favoured a liberal-Islamic outlook. Interestingly, however, initially General Musharraf avoided openly steering the country away from the orthodox interpretations of Islam. . . .

It was, however, not until the terrorist attacks on the United States on 11 September 2001 that the General gained an opportunity to openly address the issue of rampant orthodoxy and Islamic militancy.

The terrorist attacks placed Pakistan in an unenviable position of being the only state that had not only sponsored the Taliban but had also maintained close contacts on the ground with the ultra-orthodox regime. Paradoxically, these links and the geographical realities turned Pakistan into the front-line state against the Taliban regime and the al-Qaeda based in Afghanistan. Faced with a possible choice between joining the US 'War on Terrorism' or being 'sent back to the stone age', General Musharraf opted for the former option. He agreed to provide logistical facilities and access to airspace to the US forces on the condition that Indian and Israeli troops would not be involved in any planned strikes against Afghanistan. The decision inflamed the Islamic orthodox groups in Pakistan. . . .

While Islamic groups threatened jihad, joined the Taliban in Afghanistan, and organised demonstrations, the military regime became the harbinger of liberal Islamic values. The rapid demise of the Taliban regime after the US attacks further paved way for the liberal Islamic agenda. Against the background of the rising tensions with India after the attack on the Indian parliament on 13 December 2001, General Musharraf adopted a more aggressive strategy targeting Islamic orthodoxy and militancy in Pakistan. He banned the Islamic militant groups in Pakistan on 12 January 2002. This decision directly targeted groups like Lashkar-i Taiba, Jaish Muhammad and Harkatul Mujahedden which had been operating from within Pakistan with assistance from groups within the army. But realising that the militant groups had found a fertile ground in the dini madaris, the General also targeted the religious schools. Instead of closing them down, he argued for madaris that took into account the requirements of the modern era and educated their students accordingly. The demand for a revision of the curriculum was accompanied by the requirements of making these institutions more transparent. The suggestion that Muslims need to take into account changed circumstances, however, was not restricted to the dini madaris alone. General Musharraf has argued that the Muslim *umma* needs to revert back to the liberal, enlightened past in which Muslims played a major role in various fields. The language being used for this, however, is conciliatory: instead of drawing a distinction between liberal and orthodox approaches, General Musharraf has been arguing for the 'middle way' where Muslims shun extreme modernism as well as militancy. The military regime in Pakistan, after a lapse of more than two decades, has emerged as an agent for liberal Islamic values in Pakistan.

Chapter 3

Islamic Terrorism

Turning Points

IN WORLD HISTORY

Islamic Fundamentalists' Increasing Use of Suicide Attacks

Shaul Shay

Islamic fundamentalism has inspired a great deal of terrorist activity, including suicide attacks. Militants find recruits to carry out these attacks by promising them entry into the Garden of Eden after their death. As Shaul Shay explains in this selection, the theological justifications for suicide attacks were pioneered by Iran's Ayatollah Khomeini and his fellow Shiite clerics during Iran's desperate war with Iraq in the 1980s. Both suicide and attacks on citizens are expressly prohibited by the Koran, so Khomeini had to use novel and convoluted arguments to justify his support of them. Khomeini's ideology was adopted by religious clerics and the radical Shiite terrorist group Hizballah in Lebanon. Since the early 1990s Palestinian fundamentalists have also carried out many suicide attacks against Israelis. Shay served as a senior career officer in the military intelligence division of the Israeli Defense Forces (IDF). He is the author of *Endless Jihad: The Mujahidin, the Taliban and Bin Laden* and *The Shahids: Islam and Suicide Attacks*.

Following the [1979] Islamic revolution in Iran, and since the beginning of the 1980s, suicide attacks perpetrated by Shiite and Iranian entities have become a prominent characteristic of Shiite terror. These attacks took a high toll and proved to have an impressive psychological impact, particularly vis-à-vis Western countries and Israel, which served as central targets for these attacks.

Shaul Shay, *The Shahids: Islam and Suicide Attacks*, trans. Rachel Lieberman. Piscataway, NJ: Transaction Publishers, 2004. Copyright © 2004 by The Interdisciplinary Center for Herzliya Projects. Reproduced by permission of Transaction Publishers, conveyed through Copyright Clearance Center, Inc.

Khomeini's Religious Justification for Suicide Attacks

The outlook of the leader of the Iranian Islamic revolution, the Ayatollah Khomeini, was structured on his interpretation of several key issues in Shiite Islam and on adapting the solutions to the reality of the twentieth century. In the center of his theory there stands the necessity for an activist approach to promote the goals of Islam and achieve redemption. Khomeini's theory grew and spread against the background of the Shiites' historical frustration, a difficult socioeconomic situation, and the escalation of fundamentalist thinking in the Muslim world.

Khomeini regarded "revolutionary violence" as a central tool for the solution of the problems in Islamic society, as well as the resolution of the individual's problems. The struggle is first and foremost directed at the purification of Islamic society from within, starting with the Shiite community and subsequently expanding to the wider Islamic circle. The struggle does not cease in the Islamic arena; it is designated to crush the "evil root"—the superpowers that cause world destruction. Thus, the revolutionary message transmitted by Khomeini is universal, with the Shiites representing the downtrodden of the entire world.

Khomeini provided the religious/ideological and rational justifications for the use of violence to promote the goals of Islam, and placed the Jihad and "self-sacrifice" at the forefront of his philosophy. This fact gave the Shia a worldwide reputation of a fanatic religion that demands martyrdom of its believers in the name of its goals. One of the prominent innovations in Khomeini's theory was the permission to sacrifice an individual's life for the realization of the goals of Islamic society, in contrast to the accepted Islamic ruling that prohibits suicide.

Khomeini used several arguments to justify his stance: First, as he believed that the individual lives in a corrupt society whose main role is to meet material needs, therefore when the individual sacrifices himself he is sacrificing something material for an elevated spiritual goal (sacrifice of the "materialistic I" for the "spiritual I"). Khomeini regarded the story of the death of the Imam Hussein [A.D. 626–680] as the main argument justifying martyrdom in the name of Islam. When Hussein set out on his long journey from Hejaz to Karbala, according to this interpretation, he knew that he would not return from his travels and that he would die a cruel death. But his martyrdom was important to the Shiite community because it enabled the latter to endeavor to claim the Islamic throne of leadership. Hussein's death is reconstructed every year at the Ashura ceremonies, but Khomeini claimed that this could not suffice, and stated that Hussein's martyrdom must be relived through its practical implementation via daily self-sacrifice in the name of Islam.

The issue of martyrdom is also closely linked with the concept of Jihad [holy war]. According to Islamic religious rulings, there are two types of Jihad: defensive and offensive. The defensive Jihad refers to the defense of Muslim territory conquered by infidels. The goal of offensive Jihad is the enforcement of Islamic rule in parts of the world that have not yet submitted to its reign. Falling in battle during the Jihad, including martyrdom in the battlefield, is a lofty commandment that entitles the martyr to the parting of the gates of the Garden of Eden in welcome.

According to the time-honored concept of the Shia, only the "vanished Imam" may declare a Jihad, and thus until his return the duty of Jihad does not fall on the Shiite believers. Khomeini objected to this approach and claimed that until the return of the "vanished Imam," the responsibility for the leadership of the flock of believers falls upon the *mujtahad*, which is also permitted to declare a Jihad. During the 1980s, the encouragement of martyrdom became a central theme in Shiite combat, both in the framework of the war against Iraq and in the framework of the struggle of extremist Shiite organizations against Israel and Western targets in Lebanon.

Keys to the Garden of Eden

In 1983, Khomeini gauged the tremendous attraction that war presented for Iranian youth and passed a religious ruling permitting boys over the age of twelve to volunteer to fight at the front even without their parents' permission. The young volunteers turned into the Imam's protégés and they were promised entry to the Garden of Eden if they fell in battle. Tens of thousands of youthful volunteers received the "key to the Garden of Eden" (a plastic key made in Taiwan) and purple headbands bearing the slogan "long live Khomeini," after which they were thrust into the battlefield. The willingness to "die a 'martyr's' death" motivated the Iranians to use special tactics during the Iran-Iraq war such as dispatching human waves to face the enemy, clearing minefields by having young boys run across them, and suicide attacks against fortified targets and Iraqi tanks.

Most of the "volunteers" wrote wills prior to their departure to battle through special messengers who were sent to the front for this purpose. The wills were worded as letters addressed to the Imam or the mothers of the soldiers. "How miserable, how unfortunate, how ignorant was I during all of my fourteen regrettable years, which passed by without my knowing Allah. The Imam opened my eyes. . . . How sweet, sweet, sweet is death, it is like a blessing that Allah has bestowed upon his beloved."

The Iranian press published the wills of the shahids daily, in which they expressed their aspirations—before leaving for action from which they never returned—to be at peace and reach the shaded shelter of Allah's wings. In most of these wills there was idealization of death as a lofty value. Many of them ended with the verse from the Koran: "Do not think that the shahids are dead; they live and flourish in the shaded shelter of Allah's wings." Some closed with quotations from Islamic sources and Khomeini's letters, which describe the delightful eternal life of the shahids in the Garden of Eden, and promise that this is the destiny of anyone who lays down his life in a holy war. As to the injured, in one of his speeches Ali Khamenar [who became prime minister of Iran in 1981] promised that they would not feel their amputated limbs when they reach the Garden of Eden. . . .

The Shiites in Lebanon and Suicide Attacks

The link between Iran and the Shiites in Lebanon was expressed in the adoption of Khomeini's ideology and rulings by religious clerics and Hizballah [a radical Shiite Islamic organization] activists in Lebanon. The operational link between the Shiites in Lebanon and Iran lies in the connection of a spiritual authority and obedience to the Imam by his "soldiers in Lebanon," which is perpetuated through religious clerics of the Hizballah. The latter were responsible for interpreting Khomeini's rulings, which were perceived as operational orders, and provided inspiration and permission for violent actions perpetrated by Shiites against foreigners.

The issue of suicide attacks was also given due consideration by Shiite philosophical circles in Lebanon. Sheikh Fadallah, the spiritual leader of Hizballah, claimed that in the absence of the "Vanished Imam," the mujtahid is permitted to declare only a defensive Jihad. But he maintained that the struggle underway in Lebanon and Palestine was a defensive Jihad whose goal was to liberate conquered Muslim territory, and therefore martyrdom as part of the struggle against the invaders is allowed according to Islamic ruling. The Sheikh Hassan Trad, one of Hizballah's clerics, also clarified this matter:

> Lebanon would not have been liberated if not for the Jihad of Iran. Lebanon was only liberated thanks to the "istashad" (martyrdom) actions, and the only one who gave them his blessing was the Imam Khomeini. Bilal Pahatz, who became a symbol of the opposition, wrote me a letter as follows: "I am a *mukalid* (follower) of the Imam Khomeini who instructed to carry out *istashad* and strike out at the enemy and I answered him (positively) based on the rulings of his *marjha taklid* (source of authority), the Imam Khomeini.". . .

Suicide Attacks Against "Western" Targets in Lebanon and Kuwait

The suicide attack against the U.S. Embassy in Lebanon. On April 18, 1983, the Hizballah perpetrated its first suicide attack. A van loaded with about 400 kilograms of explosives and driven by a suicide terrorist exploded near the structure of the U.S. Embassy in Beirut. As a result of the explosion, part of the building collapsed, leaving sixty-three dead and

120 wounded, including most of the employees at the Embassy and at the branch of the CIA in Lebanon. The Islamic Jihad organization claimed responsibility for the attack (subsequently, the Hizballah continued to use this name in order to claim responsibility for attacks). As a result of the blast, the American Embassy was moved to Achar, north of Beirut.

On September 20, 1984, another suicide attack was carried out against the U.S. Embassy in Achar. A truck bomb driven by a suicide attacker exploded near the Embassy. In this attack eleven people were killed and fifty-eight were wounded. Here, too, the Islamic Jihad claimed responsibility for the attack.

The suicide attack against the headquarters of the U.S. Marines in Beirut. On the morning of October 23, 1983 (at 06:22), a Mercedes truck loaded with explosives and driven by a suicide terrorist exploded near the building that housed the Marines Headquarters at the Beirut airport. The truck rammed through the gate and exploded in the courtyard near the headquarters. The four-story building, which served as both headquarters and barracks for the Marines, collapsed as the result of the explosion. Two hundred and forty-one people were killed and eighty were injured, most of whom were U.S. Marines serving in the multinational force in Lebanon.

This was the terror attack to take the heaviest toll on the United States until the attacks of September 11, 2001. To quote the commander of the U.S. Marines Corp General Kelly:

> It was the largest terrorist act in United States history.... When 220 Marines died on October 23, 1983, the day became the Corps' bloodiest since February 1945, when Marines fought to secure Iwo Jima. October 23, 1983 surpasses even the Corps' bloodiest days during the Vietnam and Korean Wars....

Suicide Attack Perpetrated by the Hizballah in Buenos Aires, Argentina

In the beginning of the 1990s, the Hizballah, with Iranian assistance, perpetrated two suicide attacks in Buenos Aires against Israeli and Jewish goals.

- On March 17, 1992, a suicide attack was perpetrated against the Israeli Embassy in Buenos Aires.
- On July 18, 1994, a suicide attack was perpetrated against the Jewish cultural center (AMIA) in Buenos Aires.

The Attack against the Israeli Embassy in Buenos Aires

On March 17, 1992, a powerful explosion shook the Norte Quarter of Buenos Aires; a car bomb had detonated in front of the Israeli Embassy, demolishing the six-floor building. Twenty-nine people were killed including four Israelis and five Jews, all embassy employees. Two hundred and twenty-four individuals were wounded, including eight Israelis.

The Argentinean government immediately launched an investigation of the incident and the Israeli government dispatched a special team in order to investigate how the attack had happened and who bore responsibility for it.

The Islamic Jihad Organization (Hizballah had used this name in the past to claim responsibility for attacks) claimed responsibility immediately after the attack. However, out of fear of Israeli and international reprisals, the organization retracted its original announcement (on March 19), subsequently reassuming responsibility for the attack (on March 23). The attack, which was apparently carried out by the Hizballah with Iranian assistance, was launched in reprisal against the termination of the secretary general of the Hizballah, Abas Musawi, by Israeli attack helicopters. . . .

The Attack against the Jewish Cultural Center (AMIA) in Buenos Aires

On July 18, 1994, at about 7:00 a.m., a car bomb exploded near a seven-story building that served as the cultural center of the Jewish community in Buenos Aires. There were ninety-seven fatalities and 230 casualties, most of whom were Jewish Argentineans. The "Islamic Commando— Hizballah Argentina" claimed responsibility for the attack.

Following the attack, on July 19, an IDF [Israeli Defense Force] rescue and evacuation team left for Argentina in order to assist the local authorities in handling the consequences of the attack against the Jewish community structure. During their work at the site, delegation members extricated sixty bodies of people who had been trapped in the rubble and eighteen body parts. The delegation returned to Israel on July 27, 1994. . . .

Suicide Attacks by Palestinians

The phenomenon of suicide attacks, which until 2001 was an operational tool exclusive to the Islamic terror organizations, that is, the Hamas and Islamic Jihad, currently serves all of the different types of organizations including secular organizations such as the Fatah (and its various factions) and the Popular Front for the Liberation of Palestine. Moreover, suicide attacks have become a norm in Palestinian society.

As stated in the Israeli daily newspaper *Maariv:* "Today suicide attacks are no longer perceived as an act of desperation, disappointment or revenge but rather as hopeful attacks. The goal of the attack is not killing for killing's sake but rather a means to break Israel's staying power—to destroy the society and crush its economy. . . . "

An interesting expression of these ideas can be gleaned from an article by Amira Hess entitled "The suicide attacker is a happy person who loves life." The article contains an interview with Osama Mazini, a Ph.D. in psychology at the Islamic University in Gaza. Mazini claims that personal desperation is not what impels the suicide attackers, but rather a national objective. The feeling of general fury and the patriotic desire to facilitate the struggle for liberation and independence are the main motives for the suicide attacks. Mazini states: "Psychologically one must differentiate between someone who puts an end to his life because of emotional suffering and the istashad who is a happy person that loves life, an individual with inner strength.". . .

"Anyone going out to fight an Israeli soldier," explained Mazini "knows that chances are that he will never return, because the Israeli soldier is trained, skilled and has more weapons. Thus, psychologically, anyone who goes out to fight a soldier wearing a belt bomb—there is the similarity. They are similar in the tension that impels them to endanger themselves." Mazini claims, "The Israelis have a central role in impelling the young men to choose a martyr's death. The random deaths that we have experienced during the months of the Intifada have caused each young man to say 'if I am doomed to die arbitrarily, why shouldn't I go and die honorably?' This inner discussion has generated tension, and the tension awakens excitement to the point that thought is neutralized. Thus, the will to take risks grows."

Mazini adds that the religious promise of eternal life in the Garden of Eden plays a central role. "Life on earth is dear to every person, so it is not easy to relinquish it for happiness in the world to come. He who chooses to be a martyr is not ending his days but rather extending them, and therefore the martyrdom (perishing in the name of Allah) is really a love of life."

The Hizballah Terrorist Group Develops in Lebanon

Hala Jaber

In June 1982 Israel invaded Lebanon, a deeply divided country in which Shiite Muslims and Maronite Christians, among other groups, contended for control. Israel's immediate intention was to expel the Palestine Liberation Organization (PLO), which had been using southern Lebanon as a base for attacks against Israel. Its suspected long-term intention was to bring an Israel-friendly Christian Maronite government to power and to secure access to water resources in Lebanon. Many Shiites in southern Lebanon were frustrated and unhappy with the PLO and were not sorry to see them driven out. However, Israeli forces stayed on after the PLO had been driven out, and Lebanon became fertile ground for a resistance movement whose genesis is described in this selection by freelance journalist Hala Jaber. A new Shiite Islamic fundamentalist group, Hizballah ("Party of God"), used such tactics as truck bombings and suicide attacks in an effort to drive the Israelis out of Lebanon and to make the country a Shiite fundamentalist state like Iran.

Today Hizballah continues to fight the influence of Western countries, which it believes act only out of self-interest and the desire to control the Middle East's oil supplies. Hizballah also continues to sponsor anti-Israel terrorist attacks. Jaber has written for the Associated Press and Reuters. She is the author of *Hezbollah: Born with a Vengeance*.

When Israel launched its invasion in June 1982, Lebanon's leading Shia Muslim clerics were in Tehran, attending the annual Islamic Conference. The timing was fateful: Iran immediately volunteered to help its Lebanese brethren and the Iranian Revolutionary Guards were swiftly dispatched to Baalbeck in the Bekaa Valley. . . . Hezbollah had been conceived.

Those were heady days in Lebanon. At least twenty-five different groups and militias were locked in a continuous round of fighting. The emergence of yet another entity did not spark great enthusiasm amongst the war-weary people nor attract much attention. The West's intelligence services, who boasted about their close monitoring of Iran's movements at the time, failed to recognise the shoots of the new group. It was an oversight in those first, highly sensitive months that would eventually exact a high cost.

In the long, hot summer days and stifling nights of 1982, Baalbeck hosted scores of feverish, secret meetings in the homes of young Shiite men and revolutionary clerics. All were still inspired by the success of the Iranian Revolution and they spent months discussing the nature of the emerging party. They were devout Muslims, disillusioned by the established parties' political ideology and intent on going back to basics by creating an entity which would conform to Islamic *sharia*, Islamic law, and the word of the Almighty Allah.

The model of Iran's Islamic Republic had rekindled their own revolutionary spirit. They pledged their theological allegiance to [Iran's radical Shiite leader, the Ayatollah] Khomeini and harboured the dream of instigating a similar revolt in Lebanon in the hope of transforming the multi-confessional state into an Iranian-style Islamic country. Sheikh Naiim Qassem, who had been a cleric in Amal and became Hezbollah's deputy secretary-general, summarised the feelings amongst those who strove to form Hezbollah at the time. Qassem is a gentle, handsome man and an eloquent spokesman. His green eyes are framed by thick, dark lashes and he has long elegant hands. Beneath the customary black cloak worn by Hezbollah's clerics, it is surprising to see his Western footwear: socks and moccasins.

> The common denominator among those people was the strong feeling that what was present in the arena in the form of parties and organizations did not express their [political]

proposals nor the structural format they sought. What contributed also was the breaking of the Iranian Revolution in 1979. This inspired these men to establish relations with the Revolution and to benefit from its experiences. So, from 1979 until 1982, there was only a general desire to create something that would translate the interests of our Islamic proposals. There was a need to develop a force which would also enjoy a popular political extension, something that was not available from any of the organisations and personalities on the ground.

But having a desire to start something could only be achieved if the right circumstances prevailed. That only came about when Israel invaded Lebanon. That provided the conditions to realise the already present desire. With the willingness of the Islamic Republic to support the motives of this alliance, Hezbollah's take-off occurred.

The group of clerics began to form the backbone of Hezbollah, making frequent visits to their Iranian mentors, both in Tehran and Damascus where Iran has one of its largest embassies. The Party of God's current leader, Suyyed Hassan Nasrallah, was among the clerics. He had been a member of Amal's politburo and it was disillusionment with Amal's secular course under Nabih Berri that caused him to leave the group. At the age of sixteen, Nasrallah had travelled to Najaf, Iraq, to pursue his theological studies and he became one of several protégés of his predecessor Sheikh Abbas Musawi. Following Musawi's murder, Nasrallah was elected as Hezbollah's secretary-general at the age of thirty-two and became the youngest leader ever to run the Party of God. He described the group's priorities and activities in its first months of formation in an interview with the newspaper *Al-Safir*:

> The main effort at the time went into mustering and attracting young men and setting up military camps where they could be trained and organised into small groups capable of carrying out resistance attacks against the occupying force. There were no institutions like now, no large organisation or specialised departments. There was only a group effort con-

centrating on two main issues. The first being the banding together of young men, training and organising them into small groups and then dispatching them to the occupied areas from where they were instructed to carry out attacks.

The second effort was spreading the word among the people, first, in a bid to raise their morale, and second to instil in them a sense of animosity towards the enemy, coupled with a spirit of resistance in the face of the occupying forces. This required us to use a language of indoctrination rather than realpolitik. People then were not in need of political analysis, they were in need of being incited and goaded. They did not need to be lectured, they needed to be freed.

The Party of God [Hezbollah] had quickly registered the tolerance of many Shiite Muslims towards the Israeli army and immediately sought to bring its influence to bear. To assert that the soldiers were occupiers and not their saviours was imperative, not only for the Party of God's initial recruitment programme, but for the success and continuity of the struggle. . . .

Nabih Berri [leader of Amal, a secular resistance group that Lebanese Shiites supported] meanwhile came close to losing his hold over the Shiite movement. In the eyes of many Shiites, he had made the unforgivable error of participating in the National Salvation Committee, an emergency executive which brokered the 17 May 1983 accord between Lebanon and Israel. The accord was sponsored by the United States, which was keen to push through a second Arab-Israeli peace treaty following Camp David.[1] Muslims and Druze[2] considered it to be a vehicle for securing Israel's dominance in Lebanon. Its terms allowed Israel's proxy Christian militia to control a 30-mile area in South Lebanon and permitted its army to conduct patrols with the Lebanese army as far as the Awali River, north of Sidon. When Berri refused to join the National Salvation Front, which had been instigated by Syria to sabotage the 17 May accord, it was the

---

1. the 1978 Camp David Accords between Egypt and Israel   2. a small religious community whose members live mainly in Lebanon, Israel, Syria, and Jordan

last straw. His stance was considered by the Muslim extremists to be an acceptance of US mediation in Lebanon.

With Iran's Help

Hezbollah had few arms at the beginning and it lacked the means for mass communication. It did, however, have important elements necessary for a *jihad:* Iranian money at its disposal and, on its doorstep, Iranian Revolutionary Guards expert in the art of warfare. The Iranian Revolutionary Guards took charge of Hezbollah's security and resistance operations. Iran's backing, combined with the presence of a core of dedicated men and an increasing number of warriors graduating from the Iranian Revolutionary Guards' military training programmes, set the group forth on its long, deadly and often chilling journey. The clerics used every opportunity to spread their word and ideology. They preached tirelessly in mosques, Husseiniyahs [Shiite religious schools], at funerals and anywhere a crowd could be found. Their style was simple, but direct. They fed on Israel's mistakes, the Lebanese government's impotence and the West's blunders. Over the next two years, Hezbollah continued to operate underground from its main base, Baalbeck, in the eastern Bekaa Valley. Baalbeck was not under Israeli occupation and provided the group and the Iranian Revolutionary Guards with a safe haven from which to work and organise the movement. It was also close to Syria, giving Hezbollah the freedom of movement to travel to Iran. Its fighters worked under the banner of the Lebanese National Resistance and did not claim credit for any of the new, daring attacks that had started to make an impact among the Israeli soldiers. They concealed their joy when operations went well and hid their anguish when they failed.

From the very beginning, the United States and Israel searched in vain for the individuals within the new movement who were responsible for the group's attacks. They assassinated and kidnapped the group's officials in the belief that they had captured the ringleaders. To date, they have failed to grasp that the Party of God's chain of command has a structure which ensures that, even if its head is eradicated, the group can successfully continue. The group's decision-making policy is run in a manner whereby no single individual is ever solely responsible for making key decisions. Its history has proved that the killing of its leader does not necessarily warrant a change in its policies nor guarantee a moderate replacement. On the contrary, such events have, if anything, usually brought forth a more radical commander and an increase in militant tactics.

While the West searched for answers, Hezbollah's cadres grew secretly. Between 1982 and 1985, the Party of God was training hundreds of young men, spreading the word amongst the population and working on creating a political agenda of its own. It had also established several social services for the inhabitants of its main base in the Bekaa Valley and in the city of Baalbeck. . . .

Hezbollah Takes Hold

By the end of 1983, it was becoming more noticeable that a new force was in town. Few Lebanese had yet comprehended the nature of the force, but late that year and in early 1984, West Beirut was turning into a bleak and frightening city. The face of the once famously cosmopolitan capital was undergoing a swift transformation. With the Shiite takeover of West Beirut, heavily bearded Hezbollah militiamen became increasingly visible in the city's battered streets. They wore green bands around their heads bearing inscriptions such as 'Allahu Akbar', 'God is Greater', and 'Qaaidouna Khomeini', 'Our leader is Khomeini'. The Ayatollah became a prominent image on many of the city's streets; posters of the Iranian leader were plastered on the walls of shops, boutiques, banks and even hospitals. Schoolgirls, some as young as seven, replaced their jeans and T-shirts with long-sleeved shirts and skirts and wore their hair concealed under tightly knotted black or white scarves. Women who were considered to be dressed in an improper manner were often harassed by the radical newcomers and rumours circulated that acid had been thrown at girls dressed in an 'un-Islamic' way as a lesson to others. These stories were never verified, but for a long time afterwards many felt uneasy walking the streets of West Beirut.

Shops selling alcohol were sometimes sent a warning in the form of a few sticks of dynamite hurled at their front doors. On other occasions they were raided by unknown militiamen who took to smashing the bottles of alcohol on display after lecturing the owners on the vices of their commodities. The attacks were intended to be messages and they usually occurred late at night and after closing hours. Those who continued to sell alcohol did so secretly and customers disguised their heavily wrapped purchases in inconspicuous carrier bags. The few popular restaurants which remained open hung signs on their entrances with the words 'Family restaurants only' insinuating that they were 'dry' premises. Even the famous Commodore Hotel, home to most of the hard-drinking foreign press corps, had to play the game. During the Muslims' holy month of Ramadan the bar was emptied of all its stock apart from soft drinks. The remaining 'prohibited' drinks were transferred to a suite on another floor.

By late 1984, Hezbollah's militiamen were out in the open, but very little was known about its leaders and hierarchy. The group had by then become an umbrella for most of the Muslim factions around, ranging from Islamic Amal to the al-Dawa party and the Islamic Students' Union. Islamic Amal had been started by Hussein Musawi in 1982, following Musawi's objections to Nabih Berri's political stance towards the Israeli invasion. Musawi was one of the few visible radicals in the early eighties. He was one of the many militants who held America responsible for encouraging and allowing Israel to invade and occupy Lebanon. His continuous denunciation of the West and his close relations with Iranian radicals made him a prime suspect during the West's desperate search for the names behind the new, invisible Islamic phenomenon. . . .

Hezbollah Declares Itself

On 16 February 1985, Hezbollah made its public debut to the world. The group's manifesto was declared by Hezbollah's spokesman, Sheikh Ibrahim al-Amin, who was one of the three official clerics who had been dispatched to Beirut to spread the Party of God's agenda to the people of the suburbs. . . .

The contents of the booklet came under twenty-five headings which explained the Party of God's message in detail and set forth its Iranian orientation:

> We, the sons of Hezbollah's nation in Lebanon, whose vanguard God has given victory in Iran and which has established the nucleus of the world's central Islamic state, abide by the orders of a single wise and just command currently embodied in the supreme exemplar of Ayatollah Khomeini.
>
> From this basis, we in Lebanon are not a closed organisational structural party, nor are we a narrow political framework, but we are a nation interconnecting with all Muslims of the world. We are linked by a strong ideological and political connection—Islam.
>
> From here, what befalls the Muslims in Afghanistan, Iraq, the Philippines or anywhere else verily afflicts the body of our Islamic nation of which we are an inseparable part, and we move to confront it on the basis of our main legal obligation and in the light of a political view decided by our leader the *Wilayat al-Faqih* [Ayatollah Khomeini].
>
> As for our learning, this is primarily derived from the Holy Quran, and the infallible Sunnah [model of the ways of the Prophet], as well as the laws and edicts emanating from the Faqih.
>
> No one can begin to imagine the scope of our military strength and capability. No one can even fathom its size. For we do not have a separate military wing which is independent from the parts of our bodies. Everyone of us is a fighting soldier when a call for *jihad* arises and each one of us carries out his mission in battle on the basis of his legal obligations. For Allah is behind us supporting and protecting us while instilling fear in the hearts of our enemies.

The manifesto described the West as the 'tyrannical world set on fighting us'. It accused the West of collaborating with the Soviet Union and waging war against the Muslims, charging that they had purposely defamed Hezbollah's reputation by labelling it as terrorist to 'stunt and deform our great achievements with regard to confrontations with the United States'. Hezbollah regards the West, and particularly the United States, as its staunchest enemy after Israel.

Hezbollah associates the West with European imperialism and the struggle for independence from colonial rule. It traces the antagonism between Christendom and Islam back to the Crusades: Hezbollah believes that the West's opposition to its vision springs from this ancient religious rivalry. Although it recognises that there are political differences between Western countries, it none the less considers that they unite collectively in their hostility towards Islam and that Muslims must therefore similarly unite to confront them.

The militant group has modified its definition of confrontation with the West since the publication of the manifesto. In its early years, Hezbollah aimed at removing the Western presence from Lebanon and the group incited war against Western targets, both locally and abroad. The Party of God currently speaks of resisting the West on 'cultural and political levels.' From his modest office in Hezbollah's heavily guarded headquarters in the midst of the teeming southern suburbs of Beirut, Naimim Qassem, Hezbollah's deputy secretary-general, explained the source of confrontation with the West.

'In our region we have a problem with the West which at one time placed us under the French mandate, at other times under the British mandate and over certain periods we were politically governed by the whims of the United States.' Hezbollah regards itself as occupying the opposite end of the spectrum to the West's concept of capitalism. 'There are contradictions between capitalism and Islam, there is a mental conflict between them,' Qassem argued, and went on:

> When the West moves into a region, it does so with the intention of marketing its principles. It establishes schools, its own educational curriculum, Western cultural institutions, its own media, practically its own way of life and thinking. All of this, in a bid to impose its own ideologies in our region.

> So when the West, for example, speaks of women in our areas it wants them to be prototypes of theirs in the way they think and behave. When they speak of economic markets, they do

so according to their outlook on things. In other words, they seek to impose their own Western principles, not taking ours into consideration, in an attempt to suck us into their own agenda. From here we consider that there is a cultural conflict between us and the West and it is our job to invalidate their concepts here, to prove their evil and to spread our vision instead. If we succeed we will have obstructed their political agenda and this is our first kind of confrontation.

Hezbollah argues that the West's intentions in the Middle East are primarily based on self-interest. It perceives its presence in the region as an attempt to control the area's economic infrastructure and it condemns the Arab world, especially Saudi Arabia and the oil-rich Gulf states, for having fallen under Western influence. The Party of God regards the United States as the main player in the region and lays much of the blame at its doorstep. America, it claims, is expanding exclusively in the Middle East and imposing its political might and economic policies on Arab countries, while blocking other Western countries from having any influence in the area.

In its manifesto, Hezbollah blames the United States for all the region's catastrophes, describing it as the foremost enemy of all the Muslims of the world. 'We shall proceed to fight the vice at its very roots . . . the first roots of such vice being the United States.' The manifesto calls on its people to remember that 'the leader Imam Khomeini emphasised on many occasions that America is the cause of all our calamities and that she is the mother of all malice. If we fight her we will in effect only be exercising our just rights in defending our Islam and the honour of our nation.'

Osama bin Laden Creates an International Terror Movement

National Commission on Terrorist Attacks upon the United States

The Islamic extremist group al Qaeda, led by Osama bin Laden, has been responsible for many large-scale acts of terrorism, including the attacks that destroyed the World Trade Center and killed nearly three thousand people on September 11, 2001. This excerpt from the *Report of the National Commission on Terrorist Attacks upon the United States* (*The 9/11 Commission Report*) describes how Bin Laden developed al Qaeda after the Afghan war against the Soviet Union in the 1980s, during which mujahideen, or "holy warriors," from all over the Arab world came to fight the Communists. The struggle gave al Qaeda's future leaders and members combat experience and an inspiring example of a victory against a superpower (Russia's demoralizing experience in Afghanistan is often given credit for the breakup of the Soviet Union). According to the report, Bin Laden has been able to win thousands of followers by promising to restore Islam's former glory and to avenge Muslims who believe they are the victims of "foreign masters," particularly the United States. His message appeals to people who have suffered from the many political and economic problems in the Middle East. Al Qaeda has been unofficially supported at one time or another by many countries in the region, including Sudan, Afghanistan, and Pakistan. In the 1990s it was responsible for a series of attacks on U.S. targets, including the 1998 bombing of the U.S. embassy in Nairobi, Kenya, which killed 213 people and injured five thousand. The commission released its public report on July 22, 2004.

National Commission on Terrorist Attacks upon the United States, "The Foundation of the New Terrorism," in *Report of the National Commission on Terrorist Attacks upon the United States*, July 2, 2004.

In February 1998, the 40-year-old Saudi exile Usama Bin Ladin and a fugitive Egyptian physician, Ayman al Zawahiri, arranged from their Afghan headquarters for an Arabic newspaper in London to publish what they termed a fatwa issued in the name of a "World Islamic Front." A fatwa is normally an interpretation of Islamic law by a respected Islamic authority, but neither Bin Ladin, Zawahiri, nor the three others who signed this statement were scholars of Islamic law. Claiming that America had declared war against God and his messenger, they called for the murder of any American, anywhere on earth, as the "individual duty for every Muslim who can do it in any country in which it is possible to do it."

Three months later, when interviewed in Afghanistan by ABC-TV, Bin Ladin enlarged on these themes. He claimed it was more important for Muslims to kill Americans than to kill other infidels. "It is far better for anyone to kill a single American soldier than to squander his efforts on other activities," he said. Asked whether he approved of terrorism and of attacks on civilians, he replied: "We believe that the worst thieves in the world today and the worst terrorists are the Americans. Nothing could stop you except perhaps retaliation in kind. We do not have to differentiate between military or civilian. As far as we are concerned, they are all targets."

Though novel for its open endorsement of indiscriminate killing, Bin Ladin's 1998 declaration was only the latest in the long series of his public and private calls since 1992 that singled out the United States for attack.

In August 1996, Bin Ladin had issued his own self-styled fatwa calling on Muslims to drive American soldiers out of Saudi Arabia. The long, disjointed document condemned the Saudi monarchy for allowing the presence of an army of infidels in a land with the sites most sacred to Islam, and celebrated recent suicide bombings of American military facilities in the Kingdom. It praised the 1983 suicide bombing in Beirut that killed 241 U.S. Marines, the 1992 bombing in Aden, and especially the 1993 firefight in Somalia after which the United States "left the area carrying disappointment, humiliation, defeat and your dead with you."

Bin Ladin said in his ABC interview that he and his followers had been preparing in Somalia for another long struggle, like that against the Soviets in Afghanistan, but "the United States rushed out of Somalia in shame and disgrace." Citing the Soviet army's withdrawal from Afghanistan as proof that a ragged army of dedicated Muslims could overcome a super-power, he told the interviewer: "We are certain that we shall—with the grace of Allah—prevail over the Americans." He went on to warn that "If the present injustice continues . . . , it will inevitably move the battle to American soil."

Plans to attack the United States were developed with un-wavering single-mindedness throughout the 1990s. Bin Ladin saw himself as called "to follow in the footsteps of the Messenger and to communicate his message to all nations," and to serve as the rallying point and organizer of a new kind of war to destroy America and bring the world to Islam.

Bin Ladin's Appeal in the Islamic World

It is the story of eccentric and violent ideas sprouting in the fertile ground of political and social turmoil. It is the story of an organization poised to seize its historical moment. How did Bin Ladin—with his call for the indiscriminate killing of Americans—win thousands of followers and some degree of approval from millions more?

The history, culture, and body of beliefs from which Bin Ladin has shaped and spread his message are largely unknown to many Americans. Seizing on symbols of Islam's past great-ness, he promises to restore pride to people who consider themselves the victims of successive foreign masters. He uses cultural and religious allusions to the holy Qur'an and some of its interpreters. He appeals to people disoriented by cyclonic change as they confront modernity and globalization. His rhetoric selectively draws from multiple sources—Islam, his-tory, and the region's political and economic malaise. He also stresses grievances against the United States widely shared in the Muslim world. He inveighed against the presence of U.S. troops in Saudi Arabia, the home of Islam's holiest sites. He spoke of the suffering of the Iraqi people as a result of sanctions imposed after the Gulf War [waged in 1991 after Iraq's inva-sion of Kuwait], and he protested U.S. support of Israel. . . .

Bin Ladin's Worldview

Despite his claims to universal leadership, Bin Ladin offers an extreme view of Islamic history designed to appeal mainly to Arabs and Sunnis.[1] He draws on fundamentalists who blame the eventual destruction of the Caliphate[2] on leaders who abandoned the pure path of religious devotion. He repeatedly calls on his followers to embrace martyrdom since "the walls of oppression and humiliation cannot be demolished except in a rain of bullets." For those yearning for a lost sense of order in an older, more tranquil world, he offers his "Caliphate" as an imagined alternative to today's uncertainty. For others, he offers simplistic conspiracies to explain their world. . . .

The Rise of Bin Ladin and al Qaeda

A decade of conflict in Afghanistan, from 1979 to 1989, gave Islamist extremists a rallying point and training field. A Communist government in Afghanistan gained power in 1978 but was unable to establish enduring control. At the end of 1979, the Soviet government sent in military units to ensure that the country would remain securely under Moscow's influence. The response was an Afghan national resistance movement that defeated Soviet forces.

Young Muslims from around the world flocked to Afghanistan to join as volunteers in what was seen as a "holy war"—*jihad*—against an invader. The largest numbers came from the Middle East. Some were Saudis, and among them was Usama Bin Ladin.

Twenty-three when he arrived in Afghanistan in 1980, Bin Ladin was the seventeenth of 57 children of a Saudi construction magnate. Six feet five and thin, Bin Ladin appeared to be ungainly but was in fact quite athletic, skilled as a horseman, runner, climber, and soccer player. He had attended Abdul Aziz University in Saudi Arabia. By some accounts, he had been interested there in religious studies, in-

1. members of the largest branch of Islam, the second-largest being Shiites   2. the institution of leadership of Islam by successors to Muhammad, officially ended by a modernizing Turkish government in 1924

spired by tape recordings of fiery sermons by Abdullah Azzam, a Palestinian and a disciple of [the Islamic fundamentalist writer Sayyid] Qutb. Bin Ladin was conspicuous among the volunteers not because he showed evidence of religious learning but because he had access to some of his family's huge fortune. Though he took part in at least one actual battle, he became known chiefly as a person who gen-

The Fundamentalist Conspiratorial Thesis

Conspiracy theorists believe that political events are shaped by the dark plots of a group of people. As Middle East expert Daniel Pipes argues below, Islamic fundamentalists are conspiracy theorists who view modern history as the story of Western plots against Islam.

Of all Middle Easterners, fundamentalist Muslims present the most cohesive conspiratorial thesis. . . .

Here, in brief, is their argument: Muslim strength follows directly from living by the sacred law of Islam (known in Arabic as the *Shari'a*). A millennium ago, when the faithful lived scrupulously by God's commandments, the Muslim world flourished, enjoying military strength, wealth, and sparkling cultural attainments. But then came external influence, Jewish according to some, European according to others, and it lured Muslims away from close adherence to Islamic ways as adumbrated in the Qur'an—or Koran—and the other guides to Islamic behavior. Zionists and imperialists targeted the *Shari'a* knowing that it underlies the Islamic way of life and that its precepts would fatally obstruct their efforts to vanquish Muslims.

Fundamentalists almost unthinkingly premise their understanding of modern history on Western plots against Islam, seeing the expansion of European power around the world resulting not from Europe's power but from the successful sabotaging of Islam. Muhammad al-Ghazali, a leading fundamentalist thinker from Egypt, explains that "there is a conspiracy against Islam . . . by Western secularism because it claims that Islam is a dangerous religion." [Iran's Ayatollah] Khomeini, as ever, goes further, writing that "In the interest of the Jews, America, and

erously helped fund the anti-Soviet jihad. . . .

The international environment for Bin Ladin's efforts was ideal. Saudi Arabia and the United States supplied billions of dollars worth of secret assistance to rebel groups in Afghanistan fighting the Soviet occupation. This assistance was funneled through Pakistan: the Pakistani military Intelligence service (Inter-Services Intelligence Directorate, or

Israel, we [Muslims] must be jailed and killed, we must be sacrificed to the evil intentions of foreigners."

Conspirators got their way: Muslims strayed from the law. Predictably, Muslims lost their strength. They now lag the rest of the world. Regimes are undemocratic, people poor, and culture derivative. Literacy is low and life-spans short. To return to the grandeur of centuries past, fundamentalists insist, Muslims must implement the law in its entirety, thereby protecting it from foreign meddling. A wholehearted return to the *Shari'a* means extirpating foreign influence and resisting non-Muslim ways.

Fundamentalists see the need to return to the law as so self-evident that every loyal, righteous Muslim must seek this course; not to do so implies knowing treachery, a wish to enfeeble the Muslim world. A Muslim who neglects the law or, worse yet, encourages others to do so, must be working on behalf of a non-Muslim power. Promoting a secularized version of Islam or taking up antireligious credos like Marxism-Leninism point to agency for the Jews or the Europeans. Leaders who claim to be Muslim but do not apply the *Shari'a* are also traitors; thus did Ayatollah Khomeini accuse the shah of trying to eliminate Islam from Iran. . . .

Nearly all the most influential fundamentalist thinkers (Hasan al-Banna, Sayyid Qutb, Abu'l-A'la al-Mawdudi) accept the premise of anti-Islamic conspiracy by Jews and Europeans, as do most of the preachers, scholars, journalists, and politicians who follow their lead.

Daniel Pipes, *The Hidden Hand: Middle East Fears of Conspiracy.* New York: St. Martin's, 1996.

ISID) helped train the rebels and distribute the arms. But Bin Ladin and his comrades had their own sources of support and training, and they received little or no assistance from the United States.

April 1988 brought victory for the Afghan jihad. Moscow declared it would pull its military forces out of Afghanistan within the next nine months. As the Soviets began their withdrawal, the jihad's leaders debated what to do next.

Bin Ladin and Azzam agreed that the organization successfully created for Afghanistan should not be allowed to dissolve. They established what they called a base or foundation (al Qaeda) as a potential general headquarters for future jihad. Though Azzam had been considered number one in the MAK [Mektab al Khidmat, an organization that channeled anti-Soviet volunteers into Afghanistan], by August 1988 Bin Ladin was clearly the leader (*emir*) of al Qaeda. . . .

Bin Ladin Moves to Sudan

By the fall of 1989, Bin Ladin had sufficient stature among Islamic extremists that a Sudanese political leader, Hassan al Turabi, urged him to transplant his whole organization to Sudan. Turabi headed the National Islamic Front in a coalition that had recently seized power in Khartoum [capital of Sudan]. Bin Ladin agreed to help Turabi in an ongoing war against African Christian separatists in southern Sudan and also to do some road building. Turabi in return would let Bin Ladin use Sudan as a base for worldwide business operations and for preparations for jihad. While agents of Bin Ladin began to buy property in Sudan in 1990, Bin Ladin himself moved from Afghanistan back to Saudi Arabia.

In August 1990, Iraq invaded Kuwait. Bin Ladin, whose efforts in Afghanistan had earned him celebrity and respect, proposed to the Saudi monarchy that he summon mujahideen for a jihad to retake Kuwait. He was rebuffed, and the Saudis joined the U.S.-led coalition. After the Saudis agreed to allow U.S. armed forces to be based in the Kingdom, Bin Ladin and a number of Islamic clerics began to publicly denounce the arrangement. The Saudi government exiled the clerics and undertook to silence Bin Ladin by, among other things, taking away his passport. With help from a dissident member of the royal family, he managed to get out of the country under the pretext of attending an Islamic gathering in Pakistan in April 1991. By 1994, the Saudi government would freeze his financial assets and revoke his citizenship. He no longer had a country he could call his own.

Bin Ladin moved to Sudan in 1991 and set up a large and complex set of intertwined business and terrorist enterprises. . . .

Declaring War on the United States

Bin Ladin began delivering diatribes against the United States before he left Saudi Arabia. He continued to do so after he arrived in Sudan. In early 1992, the al Qaeda leadership issued a fatwa calling for jihad against the Western "occupation" of Islamic lands. Specifically singling out U.S. forces for attack, the language resembled that which would appear in Bin Ladin's public fatwa in August 1996. In ensuing weeks, Bin Ladin delivered an often-repeated lecture on the need to cut off "the head of the snake."

By this time, Bin Ladin was well-known and a senior figure among Islamist extremists, especially those in Egypt, the Arabian Peninsula, and the Afghanistan-Pakistan border region. Still, he was just one among many diverse terrorist barons. Some of Bin Ladin's close comrades were more peers than subordinates. For example, Usama Asmurai, also known as Wali Khan, worked with Bin Ladin in the early 1980s and helped him in the Philippines and in Tajikistan. The Egyptian spiritual guide based in New Jersey, the Blind Sheikh, whom Bin Ladin admired, was also in the network. Among sympathetic peers in Afghanistan were a few of the warlords still fighting for power and Abu Zubaydah, who helped operate a popular terrorist training camp near the border with Pakistan. There were also rootless but experienced operatives, such as Ramzi Yousef and Khalid Sheikh Mohammed, who—though not necessarily formal members of someone else's organization—were traveling around the world and joining in projects that were supported by or linked to Bin Ladin, the Blind Sheikh, or their associates.

In now analyzing the terrorist programs carried out by members of this network, it would be misleading to apply the label "al Qaeda operations" too often in these early years. Yet it would also be misleading to ignore the significance of these connections. And in this network, Bin Ladin's agenda stood out. While his allied Islamist groups were focused on local battles, such as those in Egypt, Algeria, Bosnia, or Chechnya, Bin Ladin concentrated on attacking the "far enemy"—the United States.

Attacks Known and Suspected

After U.S. troops deployed to Somalia in late 1992, al Qaeda leaders formulated a fatwa demanding their eviction. In December, bombs exploded at two hotels in Aden where U.S. troops routinely stopped en route to Somalia, killing two, but no Americans. The perpetrators are reported to have belonged to a group from southern Yemen headed by a Yemeni member of Bin Ladin's Islamic Army Shura; some in the group had trained at an al Qaeda camp in Sudan.

Al Qaeda leaders set up a Nairobi cell and used it to send weapons and trainers to the Somali warlords battling U.S. forces, an operation directly supervised by al Qaeda's military leader. Scores of trainers flowed to Somalia over the ensuing months, including most of the senior members and weapons training experts of al Qaeda's military committee. These trainers were later heard boasting that their assistance led to the October 1993 shootdown of two U.S. Black Hawk helicopters by members of a Somali militia group and to the subsequent withdrawal of U.S. forces in early 1994. . . .

Sudan Becomes a Doubtful Haven

Not until 1998 did al Qaeda undertake a major terrorist operation of its own, in large part because Bin Ladin lost his base in Sudan. Ever since the Islamist regime came to power in Khartoum, the United States and other Western governments had pressed it to stop providing a haven for terrorist organizations. Other governments in the region, such as those of Egypt, Syria, Jordan, and even Libya, which were targets of some of these groups, added their own pressure. . . .

In February 1996, Sudanese officials began approaching officials from the United States and other governments, asking what actions of theirs might ease foreign pressure. In secret meetings with Saudi officials, Sudan offered to expel Bin Ladin to Saudi Arabia and asked the Saudis to pardon him. U.S. officials became aware of these secret discussions, certainly by March. Saudi officials apparently wanted Bin Ladin expelled from Sudan. They had already revoked his citizenship, however, and would not tolerate his presence in their country. And Bin Ladin may have no longer felt safe in Sudan, where he had already escaped at least one assassination attempt that he believed to have been the work of the Egyptian or Saudi regimes, or both. In any case, on May 19, 1996, Bin Ladin left Sudan—significantly weakened, despite his ambitions and organizational skills. He returned to Afghanistan.

Al Qaeda's Renewal in Afghanistan

Bin Ladin flew on a leased aircraft from Khartoum to Jalalabad, with a refueling stopover in the United Arab Emirates. He was accompanied by family members and bodyguards, as well as by al Qaeda members who had been close associates since his organization's 1988 founding in Afghanistan. Dozens of additional militants arrived on later flights.

Though Bin Ladin's destination was Afghanistan, Pakistan was the nation that held the key to his ability to use Afghanistan as a base from which to revive his ambitious enterprise for war against the United States.

For the first quarter century of its existence as a nation, Pakistan's identity had derived from Islam, but its politics had been decidedly secular. The army was—and remains—the country's strongest and most respected institution, and the army had been and continues to be preoccupied with its rivalry with India, especially over the disputed territory of Kashmir.

From the 1970s onward, religion had become an increasingly powerful force in Pakistani politics. After a coup in 1977, military leaders turned to Islamist groups for support, and fundamentalists became more prominent. South Asia had an indigenous form of Islamic fundamentalism, which had developed in the nineteenth century at a school in the Indian village of Deoband. The influence of the Wahhabi school of Islam had also grown, nurtured by Saudi-funded institutions. Moreover, the fighting in Afghanistan made Pakistan home to an enormous—and generally unwelcome—population of Afghan refugees; and since the badly strained Pakistani education system could not accommodate the refugees, the government increasingly let privately funded religious schools serve as a cost-free alternative. Over time, these schools produced large numbers of half-educated young men with no marketable skills but with deeply held Islamic views.

Pakistan's rulers found these multitudes of ardent young Afghans a source of potential trouble at home but potentially useful abroad. Those who joined the Taliban movement, espousing a ruthless version of Islamic law, perhaps could bring order in chaotic Afghanistan and make it a cooperative ally. They thus might give Pakistan greater security on one of the several borders where Pakistani military officers hoped for what they called "strategic depth."

It is unlikely that Bin Ladin could have returned to Afghanistan had Pakistan disapproved. The Pakistan military intelligence service probably had advanced knowledge of his coming, and its officers may have facilitated his travel. During his entire time in Sudan, he had maintained guesthouses and training camps in Pakistan and Afghanistan. These were part of the larger network used by diverse organizations for recruiting and training fighters for Islamic insurgencies in such places as Tajikistan, Kashmir, and Chechnya. Pakistan intelligence officers reportedly introduced Bin Ladin to Taliban leaders in Kandahar, their main base of power, to aid his reassertion of control over camps near Khowst, out of an apparent hope that he would expand the camps and make them available for training Kashmiri militants. . . .

Bin Ladin appeared to have in Afghanistan a freedom of movement that he had lacked in Sudan. Al Qaeda members could travel freely within the country, enter and exit it without visas or any immigration procedures, purchase and import vehicles and weapons, and enjoy the use of official Afghan

Ministry of Defense license plates. Al Qaeda also used the Afghan state-owned Ariana Airlines to courier money into the country.

The Taliban [Islamic extremist regime that came to power in Afghanistan in 1996] seemed to open the doors to all who wanted to come to Afghanistan to train in the camps. The alliance with the Taliban provided al Qaeda a sanctuary in which to train and indoctrinate fighters and terrorists, import weapons, forge ties with other jihad groups and leaders, and plot and staff terrorist schemes. While Bin Ladin maintained his own al Qaeda guesthouses and camps for vetting and training recruits, he also provided support to and benefited from the broad infrastructure of such facilities in Afghanistan made available to the global network of Islamist movements. U.S. intelligence estimates put the total number of fighters who underwent instruction in Bin Ladin–supported camps in Afghanistan from 1996 through 9/11 at 10,000 to 20,000. . . .

The February 1998 fatwa thus seems to have been a kind of public launch of a renewed and stronger al Qaeda, after a year and a half of work. Having rebuilt his fund-raising network, Bin Ladin had again become the rich man of the jihad movement. He had maintained or restored many of his links with terrorists elsewhere in the world. And he had strengthened the internal ties in his own organization.

Chapter 4

The Future of Islamic Fundamentalism

Turning | Points

IN WORLD HISTORY

Islamic Fundamentalists Must Be Encouraged to Participate in International Politics

Robin Wright

In the following selection Robin Wright argues that despite its discomfort with radical Islam, the United States needs to encourage Islamic fundamentalists to participate in the international political process. Rather than alienating Muslims by excluding them from international politics, she asserts, the U.S. government needs to find ways to include and work with them to promote transformation and democracy. She suggests several ways to foster the participation of Islamic countries: The United States could have an authentic dialogue with jihadists; the United States could encourage Muslim countries to support the rule of law by offering them membership in the World Trade Organization as an incentive; and the United States could work to ensure that Muslims who live in the United States do not feel they are living on the fringe of society. When Islamists have a peaceful means to influence the political process, they will lose their reasons for practicing jihad against their own governments and against the West, Wright asserts. Wright is the author of *Sacred Rage: The Wrath of Militant Islam* and *The Last Great Revolution: Turmoil and Transformation in Iran.*

Once familiar to most Americans mainly from seventh grade social studies, Islam has now become synonymous in the minds of many with the biggest post–Cold War threat. Even as we struggle to understand it, we're afraid of it. And because of that fear, we're drawing a Green Curtain around the Muslim world, creating an enduring divide.

Robin Wright, "After Grief, the Fear We Won't Admit," *Washington Post*, September 12, 2004, p. B01. Copyright © 2004 by Washington Post Book World Service/ Washington Post Writers Group. Reproduced by permission.

Figuring out Islam's role in the 21st century is an existential challenge, but one many of us are emotionally unprepared to face. We pretend that we're not prejudiced, that we understand that most Muslims don't support the horrific bloodshed of bin Ladenism. Yet we still view 1.2 billion Muslim people spread throughout 53 countries as a threatening monolith. As long as we make that mistake, America and its allies won't feel safe, no matter how many billions of dollars are poured into security precautions.

Aside from the vital mission of tracking down bin Ladenists, military muscle is not always an effective instrument for moving forward. Nor are tepid diplomatic initiatives aimed at coaxing authoritarian governments into adopting change at a pace and in a manner that they control. There's another strategy that's gaining favor among Mideast experts: Bring Islamic movements and groups into the political process. Give Islamist parties new political space—wide open space—to absorb passions and sap anger.

Islam Is the Solution, Not the Problem

That means accepting, even embracing, the idea that Islam is not the problem, but the way out of a political predicament that has been building quietly for decades. It means not only supporting nationalists, liberals and nascent democrats already on our side in the quest to transform the Middle East but also encouraging Islamists and their parties to participate. Basically, it means differentiating between Islamists and jihadists, and accepting anyone willing to work within a system to change it rather than work from outside to destroy it.

"It's hard to imagine political evolution in the next 20 years that does not include the Islamists," says Ellen Laipson, president of the Stimson Center, a Washington think tank that studies international security issues. "They have established legitimacy and a following and you won't make them disappear overnight by supporting the activities of a small elite of secular modernists. . . . You have to imagine a political space that has both."

Mideast scholars say it's too late to do anything less. The

alternative is alienating even more Muslims by excluding them. And alienation—from closed political systems and corrupt economies—is what originally drove many Muslims to seek refuge in their mosques.

Including Islamists in government is an uncomfortable idea for those of us in secular societies. It summons up haunting images of Iranian clerics and American hostages, oppressed women and antiquated laws. That's why for years, U.S. governments have accepted Algeria's military, which voided free elections won by Islamic parties, and [Egyptian president] Hosni Mubarak's suppression of Egypt's Muslim groups. That's shortsighted because perpetuating the status quo will be worse. Now that Islamists have moved from the fringe to the center of political activity, a trend that has accelerated since the U.S. invasion of Iraq, they can no longer be excluded.

We have to think outside the prism of the war on terrorism. "Even as it wages a resolute campaign against international terrorism, America should not believe that it is engaged in a fight to the finish with radical Islam," Robert Hutchings, chairman of the National Intelligence Council, wrote in a recent issue of *Foreign Policy* magazine. "This conflict is not a clash of civilizations, but rather a defense of our shared humanity and a search for common ground, however implausible that may seem now.". . .

America Should Help Islamists Get Access to the Political Process

What can America do? A growing number of voices on both the right and the left have been emboldened to shape proposals in a broader context.

The United States has tipped its hat to political change with initiatives to promote democracy. As President Bush said in a June [2004] speech in Istanbul, "Democratic societies should welcome, not fear, the participation of the faithful."

Yet in practice, the United States still veers away from Islamists. In Iraq, which Washington seeks to turn into a model for the region, U.N. and U.S. envoys deliberately picked politicians mainly from secular parties to assume power after the formal end of the U.S.-led occupation. Despite strong support in opinion polls, Islamist parties were marginalized. Analysts now predict they'll make a comeback in next year's [2005] elections and the United States would be wise not to try to prevent it.[1]

"Political debate must encompass Islam if the debate is to be meaningful. Exclusion of the Islamic factor in Arab politics will simply be one-sided and unrealistic in its exclusion of the single greatest force within politics," writes Graham Fuller, a former senior intelligence analyst, in a paper released this month [September 2004], by the Carnegie Endowment for International Peace. The same applies to the wider Islamic world that constitutes 18 percent of the world's people.

In the race to capture the imagination of the vast, alienated middle, hard-line groups need to be operating under the same legal umbrella as more moderate groups—or they will try to lure the faithful through other means. "It's hard to hand over individual authority to people who are illiberal. What you have to realize is that the objective is to defeat bin Ladenism and you have to start the evolution. Moderate Muslims are not the answer. Shiite clerics and Sunni fundamentalists are our salvation from future 9/11s," says Reuel Marc Gerecht, a Middle East expert and senior fellow at the American Enterprise Institute.

A Risk Worth Taking

Transitions away from authoritarian regimes may be messier and more volatile than political transformations elsewhere over the past quarter century. But "Let it roll," Gerecht advises. "Don't walk away. It's part of the process. It's trying to ensure the system is sufficiently open that fundamentalists burn themselves out. You have to rob bin Ladenism of that

---

1. In Iraq's January 2005 elections, Shiites received 48 percent of the votes, the Kurdish alliance won 25 percent of the votes, and a bloc led by interim prime minister Ayad Allawi received about 14 percent of the votes. The Shiite parties, backed by the country's most influential religious leader, the Ayatollah Sayyed Ali al-Sestani, thus won the greatest number of votes, though not the majority landslide that some had predicted.

virulent elixir. If we don't go in that direction, we know all other roads go back to 9/11."

"You want in a Machiavellian way to have fundamentalists do the dirty work," he says. "You want them to take care of the people who slaughtered the children [in Beslan, Russia]. The only way to do that is to have them compete in the political system. It may come off the rails for a while in some places, but even if it does, you will be better off. You don't want fundamentalists to take states by coups d'etat."

The premise behind the new ideas is that activists inspired or protected by religion have stood in for jailed or exiled secular opposition figures in many societies. "Rebellion to tyrants is obedience to God," Benjamin Franklin once said. And more recently, liberation theologians in Latin America, Jewish refuseniks in the Soviet Union, South Africa's Anglican Archbishop Desmond Tutu and Catholic priests in Poland and the Philippines have played pivotal roles in political transformations.

"Conservative and even fundamentalist views of religion are manageable in a plural environment, as shown by a host of Protestant, Catholic and Jewish cases," wrote French scholar Olivier Roy in the new anthology "A Practical Guide to Winning the War on Terrorism." "A pluralist approach allows civil society to reach the cadres of youth who could be ideal targets for radicals and neo-fundamentalist groups."

Attempts to control the pace of change or choose the participants in the political process could invite an even deeper backlash than we face now. America cannot want less for Muslim countries than it wants for the rest of the world. And Muslims must not feel they are bystanders. "In the end, you have to treat Muslims as adults. They have to become responsible for their own fate," says Gerecht.

Three Things the United States Could Do

Based on conversations with Mideast experts, it appears that in the meantime, the United States could do three things. First, hold a genuine two-way dialogue. For all the hand-wringing about ending hatreds, that essential element is missing.

In a speech at the U.S. Institute of Peace last month [August 2004], national security adviser Condoleezza Rice said that the United States must do more with the Islamic world to dispel "destructive myths" about America and to support "voices of moderation." The most striking thing about the speech was that she gave it to an American audience. Asked why no senior U.S. official had given a similar speech in any of the five largest Muslim countries in the three years since Sept. 11, she replied, "That's a good question. Maybe we should."

Dialogue must not just engage people listed in the local U.S. embassy's Rolodex. We need to listen to the bad guys too to understand where the fissures—and opportunities— might be.

"Even the hard-core jihadis are having big debates about who exactly the enemy is and . . . about their tactics," says Princeton University Mideast expert Michael Doran, who gets up early each morning to research Islamist and jihadi Web sites. When U.S. contractor Paul Johnson was beheaded in Saudi Arabia [in 2004] "some said it was wrong. Others said, 'Our violence makes us look bad.' One of the most important ideologues, Abu Baseer, a cleric who was an Afghan jihadist, said 'Westerners in our society have protection.' The radicals countered that an apostate state—Saudi Arabia—can't grant immunity. But Baseer said, 'That's not right, we haven't thrown traditions out.' Three years after Sept. 11 . . . the debate among them is totally unknown."

A second course of U.S. action would be to use economic tools. Several Muslim countries, including Algeria, Lebanon, Saudi Arabia, Yemen, Libya, Iran and Iraq, are seeking membership in the World Trade Organization [WTO]. The United States could use WTO membership to induce change and force countries to embrace the rule of law.

Finally, we can embrace our own Islamic identity. Islam, the fastest-growing religion in the United States, is expected to become the second-largest faith in six years. Yet Muslims remain on the fringe. Just ask women who cover their heads or men with beards waiting in the boarding areas of airports.

Immediately after 9/11, Bush visited the Islamic Center in Washington and said Islam was not the enemy. This is a noble sentiment, but Muslims must also become part of the mainstream—a challenge faced throughout the West. For Europeans, the most important battle for Muslim hearts and minds over the next decade will not be fought in the Middle East but in European cities where the numbers of Muslims are growing as Gilles Kepel, a French expert on Islam, says in his new book "The War for Muslim Minds: Islam and the West." "If European societies are able to integrate these Muslim populations . . . this new generation of Muslims may become the Islamic vanguard of the next decade," he writes.

The unspoken undercurrent behind our failure to do more over the past three years is what former [Soviet] national security adviser Zbigniew Brzezinski calls "a fear that periodically verges on panic that is in itself blind." As we look beyond our grief [over the 9/11 attacks] we must also get beyond our prejudice and fear.

Islamic Societies Must Be Reformed

Ibn Warraq

Most Westerners writing about Islamic fundamentalism make a distinction between ordinary Muslims and jihadists. Those who condemn radical Islamists are generally careful not to criticize Islam itself, a religion practiced by 1.2 billion people around the world. Ibn Warraq, however, argues that Islam is an "irreformably fascist ideology." In the next selection he argues that because Islam is based on the Koran, which contains many verses that are "intolerant, bellicose, and misogynist," a society based on its laws can never be moderate or respect human rights. Warraq states that Islamic societies must have secular governments so that their citizens can enjoy freedom of thought and expression and an end to cruel punishments. Such a reformation, Warraq argues, will require that Islamic societies adopt modern principles of human rights, such as those laid out by the United Nations Universal Declaration of Human Rights. People will still be free to practice Islam, but their religious choices will be private rather than dictated by the state. Ibn Warraq is a research fellow in Islamic secularism at the Center for Self-Inquiry International and a member of the center's Committee for the Scientific Examination of Religion. He is also the author of *Why I Am Not a Muslim*.

To ask whether Islam can come into the twenty-first century is to ask whether Islam can be divorced from Islamic fundamentalism. Yet the root cause of Islamic fundamentalism is Islam itself.

Ibn Warraq, "Yes! Islam Can Be Reformed," *Free Inquiry Buffalo*, vol. 24, April/May 2004. Copyright © 2004 by Council for Democratic and Secular Humanism, Inc. Reproduced by permission.

Poverty is not the root cause of Islamic fundamentalism. Modern Islamists are mostly middle-class young men who are highly motivated, upwardly mobile, and well-educated. Often they hold science or engineering degrees. Islamists themselves rarely talk of poverty. [Iran's Islamic fundamentalist leader] Ayatollah Khomeini once said, "we did not create a revolution to lower the price of melons." For Islamists, wealth is a means, not an end: if they yearn for money, it is for buying weapons, not for opulent living.

Nor is the existence of Israel the cause of Islamic terrorism. Even Benjamin Netanyahu [Israeli prime minister from 1993 to 1996] admits, "The soldiers of militant Islam do not hate the West because of Israel, they hate Israel because of the West." This is confirmed by Wagdi Ghuniem, a militant Islamic cleric from Egypt: "Suppose the Jews said 'Palestine—you [Muslims] can take it.' . . . What would we tell them? No! The problem is belief; it is not a problem of land." Nor is Islamic terrorism caused by American foreign policy. If anything, U.S. policy toward the Arab and Muslim world prior to 2003 has been accommodating toward Muslim interests: American arms protected Afghanistan from the Soviets, Saudi Arabia and Kuwait from Iraq, Bosnia and Kosovo from Yugoslavia, and (to some degree) Somalia from the warlord Muhammad Farah Aidid. And what had U.S. foreign policy to do with the deaths of 150,000 Algerians at the hands of Islamist fanatics? That's 15,000 murders per year for a decade—a World Trade Center atrocity every two-and-a-half months for ten years—with no conceivable link to American conduct.

Ten years ago [in 1994] I wrote that the principal victims of Islamic fundamentalism are Muslims: men, women, children, writers, intellectuals, and journalists. That's still true—as it is true that the theory and practice of jihad was not concocted in the Pentagon but derived directly from the Qur'an and Hadith, from Islamic tradition.

Unfortunately, Western liberals and humanists find this hard to accept. They are pathologically nice: they believe that everyone thinks as they do. They assume that all people, Islamists included, have the same desires and goals in life.

Contrary to this naive view, Islamic fundamentalists are the-outopian visionaries. Their goal is to replace Western-style liberal democracy with an Islamic theocracy, a fascist system of thought that aims to control every single act of every single individual. Asked what lesson he had learned from his experience, one survivor of the Holocaust replied, "If someone tells you that he intends to kill you, believe him." This is a harsh lesson that members of the humanist movement desperately need to learn.

Jihad and Its Qur'anic Roots

The four greatest influences on the rise of contemporary militant Islam have been Egypt's Hassan al-Bana (1906–1949); Sayyid Qutb (1906–1966), founder of the Muslim Brethren; Indo-Pakistani scholar-activist Sayeed Abdul a'la Maududi (1903–1979); and Iran's Ayatollah Ruhollah Khomeini (1900–1989). They all repeat the same message, derived from classical writers like Ibn Taymiyyah (1268–1328) and ultimately from the Qur'an and Hadith: it is the divinely ordained duty of all Muslims to fight non-Muslims in the literal sense until man-made law has been replaced by God's Law, the Sharia—until Islam has conquered the entire world. In Maududi's words:

> In reality Islam is a revolutionary ideology and programme which seeks to alter the social order of the whole world and rebuild it in conformity with its own tenets and ideals. . . . Islam wishes to destroy all states and governments anywhere on the face of the earth which are opposed to the ideology and programme of Islam regardless of the country or the nation which rules it. The purpose of Islam is to set up a state on the basis of its own ideology and programme, regardless of which nation assumes the role of the standard bearer of Islam or the rule of which nation is undermined in the process of the establishment of an ideological Islamic State.

Here is Khomeini:

> . . . Islam makes it incumbent on all adult males, provided they are not disabled and incapacitated, to prepare themselves for the conquest of [other] countries so that the writ of

Islam is obeyed in every country in the world. But those who study Islamic Holy War will understand why Islam wants to conquer the whole world. . . . Those who know nothing of Islam pretend that Islam counsels against war. Those [who say this] are witless. Islam says: Kill all the unbelievers just as they would kill you all! . . . There are hundreds of other [Koranic] psalms and Hadiths [sayings of the Prophet] urging Muslims to value war and to fight. Does all that mean that Islam is a religion that prevents men from waging war? I spit upon those foolish souls who make such a claim.

Instead of confronting these facts, too many humanists wallow—better, choke, to use [writer] Howard Jacobson's word—on the stink of their own self-hatred. To quote Jacobson fully:

Utterly obscene, the narrative of guilty causation which now waits on every fresh atrocity—"What else are the dissatisfied to do but kill?" etc.—as though dissatisfaction were an automatic detonator. . . . Obscene in its self-righteousness, mentally permitting others to pay the price of our self-loathing. Obscene in its ignorance . . . encouraging those who hate us only to hate us more, since we concur in their conviction of our detestableness. Here is our decadence: not the nightclubs, not the beaches and the sex and the drugs, but our incapacity to believe we have been wronged. Our lack of self-worth. . . .

Self-criticism is one of the glories of Western civilization; both democracy and progress in science depend on it. Self-loathing in modern times is one of its weaknesses.

Dare We Hope for an Islamic Reformation?

Can Islam come into the twenty-first century? How would we know if it did? In essence we are speaking of what amounts to a modern-day Islamic Reformation, a Second Vatican Council for Islam. Can such a thing be a realistic hope?

First, we must define what an Islamic Reformation might consist of. It might be argued that since Islam has no pope or even, in principle, a centrally organized clergy, there is no sure way to verify that such a reformation had occurred. One Muslim's reformation would be another Muslim's decadence. I would suggest that the United Nations Universal

Declaration of Human Rights (UDHR) (1948) provides a metric by which any Islamic Reformation might be measured. Granted, many Muslims do not accept the UDHR. Indeed, in 1981 several Muslim countries issued their own Universal Islamic Declaration of Human Rights, which denies many of the individual freedoms guaranteed under UDHR, especially the right of any individual to change his or her religion as established in UDHR's Article 18.

Still, I think most observers who do accept UDHR would agree that a de facto reformation would take place in an Islamic society like that of Pakistan or Egypt if the UDHR's major articles began to enjoy respect:

1. The rights of women.

2. The rights of non-Muslims.

3. The rights of individuals regarding freedom of thought, conscience, expression, and religion, including the right to change one's religion and the right not to believe in any deity.

4. The cessation of cruel punishments such as mutilation of limbs for theft and stoning to death for adultery.

5. The freedom of inquiry for which one measure might be whether copies of [writer] Salman Rushdie's *The Satanic Verses* and my own *Why I Am Not a Muslim* are freely available.

Is such a reform likely? Can Islam institute such reforms and still be Islam? At this point, some misguided liberal Muslims will offer a have-your-cake-and-eat-it-too argument. On their view, the real Islam is compatible with human rights; the real Islam is feminist, egalitarian, tolerant of other religions and beliefs, and so on. They then proceed to re-interpret the many embarrassing, intolerant, bellicose, and misogynist verses of the Qur'an in wildly creative ways. But intellectual honesty demands that we reject such dishonest tinkering. The holy text may be open to some re-interpretation, but it is not infinitely elastic. Sooner or later we must come to terms with what the Qur'an actually says.

In any case, any strategy that ultimately reduces to trading verses with the fundamentalists does battle on the fanatics' terms, on the fanatics' ground. For every text liberal Muslims can produce, the mullahs will adduce dozens of counter-examples of greater exegetical, philological, and historical legitimacy. Liberal reformists cannot escape the simple fact that orthodox Islam is incompatible with modern concepts of human rights. On the contrary, every tenet of Islamic fundamentalism derives directly and altogether legitimately from the Qur'an, the Sunna, and the Hadith. Moderate Muslims there may be, but Islam itself is not—can never be—moderate.

Islam itself is an irreformably fascist ideology.

If Islamic societies are to be reformed, this must occur in spite of Islam, not in harmony with it. Questions of human rights must be brought out of the sphere of religion and into the sphere of the civil state. In other words, religion and state must be separated. Unavoidably, any separation effort will at some point have to confront Sharia, the Islamic law. Why have a separation, Islamists will demand, when Islam is such a perfect religion that provides answers for even the most mundane of problems? If forced to concede that Islam does not provide answers for all possible problems, nonetheless they will ask, Why not keep Islamic law in all those arenas of life for which it claims to offer solutions? Why not maintain, for instance, stoning for adultery? At that point, someone in the reformist camp will have to assert that such punishments are barbaric and incompatible with human rights as envisaged in the UDHR. He or she will need to argue that the demands of reason and common humanity override the dictates of revelation. At that point the battle between Islam and modernity—a battle that could never be prevented, only delayed—will at last be joined in earnest.

When such a Reformation is complete, Islam would exist within a secular state, relegated to the realm of the personal where it would wield limited power but could nonetheless continue to provide consolation, comfort, and meaning to millions of individuals.

Secularization: Difficult but Possible

Can any such reformation occur? In other words, can Islamic societies be secularized? There are many reasons to suppose they can.

Since September 11, 2001, it has become a commonplace

[observation that] Islam knows no separation between mosque and state, indeed that classical Arabic contains no word pairs corresponding to lay and ecclesiastical, spiritual and temporal, secular and religious. All of this is true, and yet Islamic history does not chronicle a series of relentless Muslim theocracies. On the contrary, as [the author] Carl Brown has recently demonstrated, Muslim history has been marked by a nondoctrinal, de facto separation of state and religious community. Rule was mainly by decree, those decrees being given ex post facto religious sanction by the jurists.

Most of today's culturally Islamic countries were founded or sweepingly reformed by secularists. Consider Muhammad Ali Jinnah of Pakistan, Nasser of Egypt, Sukarno of Indonesia, Bourguiba of Tunisia, Sultan Muhammad V of Morocco, Riza Shah and his son Muhammad Riza Shah plus Muhammad Musaddiq in Iran, and so on. Only after the secularizers discredited themselves through corruption, nepotism, and incompetence were the Islamists able to exploit popular discontent and compel the re-introduction of Islam into public life.

Finally, consider the Islamic Republic of Iran. Iran has adopted many Western democratic institutions such as popular elections, a constituent assembly, a parliament, and even a constitution, inspired by France's constitution of 1958. None of these have any doctrinal or historic link to Islam, yet a putatively hardcore Islamist regime has made no attempt to jettison them. Iran even has a student protest movement that even now is demonstrating to demand a secular republic.

Yet there are also good reasons to admit that, if Islamic secularization is possible, it will not be easy. With the partial exception of Turkey, the Islamic world contains not a single stable democracy. It is not surprising that Muslims living under repressive regimes turn to Islamists for support, both moral and economic. Even if free and fair elections occur, they will not necessarily lead to secular governments, as Islamist electoral victories in Algeria, Pakistan, and Turkey demonstrate.

Today's Middle East offers a hostile environment in which

to nurture democratic institutions. Studies by Human Rights Watch, the United Nations Development Program, and others document disheartening social stasis, institutional underdevelopment, and economic malaise. Across most of the region, such essential precursors of democracy as political parties and human rights organizations are hampered or banned outright, usually by governments in the thrall of conservative Islamic clergy.

A Difficult Blueprint for Reform

If secularizing reformation is to occur in the Muslim world, we in the West cannot escape the need to confront Islam openly. First, we who enjoy freedom of expression and scientific inquiry should encourage Muslims to take a rational look at Islam. We should especially encourage Qur'anic criticism, which can help Muslims to look at their scripture and ultimately their faith in a more rational and objective way. It makes no sense when the same persons who lament the lack of an Islamic Reformation disparage books like *Why I Am Not a Muslim* or cry "Islamophobia!" each time Islam is criticized. Western political leaders, journalists, and scholars need to overcome their fondness for protecting tender Muslim sensibilities. We do Islam no favors by delaying its encounter with Enlightenment values.

Second, simply by protecting non-Muslims in Islamic societies we are encouraging religious pluralism, from which can one day blossom pluralism in general. Just by insisting on article 18 of the UDHR, which states, "Everyone has the right to freedom of thought, conscience and religion; this right includes freedom to change his religion or belief . . ." we loosen the grip of fanatics and encourage what [scholar] Owen Chadwick called a free market in all opinions—in other words, democracy.

Third, we can encourage rationality by secularizing education across the Muslim world. Secular education will mean closing the religious madrassas where young children from poor families memorize the Qur'an and learn only jihad—in short, where they learn to be fanatics. There must be a wholesale rewriting of school texts, which at present preach intolerance of non-Muslims, particularly Jews. Critical thinking and rationality must be encouraged, not denigrated. Pluralism would be further encouraged by teaching the glories of pre-Islamic history to all children. Advances in education must be matched by genuine economic opportunity, lest schools create impossible expectations whose frustration feeds the Islamists' agenda.

Fourth, there must be broader self-criticism and a retreat from self-pity. Islamic countries will never progress while they blame all their ills on the West; whining about U.S. imperialism or some putative Zionist conspiracy will only perpetuate the current stasis. Islamic countries need charismatic leaders capable of self-criticism—leaders who can say to their peoples, at the risk of misquoting Shakespeare, that "the fault is not in [the] stars [and stripes], but in ourselves, that we are underlings."

I believe that a meaningful Islamic Reformation is possible. But it will be painful and difficult. It will require Muslim—not Islamist—leaders who can guide their peoples toward democracy, leaders willing to institute civil states and uniform codes of civil laws separate from and independent of religious institutions. It will require legislation that establishes the rights of all citizens, male and female, Muslim and non-Muslim, as set forth in the Universal Declaration of Human Rights—including the right to free choice of religious belief and practice. And it will demand Western leaders who support this process wholeheartedly—or will at least get out of the way.

Is the West truly ready to encourage secularism in the Islamic world? One wonders in light of continuing U.S. support for the Saudi regime, which has largely bankrolled the spread of radical Islam. One wonders in light of the fact that George W. Bush and Tony Blair have done more than any Western leaders since 1945 to reinject religion into the public sphere. Perhaps they have forgotten the words of James Madison: "There is not a shadow of right in the general government to intermeddle with religion. Its least interference with it would be a most flagrant usurpation."

Discussion Questions

Chapter 1: The Roots of Islamic Fundamentalism

1. In his article R. Scott Appleby explores the intellectual roots of Islamic fundamentalism. Based on your reading of Appleby's article, do you believe Islamic fundamentalism is a distortion of Islam or a return to Islamic roots? According to Appleby, what traits are shared by Christian fundamentalism, Orthodox Judaism, and Islamic fundamentalism?

2. Alan Richards argues that Islamic fundamentalism is a symptom of economic modernization and that industrialization has led to ideological extremism and violence in many parts of the world. In Richards's view, why has modernization given rise to extremism and violence?

3. John L. Esposito describes the genesis of two organizations that have had a powerful influence on the culture and politics of Muslim countries in modern times. What do the Muslim Brotherhood and the Jamaat-i-Islami have in common? In Esposito's opinion, what is modern and what is traditional about the Muslim Brotherhood and Jamaat-i-Islami? Are they political organizations or religious organizations or both? Explain.

4. Mir Zohair Husain examines the effects of the Arab-Israeli conflict, and especially the 1967 Arab-Israeli War, on the growth of Islamic fundamentalism. According to Husain, why was the creation of Israel a source of so much anger in the Middle East? Why did the dramatic Israeli victory in the 1967 war discredit secular regimes in the Middle East and give strength to Islamic fundamentalists?

5. In his article Aijazz Ahmed investigates the madrassas, Islamic religious schools that are said to foster an intensely anti-Western, politicized version of Islam. In Ahmed's view, are all madrassas fundamentalist? Explain why or why not. Would madrassas be less influential if there were more secular educational opportunities in countries such as Pakistan? Explain your answer.

Chapter 2: Islamic Fundamentalism Achieves State Power

1. Joseph Nevo writes about the relationship between religion and national identity in Saudi Arabia, where a single family controls

the world's richest oil reserve and the holiest sites in Islam. What is Wahhabism, and how, according to Nevo, does it serve to legitimize the Saudi state? What are the objections of Saudi dissidents to the Saudi government? If Saudi Arabia were to become more democractic, who would benefit?

2. Gilles Kepel analyzes the religious and political forces behind the 1979 revolution, which turned Iran from an authoritarian secular state into an Islamic theocracy led by Ayatollah Khomeini. According to Kepel, how did Khomeini manipulate other groups that sought to unseat the shah? Which groups might have reduced Islamic fundamentalism's power once the shah was overthrown and why did they fail to do so?

3. Judith Miller discusses the coups that brought increasingly harsh Islamic rule to a poor African country in the grip of decades of civil war. According to her article, why has Sudan chosen a fundamentalist Islamic government when the country has many minorities with other faiths?

4. Angelo Rasanayagam describes the government of the Taliban, a group of Islamic extremists who came to power in Afghanistan in the mid 1990s. Using examples from Rasanayagam's article, explain how the war and chaos in Afghanistan helped the Taliban achieve power. Why were the Taliban so indifferent to the opinion of other governments? In retrospect, what should the international community have done about Afghanistan? Should the United Nations have acted? Would the United States have been justified in overthrowing the Taliban prior to 9/11? Why or why not?

5. Samina Yasmeen analyzes the forces that led Pakistan to foster Islamic fundamentalism at home and in the bordering country of Afghanistan. Why do relatively unstable states turn to religion as a form of political legitimacy, and what are the rewards and dangers of such an approach? Support your answer with evidence from Yasmeen's article on Pakistan and Judith Miller's article on Sudan.

Chapter 3: Islamic Terrorism

1. Shaul Shay traces the steps by which militant Islamists, whose religion specifically prohibits both suicide and killing civilians in war, made the terrorist suicide attack their major weapon. According to Shay, how were suicide attacks fostered by Iran's Ayatollah Khomeini? What effect did Iran's desperate war with

Iraq have on the growth of suicide attacks? Why were suicide attacks used as a tactic in the Palestinian-Israeli conflict?

2. Hala Jaber details the circumstances under which Hizballah, the "Party of God," was formed in Lebanon. How did the Israeli invasion of Lebanon contribute to the birth of Hizballah? What role did the Iranian invasion play? Using what you have learned from Jaber's article, explain whether you believe Hizballah is a legitimate resistance group or a terrorist group.

3. The authors of the 9/11 report trace the growth of the Islamic fundamentalist terrorist group al Qaeda under the leadership of Saudi millionaire Osama bin Laden. What role did the chaotic political situation in countries like Sudan and Afghanistan play in the development of al Qaeda? According to the report, could the United States have done anything to prevent the 9/11 attacks? Explain.

Chapter 4: The Future of Islamic Fundamentalism

1. Robin Wright argues that Islamic fundamentalists must be accepted by democratic governments in the Middle East and South Asia. Does Wright think that democratically elected Islamic fundamentalists, once in power, would permit elections that might dislodge them? Explain why or why not.

2. Ibn Warraq maintains that all Islamic beliefs are fundamentalist and that only significant reform could make Islam compatible with human rights. What are the conflicts that Ibn Warraq sees between Islam and human rights as defined by the United Nations? How does Warraq think Islam should be reformed?

Appendix of Documents

Document 1: Hasan al-Banna's Criticism of European Civilization

In 1928, several years after the breakup of the Ottoman Empire and four years after Turkey formally abolished the institution of the caliphate (a single ruler of all Islam), an Egyptian former schoolteacher named Hasan al-Banna founded the Muslim Brotherhood. This organization advocates that Muslims reject secular government and Western influences and create governments based on the precepts of the Koran. The following is a short excerpt from al-Banna's tract "Between Yesterday and Today."

The European nations, which had socialized and had come into contact with Islam and Muslims (due to their Crusades in the East, and their proximity to the Arabs of Andalus in the West), not only benefited from this in terms of a heightened awareness, cohesion, and political unification; but also in terms of a great intellectual awakening, acquiring numerous sciences and branches of knowledge. A scientific and cultural Renaissance, vast in scope, made its appearance, and the Church with all the strength at its command rose to combat this strange phenomenon. It subjected their scholars and intellectuals to the most horrific punishments: the courts of The Inquisition waged war upon them and aroused the wrath of the people against them. But this accomplished nothing, its teachings could not stand up in front of scientific realities and discoveries. The scientific Renaissance emerged victorious, and the state thereby awoke and it too fought the Church until it completely delivered European society from Church authority. Its men were driven into the shrine and the cloister, the Pope was confined to the Vatican, and the work of the clergy was limited and their efforts were confined. Christianity remained in Europe, but only to serve as a historical heirloom. It was an instrument for educating the simple minded and naive among the masses, and a mechanism for conquest, colonization, and the suppression of political aspirations. The domain of science stretched out before Europe, and the scope of invention and discovery broadened. The machine doubled production and industrialized life. All this [proceeded] hand in hand with the rise of the strong state, whose authority reached out across many lands and regions. The world eagerly welcomed the European nations and chose them as its sustainers. Wealth poured out from it in every direction. It was only natural then, that European life and culture should be based on excluding religion from all aspects of social life, especially the state, the law court, and the school; with a predominant materialistic outlook becoming the criterion for everything. As a result, the make-up of this civilization became purely materialistic, demolishing what the revealed religions had advocated and utterly contradicting the principle of uniting the spiritual and the material which Islam had laid as the foundation of its civilization. Among the most important traits of European civilization are the following:

1) Apostasy, doubt in Allah, denial of the soul, disregard as to reward or punishment in the world to come, and an obsession to limit themselves to only that which is material and tangible:

'They know something external of the life of this world, but of the world to come they are heedless.'

2) Lust, unseemly dedication to pleasure, new ways of self in-dulgence, uncontrolled freedom of the lower instincts and bodily desires, the equipment of women with every technique of seduc-tion and incitement, and the drowning into wicked practices which shatter both mind and body, destroying the integrity of the family and threatening the happiness of the home:

'Those who disbelieve take their enjoyment and eat as cattle eat, and the Fire is their dwelling place.'

3) Individual greed, for every man wants any thing good only for himself; Greed also exists in the social strata, for each strata wants to gain the upper hand over the other and seeks to secure profits for itself. Finally there is greed on a national level, for each nation is prejudiced towards its own nationality, while looking down on all others, and trying to engulf those who are weaker.

4) Usury, granting it legal recognition, regarding it as a princi-ple of general transactions, and making it a general practice among nations and individuals.

These purely materialistic traits of European society have cor-rupted the spirit, devalued morality, and made them sluggish in the war against crime, all this and the problems have multiplied, de-structive ideologies have made their appearance, devastating and damning revolutions have burst forth, economic, social, and polit-ical institutions no longer stand on firm foundations. Nations have been torn apart by sects and parties, while greed and hatred have driven people to cut each other's throats. This modern civilization has substantiated its complete impotence in securing peace, tranquillity and safety within society. It has failed to grant happiness to man, despite all the doors of science, knowledge, wealth and opulence it has left open for them, and despite the power and authority it enjoys throughout the earth, and even though it has not been in existence for so much as a century.

The Tyranny of Materialism on Muslim Land

The Europeans worked assiduously in trying to immerse (the world) in materialism, with their corrupting traits and murderous germs, to overwhelm those Muslim lands that their hands stretched out to. Under their authority the Muslims suffered an ill fate, for while they secured for themselves power and prosperity through science, knowledge, industry, and good organization, the Muslims were barred from all this. They laid the plans for this social turmoil in masterly fashion, invoking the aid of their political intellect and military might until they achieved their goal. They deluded the Muslim leaders by granting them loans and entering into financial transactions with them—An easy task which enabled them to infiltrate the economy and flood the country with their capital, their banks, and their companies; Thus they ran the economic machinery, exploiting the enormous profits and vast sums of money. All to the exclusion of the inhabitants. Hence, they were able to alter the basic principles of government, justice, and education, and infuse in the most powerful Islamic countries, their own peculiar political judicial, and cultural systems. They imported their semi-naked women into these regions, together with their liquors, their theatres, their dance halls, their amusements arcades, their stories, their newspapers, their novels, their whims, their silly games, and their vices. Here they allowed for crimes intolerable in their own countries, and beautified this tumultuous world to the deluded, naive eyes of wealthy Muslims and those of rank and authority. This was not enough for them, so they built schools and scientific cultural institutions, casting doubt and heresy within the hearts of people. They taught them how to demean themselves, to vilify their religion and their homeland, to detach themselves from their beliefs, and to regard anything Western as sacred, in the belief that only that which is European can be emulated.

Hasan al-Banna, *Five Tracts of Hasan al-Banna*, trans. Charles Wendell. Berkeley: University of California Press, 1978.

Document 2: Sayyid Qutb on the Decline of Western Civilization

Sayyid Qutb, hanged in 1966 for his opposition to the policies of Egyptian president Gamal Abdel Nasser, remains a major influence on Islamic fundamentalists today. In his book Milestones, *first published in 1964, he finds emptiness and futility in all the ideologies of the modern Western world, arguing that Islam is the only valid alternative belief system.*

Today mankind stands at the brink of a precipice, not because the danger of total extinction is hovering over its head—for this being only an apparent symptom not the real disease—but because today humanity is bereft of those values of life, which are not only instrumental to its healthy growth but also to its real evolution. This spiritual destitution has become fully evident to the people of the West, because the Western civilization has no healthy values of life to offer to humanity. Rather its spiritual decadence has reached a point that it does not have any reasonable ground or justification for its survival, which, short of all, could, at least, satisfy its own collective conscience. Democracy has proved sterile in the west, which has now been compelled to borrow Oriental thoughts and theories and ways of life. A significant example is its acceptance of economic concepts of the Eastern camp under the garb of socialism.

The condition of the Eastern Block, on the other hand, is not substantially different. Its Social theories, foremost among them Marxism, originally attracted not only the people of the East but also a considerable number from the West, for it was a way of life based on creed. But Marxism now stands defeated on the intellectual plane. It would not be an exaggeration to say that it has now become the system of a State which has not even remote connection with Marxism. On the whole this theory is the travesty of the human nature. It can only prosper in a degraded, decadent and destitute environment or in a society reconciled to the hardships of a prolonged dictatorial regime. But now its materialistic economic experience is proving infructuous even in such a downtrodden and soulless environment, although this is the only foundation on which its entire edifice rests and is a matter of pride for it. Russia, which is the leader of all communist countries is itself suffering from food shortages. Although it has been producing surplus crops even in the days of Tears, it is now importing foodstuff from abroad, and selling its gold reserves for procuring wheat. The reason is that its sytem of collective farming has met with total failure, or one can say, that a system has failed which was antagonistic to the human nature.

Need for New Leadership

Mankind now needs a new leadership. It is a fact that the leadership by the west is thoroughly on the decline, not because the Western civilization has become poor materially, or because its economic or military power has become weak. The root cause is that the Western Man has been deprived of those life-giving values which could have sustained him to the leadership of Mankind. That is why his role on the stage of history is over, and an urgent need of such leadership is felt which could preserve and further develop the material advancements acquired as a result of the creative genius of Europe and also provide mankind with such high ideals and sublime values of life which have so far remained undiscovered by mankind, and which will also acquaint humanity with a way of life, consonant with human nature and be positive, constructive and realistic. It is Islam and Islam alone which possesses these enlivening values and is the unique way of life. It would be a futile exercise to seek it from any source other than Islam.

The period of renaissance of Europe has come to an end. The movement of resurgence of science which started in the sixteenth century after Christ, and rose to its zenith in the eighteenth and the nineteenth centuries after Christ, does not possess any reviving spirit.

All chauvinistic and nationalistic ideologies which have appeared in these modern times and all those collective movements which flourished as a result of these theories are left with no other weapon. In short all the man-made individual and collective theories have one by one declared their failure.

Sayyid Qutb, *Milestones*, trans. S. Badrul Hasan. Karachi, Pakistan: International Islamic Publishers, 1981.

Document 3: Ayatollah Khomeini Announces the First Day of God's Government

In 1979 a revolution in Iran forced Shah Reza Pahlavi to abdicate and flee the country. Ayatollah Ruhollah Khomeini, a seventy-six-year-old clerical leader, was named "supreme leader" of Iran, transforming the country into an Islamist theocracy. The following excerpt is from Khomeini's speech declaring the Islamic Republic of Iran.

I offer my sincere congratulations to the great people of Iran, who were despised and oppressed by arrogant kings throughout the history of the monarchy. God Almighty has granted us His favor and destroyed the regime of arrogance by His powerful hand, which has shown itself as the power of the oppressed. He has made our great people into leaders and exemplars for all the world's oppressed, and He has granted them their just heritage by the establishment of this Islamic Republic.

On this blessed day, the day the Islamic community assumes leadership, the day of the victory and triumph of our people, I declare the Islamic Republic of Iran.

I declare to the whole world that never has the history of Iran witnessed such a referendum, where the whole country rushed to the polls with ardor, enthusiasm, and love in order to cast their affirmative votes and bury the tyrannical regime forever in the garbage heap of history. I value highly this unparalleled solidarity by virtue of which the entire population—with the exception of a handful of adventurers and godless individuals—responded to the heavenly call of "Hold firm to the rope of God, all together" (Qur'an, 3:103) and cast a virtually unanimous vote in favor of the Islamic Republic, thus demonstrating its political and social maturity to both the East and the West.

Blessed for you be the day on which, after the martyrdom of your upright young people, the sorrow of their grieving mothers and fathers, and the suffering of the whole nation, you have overthrown your ghoulish enemy, the pharaoh of the age. By casting a decisive vote in favor of the Islamic Republic, you have established a government of divine justice, a government in which all segments of the population shall enjoy equal consideration, the light of divine justice shall shine uniformly on all, and the divine mercy of the Qur'an and the Sunna shall embrace all, like life-giving rain. Blessed for you be this government that knows no difference of race, whether between black and white, or between Turk, Persian, Kurd, and Baluch. All are brothers and equal; nobility lies only in the fear of God, and superiority may be attained only by acquiring virtues and performing good deeds. Blessed for you be the day on which all segments of the population have attained their legitimate rights; in the implementation of justice, there will be no difference between women and men, or between the religious minorities and the Muslims. Tyranny has been buried, and all forms of transgression will be buried along with it.

The country has been delivered from the clutches of domestic and foreign enemies, from the thieves and plunderers, and you, courageous people, are now the guardians of the Islamic Republic. It is you who must preserve this divine legacy with strength and determination and must not permit the remnants of the putrid regime of the Shah who now lie in wait, or the supporters of the international thieves and oil bandits, to penetrate your serried ranks. You must now assume control of your own destiny and not give the opportunists any occasion to assert themselves. Relying on the divine power that is manifested in communal solidarity, take the next steps by sending virtuous, trustworthy representatives to the Constituent Assembly, so that they may revise the Constitution of the Islamic Republic. Just as you voted with ardor and enthusiasm for the Islamic Republic, vote, too, for your representatives, so that the malevolent will have no excuse to object.

This day of Farvardin 12, the first day of God's government, is to be one of our foremost religious and national festivals; the people must celebrate this day and keep its remembrance alive, for it is the day on which the battlements of the twenty-five-hundred-year-old fortress of tyrannical government crumbled, a satanic power departed forever, and the government of the oppressed—which is the government of God—was established in its place.

Ayatollah Ruhollah Khomeini, speech delivered in Qum, Iran, on April 1, 1979.

Document 4: Ayatollah Khomeini Urges Iranians to Export Their Revolution

The United States was conciliatory to Iran's revolutionary Islamic regime when it took power in 1979, and continued to attempt to work with "moderates" within the regime throughout the 1980s. However, Ayatollah Khomeini made the fear of American intervention a source of solidarity among his people, as can be seen in this excerpt from his speech delivered in Tehran on the occasion of the Iranian New Year in 1980.

I offer my congratulations to all the oppressed and to the noble people of Iran on the occasion of the New Year, which coincides with the completion of the pillars of the new Islamic Republic.

God Almighty has willed—and all thanks are due to Him—that this noble nation be delivered from the oppression and crimes inflicted on it by a tyrannical government and from the domination of the oppressive powers, especially America, the global plunderer, and that the flag of Islamic justice wave over our beloved land. It is our duty to stand firm against the superpowers, as we are indeed able to do, on condition that the intellectuals stop following and imitating either the West or the East, and adhere instead to the straight path of Islam and the nation. We are at war with international communism no less than we are struggling against the global plunderers of the West, headed by America, Zionism, and Israel.

Dear friends! Be fully aware that the danger represented by the communist powers is no less than that of America; the danger that America poses is so great that if you commit the smallest oversight, you will be destroyed. Both superpowers are intent on destroying the oppressed nations of the world, and it is our duty to defend those nations.

We must strive to export our Revolution throughout the world, and must abandon all idea of not doing so, for not only does Islam refuse to recognize any difference between Muslim countries, it is the champion of all oppressed people. Moreover, all the powers are intent on destroying us, and if we remain surrounded in a closed circle, we shall certainly be defeated. We must make plain our stance toward the powers and the superpowers and demonstrate to them that despite the arduous problems that burden us, our attitude to the world is dictated by our beliefs.

Beloved youths, it is in you that I place my hopes. With the Qur'an in one hand and a gun in the other, defend your dignity and honor so well that your adversaries will be unable even to think of conspiring against you. At the same time, be so compassionate toward your friends that you will not hesitate to sacrifice everything you possess for their sake. Know well that the world today belongs to the oppressed, and sooner or later they will triumph. They will inherit the earth and build the government of God.

Once again, I declare my support for all movements and groups that are fighting to gain liberation from the superpowers of the left and the right. I declare my support for the people of Occupied Palestine and Lebanon. I vehemently condemn once more the savage occupation of Afghanistan by the aggressive plunderers of the East, and I hope that the noble Muslim people of Afghanistan will achieve victory and true independence as soon as possible, and be delivered from the clutches of the so-called champions of the working class.

The noble people should be aware that all our victories have been attained by the will of God Almighty, as manifested in the transformation that has occurred throughout the country, together with the spirit of belief and Islamic commitment and cooperation that motivate the overwhelming majority of our people.

The basis of our victory has been our orientation to God Almighty and our unity of purpose. But if we forget this secret of our success, deviate from the sacred ordinances of Islam, and embark on the path of division and disagreement, it is to be feared that God Almighty will withdraw His grace from us and the path will be open again for the tyrants to drag our people back into slavery by means of their satanic tricks and stratagems. Then the pure blood that has been spilled for the sake of independence and freedom, and the sufferings endured by old and young alike, would be in vain; the fate of our Islamic land would remain for all eternity what it was under the tyrannical regime of the Shah [Mohammad Reza Pahlavi]; and those who were defeated by our Islamic Revolution would treat us in the same way that they treat all the oppressed people of the world.

Ayatollah Ruhollah Khomeini, 1980 New Year's message, March 21, 1980.

Document 5: The Hamas Charter Accuses "Zionists" of Destroying the Caliphate

In the early 1970s, Israel began building settlements in the territories of the Gaza Strip and the West Bank of the River Jordan. These areas are inhabited by millions of Palestinian Arabs, and most governments, including the United States, do not consider them part of the state of Israel. Palestinian opposition to Israel is led by a secular organization, the Palestine Liberation Organization (PLO). Beginning in late 1980s, however, the Islamic fundamentalist group Hamas gained adherents among Palestinians. (Hamas acknowledges the leadership of the PLO.) Hamas is a major backer of suicide attacks. The next selection is an extract from the Hamas charter.

Article Twenty-two:

For a long time, the enemies [the Jews] have been planning, skillfully and with precision, for the achievement of what they have attained. They took into consideration the causes affecting the current of events. They strived to amass great and substantive material wealth which they devoted to the realisation of their dream. With their money, they took control of the world media, news agencies, the press, publishing houses, broadcasting stations, and others. With their money they stirred revolutions in various parts of the world with the purpose of achieving their interests and reaping the fruit therein. They were behind the French Revolution, the Communist revolution and most of the revolutions we heard and hear about, here and there. With their money they formed secret societies, such as Freemasons, Rotary Clubs, the Lions and others in different parts of the world for the purpose of sabotaging societies and achieving Zionist interests. With their money they were able to control imperialistic countries and instigate them to colonize many countries in order to enable them to exploit their resources and spread corruption there.

You may speak as much as you want about regional and world wars. They were behind World War I, when they were able to destroy the Islamic Caliphate, making financial gains and controlling resources. They obtained the Balfour Declaration [which established a Jewish settlement in the British Mandate of Palestine], formed the League of Nations through which they could rule the world. They were behind World War II, through which they made huge financial gains by trading in armaments, and paved the way for the establishment of their state. It was they who instigated the replacement of the League of Nations with the United Nations and the Security Council to enable them to rule the world through them. There is no war going on anywhere, without having their finger in it.

> "So often as they shall kindle a fire for war, Allah shall extinguish it, and they shall set their minds to act corruptly in the earth, but Allah loveth not the corrupt doers." (*The Table*—verse 64).

The imperialistic forces in the Capitalist West and Communist East, support the enemy with all their might, in money and in men. These forces take turns in doing that. The day Islam appears, the forces of infidelity would unite to challenge it, for the infidels are of one nation.

> "O true believers, contract not an intimate friendship with any besides yourselves: they will not fail to corrupt you. They wish for that which may cause you to perish: their hatred hath already appeared from out of their mouths; but what their breasts conceal is yet more inveterate. We have already shown you signs of their ill will towards you, if ye understand." (*The Family of Imran*—verse 118).

It is not in vain that the verse is ended with Allah's words "if ye understand."

Hamas, *The Covenant of the Islamic Resistance Movement*, August 18, 1988.

Document 6: A Saudi Radical Warns Listeners About Christian Fundamentalists

In 1992 a number of Islamic clerics opposed to the policies of the Saudi Arabian government circulated their views in the form of audiotapes. This selection is translated from an audiotape entitled The True Promise and the False One, *by Sheikh Safar al-Hawali, a lecturer at the Islamic University of Madinah's Religious Fundamentals College. Al-Hawali objected strongly to the Saudi government's cooperation with U.S. policies, especially the stationing of U.S. soldiers on Arabian soil during and after the Gulf War and the U.S. attempts to broker a Palestinian-Israeli peace settlement, which he regarded as a sellout. Here he expresses the view that American foreign policy is guided by the evangelical Christian belief that Armageddon will take place soon.*

We will now focus [our] discussion on the Christians because we, as I said, are deluded by them, and we are fooled by their discourse. We place complete confidence [in] them even though they will do with us what we shall see with our own eyes—there is no power and no strength save in God! There is a belief among the Christians which says: "The Messiah will return after a thousand years." As soon as . . . I mean, after he was raised up—may peace be upon him, they said: "the Messiah will return after a thousand years; then he will rule the world for a thousand years." Because of that, when it was the year one thousand *anno domine*—that means how long ago? About a thousand years ago, from now—the Christians in all parts of the world were waiting for the "[Second] Coming" of the Messiah. They waited and waited, but he didn't come. So, the subject fell quiet. [Then] when this century was coming, now, close to [its] end, preachings began to appear in all parts of the Christian world [to the effect] that the Messiah would return in the year two thousand. Fine! And, how would he return? They said. "When the Messiah returns, he will return in the "Kingdom of Israel" in Palestine in his original homeland. Therefore, the Christians believe that the gathering of Jews in Palestine is a precursor of the coming of the Messiah and the Millennial return of the Messiah. And, from this point the Christians adopted, four centuries ago—and not the Jews . . . the Christians before the Jews—adopted the issue—gathering the Jews in Palestine as a preparation for the return of the Messiah in the third millennium. . . .

A book has appeared in America that a man called Oral Roberts wrote. This is a very famous book; he called it *The Dream of the End of the World*. Another book, even more famous than it—it being a book which "Lindsey" wrote, is the book *The Last Days of the Late Great Planet Earth*. This book, or these two books—as examples, suppose that [by] the year two thousand, or close to it, this earthly sphere will come to a final end. . . .

How is it going to end? They have said: "All civilizations end." One of them even said: "There's no call for you to think about America's foreign debts, and there is no call to think about the future of the next generations. Do not think about rising taxes in America. The issue is [a matter] of a few years, and it will [all] end." How is it going to end? They have said: "The [final] great world struggle will happen"—the battle of Armageddon or Mageddo Plain. This battle will be between the pagans and the Christians. You must have heard much about this battle before the Gulf War and how public opinion in America was strongly prepared to believe that this war was the battle of Armageddon or Mageddo Plain. This Mageddo Plain is a small plain in Palestine; they say that the final world battle will take place in it between armies whose number will reach four hundred million even through the territory could not hold such a number. . . .

But, they say: "In these days, close to the year two thousand, this battle will occur, and it will be a nuclear war." The war will be nuclear! The Messiah will come, and he will lift those who believe in him above the clouds while the polytheist pagans will die. I mean, some of this talk . . .! Our brothers say: "Glory be to God!" This talk! The Americans believe it?! We have more than one proof [of that]. More than eleven times, President Reagan has announced his belief in this [proposition], the president of the United States! And Bush and others! Maybe we should bring out more proofs . . . except for the educated class and except for many of. . . . Of course, all men of religion believe in this matter, and [they believe] that the battle must be. They may differ on the date but this battle must happen. And, the pagans who will be killed . . . ? They are the Canaanites [Arabs].

Safar al-Hawali, "Christian Politics," in *The True Promise and the False One*. Reprinted in Peter D. Molon, *Arabic Religious Rhetoric: The Radical Saudi Sheikhs, a Reader.* Kensington, MD: Dunwoody Press, 1997.

Document 7: Human Rights Abuses in Sudan, 1994

Sudan, a country with a mixed ethnic and religious population including Muslims, Christians, and those who practice indigenous religions, has endured decades of civil war in which all sides have carried out brutal atrocities. An Islamic fundamentalist government came to power in Sudan by means of a military coup in 1989. The following excerpt is from a book-length study of human rights abuses committed by the military regime of the National Islamic Front in Sudan after it seized control of the country.

Gross human rights violations continue in Sudan five years after a military coup overthrew the elected civilian government in June 30, 1989, and brought to power a military regime dominated by the National Islamic Front (NIF), a minority party that achieved only 18.4 percent of the popular vote in the 1986 elections. The Sudanese have suffered under military rule and single-party dictatorship for twenty-seven out of the thirty-eight years since independence in 1956; they succeeded in overthrowing oppressive regimes twice in the past, in October 1964 and April 1985. Southern Sudanese continue to struggle against the present regime, as they have done against previous northern-dominated regimes for all but eleven of the thirty-eight years of independence. Massive violations of human rights and humanitarian law in the context of this civil war in southern Sudan are detailed in our July 1994 report, *Civilian Devastation: Abuses by All Parties to the War in Southern Sudan.* This report highlights human rights abuses in northern Sudan, focusing on individual testimonies to supplement the evidence of violations in the south detailed earlier.

As the current regime completes its fifth year in power, all forms of political opposition remain banned legally and through systematic terror. The regime has institutionalized changes in the character of the state through extensive purges of the civil service and by dismantling any element of civil society that disagrees with its narrow vision of an Islamic state. Political power over the whole country has been entrenched in the hands of a tiny ideological elite.

Human Rights Watch/Africa does not question the right of a people to adopt any system of law and government through the genuinely free choice of the population. This is integral to a people's right to self-government. A military regime, however, is by definition not the choice of the citizens, who had no voice in its coming to power, no participation in the formulation and implementation of its policies, and no ability to change it. Any military regime is necessarily the negation and repudiation of the national right to self government. Here the loss is more total because military rule is coupled with an exclusivist ideology, alleged to be founded on religion, that flouts minority rights.

The government of Sudan is bound by the many international human rights treaties that it has ratified or to which it has acceded. According to standards set in these treaties, the right to self-government does not mean that the majority is entitled to violate the fundamental rights and freedoms of minorities. For example, Article 26 of the International Covenant on Civil and Political Rights (ICCPR) provides:

All persons are equal before the law and are entitled without any discrimination to the equal protection of the law. In this respect, the law shall prohibit any discrimination and guarantee to all persons equal and effective protection against discrimination on any ground such as race, color, sex, language, religion, political or other opinion, national or social origin, property, birth or other status.

The government of Sudan is in clear violation of this principle. In addition, it has taken extraordinary measures to prevent the world from learning the specifics of its abysmal human rights record, harshly punishing dissidents and excluding or restricting independent observers, journalists, human rights monitors, and humanitarian organizations. After granting a visa to Human Rights Watch/Africa in June 1993, the government twice, at the last minute, postponed the visit, which, as a result, could not be made.

Sudanese who attempt to speak out on human rights issues are subjected to threats or arrest. . . .

Despite government efforts to deter scrutiny, it has become obvious that a large second-class citizenry has been created by the regime's version of an Islamic state. Public dialogue in Sudan has been silenced, even for those who share a commitment to the implementation of shari'a [religious] law but disagree with the policies and practices of the present government. All political parties remain banned, and arrests of their members continue unabated whenever they attempt any organized civic activity.

Excerpt from introduction to *Sudan 'In the Name of God': Repression Continues in Northern Sudan*, report by Human Rights Watch, 1994. www.hrw.org/reports/1994/sudan.

Document 8: Osama bin Laden Calls on All Muslims to Kill Americans

Osama bin Laden and his followers announced their intentions to kill Americans and their allies well in advance of September 11, 2001, in this fatwa published in an Arabic newspaper in 1998. A fatwa is an Islamic ruling, and is supposed to be delivered by a person qualified in Islamic law. None of the signers of this fatwa were so qualified; however, Osama bin Laden is widely regarded as a spiritual leader in the Middle East.

Praise be to God, who revealed the Book, controls the clouds, defeats factionalism, and says in His Book: "But when the forbidden months are past, then fight and slay the pagans wherever ye find them, seize them, beleaguer them, and lie in wait for them in every stratagem (of war)"; and peace be upon our Prophet, Muhammad Bin-'Abdallah, who said I have been sent with the sword between my hands to ensure that no one but God is worshipped, God who put my livelihood under the shadow of my spear and who inflicts humiliation and scorn on those who disobey my orders. The Arabian Peninsula has never—since God made it flat, created its desert, and encircled it with seas—been stormed by any forces like the crusader armies spreading in it like locusts, eating its riches and wiping out its plantations. All this is happening at a time in which nations are attacking Muslims like people fighting over a plate of food. In the light of the grave situation and the lack of support, we and you are obliged to discuss current events, and we should all agree on how to settle the matter.

No one argues today about three facts that are known to everyone; we will list them, in order to remind everyone.

First, for over seven years the United States has been occupying the lands of Islam in the holiest of places, the Arabian Peninsula, plundering its riches, dictating to its rulers, humiliating its people, terrorizing its neighbors, and turning its bases in the Peninsula into a spearhead through which to fight the neighboring Muslim peoples.

If some people have in the past argued about the fact of the occupation, all the people of the Peninsula have now acknowledged it.

The best proof of this is the Americans' continuing aggression against the Iraqi people using the Peninsula as a staging post, even though all its rulers are against their territories being used to that end, but they are helpless. Second, despite the great devastation inflicted on the Iraqi people by the crusader-Zionist alliance, and despite the huge number of those killed, which has exceeded 1 million . . . despite all this, the Americans are once again trying to repeat the horrific massacres, as though they are not content with the protracted blockade imposed after the ferocious war or the fragmentation and devastation.

So here they come to annihilate what is left of this people and to humiliate their Muslim neighbors.

Third, if the Americans' aims behind these wars are religious and economic, the aim is also to serve the Jews' petty state and divert attention from its occupation of Jerusalem and murder of Muslims there.

The best proof of this is their eagerness to destroy Iraq, the strongest neighboring Arab state, and their endeavor to fragment all the states of the region such as Iraq, Saudi Arabia, Egypt, and Sudan into paper statelets and through their disunion and weakness to guarantee Israel's survival and the continuation of the brutal crusade occupation of the Peninsula.

All these crimes and sins committed by the Americans are a clear declaration of war on God, his messenger, and Muslims. And ulema have throughout Islamic history unanimously agreed that the jihad is an individual duty if the enemy destroys the Muslim countries. . . .

On that basis, and in compliance with God's order, we issue the following fatwa to all Muslims:

The ruling to kill the Americans and their allies—civilians and military—is an individual duty for every Muslim who can do it in any country in which it is possible to do it, in order to liberate the al-Aqsa Mosque and the holy mosque [in Mecca] from their grip, and in order for their armies to move out of all the lands of Islam, defeated and unable to threaten any Muslim. This is in accordance with the words of Almighty God, "and fight the pagans all together as they fight you all together," and "fight them until there is no more tumult or oppression, and there prevail justice and faith in God."

This is in addition to the words of Almighty God "And why should ye not fight in the cause of God and of those who, being weak, are ill-treated (and oppressed)—women and children, whose cry is 'Our Lord, rescue us from this town, whose people are oppressors; and raise for us from thee one who will help!'"

We—with God's help—call on every Muslim who believes in God and wishes to be rewarded to comply with God's order to kill the Americans and plunder their money wherever and whenever they find it. We also call on Muslim ulema, leaders, youths, and soldiers to launch the raid on Satan's U.S. troops and the devil's supporters allying with them, and to displace those who are behind them so that they may learn a lesson.

Osama bin Laden, *Declaration of the World Islamic Front for Jihad Against the Jews and Crusaders*, 1998.

Document 9: President Bush Declares a "War on Terror," September 21, 2001

On September 21, 2001, in a speech to a joint session of the U.S. Congress following the September 11 attacks, President George W. Bush declared a "war on terror" and identified the enemy as Islamic extremists.

On September the 11th, enemies of freedom committed an act of war against our country. Americans have known wars, but for the past 136 years they have been wars on foreign soil, except for one Sunday in 1941. Americans have known the casualties of war, but not at the center of a great city on a peaceful morning.

Americans have known surprise attacks, but never before on thousands of civilians. All of this was brought upon us in a single day, and night fell on a different world, a world where freedom itself is under attack.

Americans have many questions tonight. Americans are asking, "Who attacked our country?"

The evidence we have gathered all points to a collection of loosely affiliated terrorist organizations known as al Qaeda. They are some of the murderers indicted for bombing American embassies in Tanzania and Kenya and responsible for bombing the USS *Cole*.

Al Qaeda is to terror what the Mafia is to crime. But its goal is not making money, its goal is remaking the world and imposing its radical beliefs on people everywhere.

The terrorists practice a fringe form of Islamic extremism that has been rejected by Muslim scholars and the vast majority of Muslim clerics; a fringe movement that perverts the peaceful teachings of Islam.

The terrorists' directive commands them to kill Christians and Jews, to kill all Americans and make no distinctions among military and civilians, including women and children. This group and its leader, a person named Osama bin Laden, are linked to many other organizations in different countries, including the Egyptian Islamic Jihad, the Islamic Movement of Uzbekistan.

There are thousands of these terrorists in more than 60 countries.

They are recruited from their own nations and neighborhoods and brought to camps in places like Afghanistan where they are trained in the tactics of terror. They are sent back to their homes or sent to hide in countries around the world to plot evil and destruction. The leadership of al Qaeda has great influence in Afghanistan and supports the Taliban regime in controlling most of that country. In Afghanistan we see al Qaeda's vision for the world. Afghanistan's people have been brutalized, many are starving and many have fled.

Women are not allowed to attend school. You can be jailed for owning a television. Religion can be practiced only as their leaders dictate. A man can be jailed in Afghanistan if his beard is not long enough. The United States respects the people of Afghanistan—after all, we are currently its largest source of humanitarian aid—but we condemn the Taliban regime.

It is not only repressing its own people, it is threatening people everywhere by sponsoring and sheltering and supplying terrorists.

By aiding and abetting murder, the Taliban regime is committing murder. And tonight the United States of America makes the following demands on the Taliban:

• Deliver to United States authorities all of the leaders of al Qaeda who hide in your land.

• Release all foreign nationals, including American citizens you have unjustly imprisoned.

• Protect foreign journalists, diplomats and aid workers in your country.

• Close immediately and permanently every terrorist training camp in Afghanistan. And hand over every terrorist and every person and their support structure to appropriate authorities.

• Give the United States full access to terrorist training camps, so we can make sure they are no longer operating.

These demands are not open to negotiation or discussion.

The Taliban must act and act immediately.

They will hand over the terrorists or they will share in their fate.

I also want to speak tonight directly to Muslims throughout the world. We respect your faith. It's practiced freely by many millions of Americans and by millions more in countries that America counts as friends. Its teachings are good and peaceful, and those who commit evil in the name of Allah blaspheme the name of Allah.

The terrorists are traitors to their own faith, trying, in effect, to hijack Islam itself.

The enemy of America is not our many Muslim friends. It is not our many Arab friends. Our enemy is a radical network of terrorists and every government that supports them.

Our war on terror begins with al Qaeda, but it does not end there.

It will not end until every terrorist group of global reach has been found, stopped and defeated.

Americans are asking "Why do they hate us?"

They hate what they see right here in this chamber: a democratically elected government. Their leaders are self-appointed. They hate our freedoms: our freedom of religion, our freedom of speech, our freedom to vote and assemble and disagree with each other.

They want to overthrow existing governments in many Muslim countries such as Egypt, Saudi Arabia and Jordan. They want to drive Israel out of the Middle East. They want to drive Christians and Jews out of vast regions of Asia and Africa.

These terrorists kill not merely to end lives, but to disrupt and end a way of life. With every atrocity, they hope that America grows fearful, retreating from the world and forsaking our friends. They stand against us because we stand in their way.

We're not deceived by their pretenses to piety.

We have seen their kind before. They're the heirs of all the murderous ideologies of the 20th century. By sacrificing human life to serve their radical visions, by abandoning every value except the will to power, they follow in the path of fascism, Nazism and totalitarianism. And they will follow that path all the way to where it ends in history's unmarked grave of discarded lies.

George W. Bush, address to a joint session of the U.S. Congress, September 21, 2001.

Document 10: Taliban Mullah Mohammad Omar Defies America, September 24, 2001

Mullah Mohammad Omar was the leader of the Taliban, a radical extremist group that controlled most of Afghanistan from the late 1990s until 2001. The Taliban encouraged Osama bin Laden and al Qaeda to use Afghanistan as their base of operations. Soon after the September 11 attacks on the World Trade Center and the Pentagon, the United States demanded that the Taliban leadership hand over Bin Laden or permit U.S. forces to arrest him. On September 22, envoys of the Taliban refused, saying they were ready for war with the United States. Two days later the Taliban leader delivered this speech.

America shouldn't be mistaken. My death or the death of Osama (Bin Laden) will not bring America out of this crisis.

If America wants to root out terrorism and intimidation, then it should withdraw its forces from the Gulf and demonstrate neutrality over the issue of Palestine.

It should release Islam, which it has taken hostage in a spiritual form and should stop further interference.

A good example of Islam as a hostage is the present situation which they (the Americans) have created in Afghanistan. They want the end of the Islamic order; they want to create disorder, and they want a pro-American government.

In this case, where will the taste of Islam be for Muslims, and how angry and in what poor conditions will Muslims be? They (the Americans) have done this in many Islamic countries.

America has no alternative in these affairs to locking itself in a bloody war in which it will burn itself and others, and which will have no result.

The American people and the government should consider this oppressive and ugly policy, which tells each Muslim: Accept my words; if not I will throw an atomic bomb on you and will close off the holes through which sustenance can reach you.

These are all facts. The distance travelled by a lie is short.

Speech by Mullah Mohammad Omar, September 24, 2001.

Document 11: Osama bin Laden Comments on the September 11 Attacks

On October 7, 2001, a videotaped statement by al Qaeda head Osama bin Laden was broadcast on the Arab television news network Al-Jazeera, which is excerpted here.

Here is America struck by God Almighty in one of its vital organs, so that its greatest buildings are destroyed. Grace and gratitude to God.

America has been filled with horror from North to South and East to West, and thanks be to God that what America is tasting now is only a copy of what we have tasted. Our Islamic nation has been tasting the same for more than 80 years, of humiliation and disgrace, its sons killed and their blood spilled, its sanctities desecrated.

God has blessed a group of vanguard Muslims, the forefront of Islam, to destroy America. May God bless them and allot them a supreme place in heaven. For He is the only one capable and entitled to do so.

When those who have stood in defence of their weak children, their brothers and sisters in Palestine and other Muslim nations, the whole world went into an uproar, the infidels followed by the hypocrites.

A million innocent children are dying at this time as we speak, killed in Iraq without any guilt. We hear no denunciation, we hear no edict from the hereditary rulers. In these days, Israeli tanks rampage across Palestine, in Ramallah, Rafah and Beit Jala and many other parts of the land of Islam, and we do not hear anyone raising his voice or reacting.

But when the sword fell upon America after 80 years, hypocrisy raised its head up high, bemoaning those killers who toyed with the blood, honour and sanctities of Muslims.

The least that can be said about those hypocrites is that they are apostates who followed the wrong path. They backed the butcher against the victim, the oppressor against the innocent child. I seek refuge in God against them and ask Him to let us see them in what they deserve.

I say that the matter is very clear. Every Muslim after this event, after the senior officials in the United States of America, starting with the head of international infidels, Bush and his staff who went on a display of vanity with their men and horses, those who turned even the countries that believe in Islam against us—the group that

resorted to God, the Almighty, the group that refuses to be subdued in its religion.

They have been telling the world falsehoods that they are fighting terrorism. In a nation at the far end of the world, Japan, hundreds of thousands young and old were killed and this is not a
world crime. To them it is not a clear issue. A million children in
Iraq, to them this is not a clear issue.

But when a few more than ten were killed in Nairobi and Dar
es-Salam, Afghanistan and Iraq were bombed and hypocrisy stood
behind the head of international infidels, the modern world's symbol of paganism, America, and its allies.

I tell them that these events have divided the world into two
camps, the camp of the faithful and the camp of the infidels. May
God shield us and you from them.

Every Muslim must rise to defend his religion. The wind of
faith is blowing, and the wind of change is blowing to remove evil
from the Peninsula of Mohammed, peace be upon him.

As to America, I say to it and its people a few words: I swear to
God that America will not live in peace before peace reigns in
Palestine, and before all the army of infidels depart the land of
Mohammed, peace be upon him.

God is the Greatest and glory be to Islam.

Statement by Osama bin Laden, October 7, 2001.

Document 12: Abu'l A'la Mawdudi on the Principles of the Islamic State

*Abu'l A'la Mawdudi was an influential thinker in the Islamic fundamen-
talist movement in the twentieth century and the founder of Jamaat-i
Islami (the Islamic Party) in Pakistan. In this extract from his tract "The
Political Theory of Islam," he provides his vision of an Islamic state.*

With certain people it has become a sort of fashion to somehow
identify Islam with one or the other system of life in vogue at the
time. So at this time also there are people who say that Islam is a
democracy, and by this they mean to imply that there is no vast difference between Islam and the democracy in vogue in the West.
Some others suggest that Communism is but the latest and revised
version of Islam and it is in the fitness of things that Muslims imitate the Communist experiment of Soviet Russia. Still others
whisper that Islam has the elements of dictatorship in it and we
should revive the cult of "obedience to the Amir" (the leader). All
these people, in their misinformed and misguided zeal to serve

what they hold to be the cause of Islam, are always at great pains to prove that Islam contains within itself the elements of all types of contemporary social and political thought and action. Most of the people who indulge in this prattle have no clear idea of the Islamic way of life. . . . As a matter of fact, this attitude emerges from an inferiority complex, from the belief that we as Muslims can earn no honour or respect unless we are able to show that our religion resembles the modern creeds and it is in agreement with most of the contemporary ideologies. . . .

The belief in the unity (*tawhid*) and the sovereignty of Allah is the foundation of the social and moral system propounded by the Prophets. It is the very starting point of the Islamic political philosophy. The basic principle of Islam is that human beings must, individually and collectively, surrender all rights of overlordship, legislation and exercizing of authority over others. . . . None is entitled to make laws on his own authority and none is obliged to abide by them. This right vests in Allah alone (the Quran says): "The Authority rests with none but Allah. He commands you not to surrender to any one save Him. This is the right way (of life)."

According to this theory, sovereignty belongs to Allah. He alone is the law-giver. . . . The Prophet himself is subject to God's commands. . . . Other people are required to obey the Prophet because he enunciates not his own but God's commands. . . . Thus the main characteristics of an Islamic state that can be deduced from (this) are as follows:

1. No person, class or group, not even the entire population of the state as a whole, can lay claim to sovereignty. God alone is the real sovereign; all others are merely his subjects;

2. God is the real law-giver and the authority of absolute legislation vests in Him. The believers cannot resort to totally independent legislation nor can they modify any law which God has laid down. . . .

3. An Islamic state must, in all respects, be founded upon the law laid down by God and His Prophet. The government which runs such a state will be entitled to obedience in its capacity as a political agency set up to enforce the laws of God and only in so far as it acts in that capacity. If it disregards the law revealed by God, its commands will not be binding on the believers.

From Abu'l A'la Mawdudi, "Political Theory of Islam," in *Islam: Its Meaning and Message*, ed. Khurshid Ahmad. London: Islamic Foundation, 1998.

Chronology

570–632
Life of Muhammad, founder of Islam.

622
Muhammad and his followers move to Medina to escape persecution. The date is the starting point of the official Islamic calendar.

640s–720s
The Arabs, united under Islam, conquer a vast empire stretching from northeastern India to the Iberian Peninsula (location of present-day Spain).

650s
Compilation of the Koran, the holy book of Islam.

661
The Umayyad dynasty begins. Islam splits into Shia and Sunni sects.

691
Abd al-Malik builds the Dome of the Rock in Jerusalem on the ruins of the Jews' Second Temple.

732
Islamic forces are stopped in Europe by Charles Martel in the Battle of Tours and Poitiers (in present-day France).

750
The Abbasid dynasty begins.

765–850
The four orthodox schools of law are established.

765
A school of medicine is established at Baghdad.

850–1055
Seljuk Turks migrate into lands of the Abbasid empire, convert to Islam, help to spread Islam as soldiers, and gradually take control of the Abbasid empire.

1055
The Abbasid caliph recognizes Seljuk leader Tughril Beg as sultan ("chieftain").

1055–1250
Islam expands under the Seljuk Turks.

1099
Crusaders capture Jerusalem and massacre many of the Jews and Muslims in the city.

1165–1227
Lifetime of the Mongol conqueror Genghis Khan.

1187
Saladin recaptures Jerusalem from the Crusaders.

1255
Genghis Khan's grandson Berke, who has converted to Islam, expands the Mongol conquests in present-day Kazakhstan, Uzbekistan, and Turkmenistan.

1258
The Mongols sack Baghdad, the Abbasid capital in Iraq, massacring more than two hundred thousand residents, and the Abbasid caliphate ends.

1295
Il-khan Ghazan, the Mongol ruler of Persia, converts to Islam, and most of the Mongols in Persia follow his example.

1360
The Turkish conquerer Timur ("Tamerlane") conquers a vast territory stretching from eastern Anatolia to the Indus River.

1400s
Christians reconquer Spain, expelling or converting all Muslims. Tartars are driven from Russia.

1453
The Ottoman Turks capture Constantinople, marking the end of the Byzantine Empire, bastion of Christianity in the East.

1492
Columbus reaches America.

1498
The Portuguese explorer Vasco da Gama arrives in India after rounding the Cape of Good Hope.

1501
Safavid Empire is founded in Persia (present-day Iran) by the young Shah Isma'il. The Safavids spread the messianic Islamic sect of Twelver Shiism in Persia.

1683
Ottoman Turks are defeated in second siege of Vienna.

1798
The French general Napoléon Bonaparte arrives in Egypt with a small expeditionary force and conquers and occupies the country. The French are driven out, not by Muslims but by a small squadron of the British Royal Navy.

1830
France seizes Algeria, an Ottoman province, on the pretext of eradicating the Barbary pirates.

1854
Britain and France declare war on Russia in order to prevent portions of the Ottoman Empire from falling into Russian hands. The Ottoman Empire is now "the sick old man of Europe."

1858
The British Parliament dissolves the East India Company, which has virtually conquered India, and institutes direct rule of India.

1881
The French take control of Tunisia, an Islamic country bordering Algeria.

1883
Lord Cromer, the British administrator, becomes the effective ruler of Egypt.

1912
Morocco becomes a French protectorate.

1914–1918
World War I results in the dismemberment of the Ottoman Empire. The Ottoman provinces are divided into French and British spheres of influence.

1917

British diplomat Arthur Balfour, in a letter known as the Balfour Declaration, pledges British support to the creation of a Jewish homeland in Palestine.

1924

Turkey abolishes the caliphate, which has (in theory though seldom in practice) ruled Islam since the 600s.

1925

Abdul Aziz al-Saud completes the unification of Saudi Arabia. Wahhabism, a fundamentalist Islamic sect, is the only version of Islam sanctioned by Saudi law.

1928

Hasan al-Banna forms the Muslim Brotherhood.

1932

Iraq becomes an independent kingdom admitted to the League of Nations. Its arbitrary borders create lasting political problems.

1941

Indian journalist Mawlana Ala Mawdudi founds the Jamaat-i-Islami.

1947

August—India becomes independent and is partitioned into Pakistan (predominantly Muslim) and India (predominantly Hindu).

1948

The State of Israel is established. Armies from Syria, Egypt, and Jordan are defeated in the first Arab-Israeli war, and an estimated 700,000 to 750,000 Palestinian Arabs become refugees.

1949

Hasan al-Banna is assassinated and the Muslim Brotherhood banned in Egypt by the government of King Farouk.

1952

A coup of Egyptian army officers dethrones King Farouk and the Muslim Brotherhood is restored.

1953

In Iran, agents of America's Central Intelligence Agency, in cooperation with the British intelligence agency MI6, engineer the overthrow of popular nationalist leader Mosaddeq, assuring decades of rule by the pro-Western shah Mohammad Reza Pahlavi.

1956
Morocco becomes independent.

1962
July—Algerians vote for independence from France after a long war marked by terrorism by the Algerian resistance and brutal repression by the French.

1966
Sayyid Qutb, Egyptian writer and Muslim Brotherhood member whose books helped to form the ideology of Islamic fundamentalism, is executed on charges of attempting to overthrow the government.

1967
June—Israel defeats Egypt, Syria, and Jordan in the Six Day War, capturing territories belonging to all three nations.

1973
Egypt, Syria, Iraq, and Jordan invade Israeli-occupied territory and are driven back after the United States resupplies Israel with modern weaponry. The Organization of Arab Petroleum Exporting Countries (OAPEC) punishes the United States with an embargo that drives up oil prices.

1977
In a military coup General Zia-ul-Haq takes power in Pakistan and seeks support from Islamic extremists.

1978
After intensive negotiations with U.S. president Jimmy Carter, Egyptian president Anwar Sadat and Israeli prime minister Menachem Begin sign a peace treaty.

1979
February 11—A revolutionary Islamic regime headed by Ruholla Khomeini assumes power in Iran.
September—Khomeini says in a speech in Qum that the whole Islamic world is caught in America's clutches.
November 4—Five hundred radical Iranian students storm the American Embassy in Iran and hold the residents hostage. Fifty-five embassy workers are held until January 1981.
November 5—Iran abrogates military agreements with the United States.
November 20—About a thousand Muslim religious radicals seize the Great Mosque in Mecca and hold it against Saudi security forces.

The radicals declare their intention to purify Islam and liberate the holy land of Arabia from the "royal clique of infidels"; that is, from Saudi Arabia's ruling family.

1979—1989
The Soviet Union invades Afghanistan to prop up a Marxist government. Young Arabs from all over the Middle East join the Afghanis in fighting the Soviets.

1980–1988
Iran and Iraq fight a devastating war that ends in a stalemate.

1981
Anwar Sadat is assassinated by extremists who hope to spark a general Islamic uprising.

1982
An uprising led by the radical Muslim Brotherhood occurs in the Syrian city of Hama. Between ten thousand and twenty-five thousand people are killed when the Syrian government suppresses the uprising, destroying a large part of the city.

1988
April—The Soviets, defeated and demoralized by their inability to win in Afghanistan, announce that they will withdraw troops within nine months.

1989
Sudanese political leader Hassan al-Turabi, an Islamic fundamentalist, invites Osama bin Laden to come with his al Qaeda organization to Sudan.

June—The National Islamic Front, an Islamic fundamentalist party led by Sudan's branch of the Muslim Brotherhood, seizes power in Sudan in a military coup d'etat.

1990
Iraqi president Saddam Hussein invades Iraq's small oil-rich neighbor Kuwait and announces its annexation.

1991
February—Saddam Hussein is defeated in the first Persian Gulf War. His defeat is a blow to secular nationalism among Islamic states.

March—Sudan's National Islamic Front introduces a broad, unusually harsh version of sharia. Renunciation of Islam is punished by death, and other offenses are punishable by amputation, crucifixion, or stoning to death.

December—Algeria's Islamic Salvation Front (FIS) does well in the first round of elections for the national assembly and seems likely to win in the second round.

1992

January—Fearing an FIS victory, the Algerian military cancels the elections and imposes a ruthless secular dictatorship (with approval from Western leaders, who fear another Islamic fundamentalist regime). A long and bitter civil war begins.

1993

Five Sudanese nationals are indicted in New York in connection with the 1993 World Trade Center bomb plots, including a scheme to blow up the United Nations and New York bridges and public buildings.

1996

A truck bomb goes off in the Khobar Towers, residence of U.S. Air Force personnel in Dhahran, Saudi Arabia. Nineteen Americans are killed and 372 are wounded. The attacks are linked to Saudi Hizballah, a group supported by Iran.

1998

February—Osama bin Laden and Ayman al-Zawahiri arrange to have a fatwa published in an Arabic newspaper in London. Their statement announces that the murder of any American, anywhere on earth, is the "individual duty for every Muslim who can do it in any country in which it is possible to do it."

August 7—Truck bombs explode almost simultaneously in the American embassies in Kenya and Tanzania, killing a total of 224 people, 12 of them Americans, and injuring around 5,000 others.

August 20—President Bill Clinton orders cruise missile strikes at Osama bin Laden's training camps in Afghanistan. Though the missiles hit their targets, no terrorist leaders are hit.

2000

October 12—The USS *Cole*, a U.S. Navy vessel, is attacked while refueling in Aden, Yemen, causing the deaths of seventeen sailors.

2001

September 11—Islamic extremists hijack four American planes. Two destroy the World Trade Center, one crashes into the Pentagon, a fourth crashes in a Pennsylvania field. Nearly three thousand people are killed.

September 20—U.S. president George W. Bush declares "war on terror."

October—The United States invades Afghanistan and overthrows the Taliban regime.

2003

The United States invades Iraq, citing, among other justifications, Saddam Hussein's possession of "weapons of mass destruction" and his collaboration with Osama bin Laden. These claims later prove unfounded.

2004

May—Abu Ghraib prison abuse scandal becomes public. Pictures of U.S. soldiers and civilians humiliating and abusing Iraqi prisoners are broadcast around the world.

May 29—Terrorists attack oil company and housing compounds in Khobar and take hostages at the Oasis housing compound. The next day Saudi commandos storm the Oasis, freeing forty-one hostages but coming too late to save twenty-two others.

June—Civilian defense contractor Paul M. Johnson is kidnapped and beheaded by Islamic terrorists, and the gruesome video of his murder is shown on the Internet. Of about thirty-five thousand Americans in Saudi Arabia at the year's beginning, ten thousand remain.

2005

January 30—Iraq, still under U.S. occupation, holds its first free elections. Turnout is high despite ongoing violence and the opposition of Iraq's Sunni minority.

May—At U.N. disarmament conference, U.S. negotiator Stephen Rademaker says that Iran is using loopholes in the Nuclear Nonproliferation Treaty to seek the means of making nuclear weapons.

For Further Research

Books

Akbar S. Ahmed, *Islam Today: A Short Introduction to the Muslim World*. London: I.B. Tauris, 1999.

———, *Islam Under Siege*. Cambridge, UK: Polity Press, 2003.

Fouad Ajami, *The Arab Predicament: Arab Political Thought and Practice Since 1967*. New York: Oxford University Press, 1981.

Tariq Ali, *The Clash of Fundamentalisms: Crusades, Jihads and Modernity*. New York: Verso, 2002.

Anonymous, *Imperial Hubris: Why the West Is Losing the War on Terror*. Washington, DC: Brassey's, 2004.

Karen Armstrong, *The Battle for God*. New York: Ballantine, 2000.

Benjamin Barber, *Jihad vs. McWorld: Terrorism's Challenge to Democracy*. New York: Ballantine, 1995.

J. Bower Bell, *Murder on the Nile: The World Trade Center and Global Terror*. San Francisco: Encounter, 2003.

John Bowker, *What Muslims Believe*. Oxford, UK: Oneworld, 1999.

Steve Coll, *Ghost Wars: The Secret History of the CIA, Afghanistan, and Bin Laden, from the Soviet Invasion to September 10, 2001*. New York: Penguin, 2004.

John L. Esposito, *The Islamic Threat: Myth or Reality?* New York: Oxford University Press, 1992.

———, ed., *The Oxford History of Islam*. New York: Oxford University Press, 2000.

Thomas L. Friedman, *Longitudes and Attitudes: Exploring the World After September 11*. New York: Farrar, Straus & Giroux, 2002.

Fred Halliday, *Two Hours That Shook the World: September 11, 2001: Causes and Consequences*. London: Saqi, 2002.

Dilip Hiro, *War Without End: The Rise of Islamic Terrorism and the Global Response*. New York: Routledge, 2002.

Johannes J.G. Jansen, *The Dual Nature of Islamic Fundamentalism*. Ithaca, NY: Cornell University Press, 1997.

Gilles Kepel, *Jihad: The Trail of Political Islam*. Cambridge, MA: Harvard University Press, 2002.

Stephen Kinzer, *All the Shah's Men: An American Coup and the Roots of Middle East Terror*. Hoboken, NJ: John Wiley and Sons, 2003.

Mark Kukis, *"My Heart Became Attached": The Strange Journey of John Walker Lindh*. Washington, DC: Brassey's, 2003.

Bernard Lewis, *The Crisis of Islam: Holy War and Unholy Terror*. New York: Modern Library, 2003.

———, *The Muslim Discovery of Europe*. New York: Norton, 2001.

Judith Miller, *God Has Ninety-nine Names: Reporting from a Militant Middle East*. New York: Simon & Schuster, 1996.

National Commission on Terrorist Attacks upon the United States, *Report of the National Commission on Terrorist Attacks upon the United States*. July 2, 2004.

Daniel Pipes, *The Hidden Hand: Middle East Fears of Conspiracy*. New York: St. Martin's, 1996.

Angelo Rasanayagam, *Afghanistan: A Modern History*. London: I.B. Tauris, 2003.

Ahmed Rashid, *Jihad: The Rise of Militant Islam in Central Asia*. New Haven, CT: Yale University Press, 2002.

Edward W. Said, *Orientalism*. New York: Vintage, 1979.

Shaul Shay, *Endless Jihad: The Mujahadin, the Taliban and Bin Laden*. Herzliya, Israel: International Policy Institute for Counterterrorism, 2002.

———, *The Shahids: Islam and Suicide Attacks*. Herzliya, Israel: International Policy Institute for Counterterrorism, 2004.

Martin Stone, *The Agony of Algeria*. New York: Columbia University Press, 1997.

Abdulkader Tayob, *Islam: A Short Introduction*. Oxford, UK: Oneworld, 1999.

Periodicals

Lisa Beyer, "The Most Wanted Man in the World," *Time*, September 24, 2001.

John F. Burns, "America Inspires Both Longing and Loathing in Muslim World," *New York Times*, September 16, 2001.

Charles W. Collier, "The Harsh Judgment of History," *Dissent*, Winter 2003.

Economist "The Gods That Failed," September 13, 2003.

Abdullahi A. Gallab, "The Insecure Rendezvous Between Islam and Totalitarianism: The Failure of the Islamist State in Sudan," *Arab Studies Quarterly*, Spring 2001.

Susan Headden et al., "The Banality of Evil: The Terrorists Hung Out, Did Laundry, Then They Murdered," *U.S. News & World Report*, October 1, 2001.

Christopher Hitchens, "Against Rationalization," *Nation*, October 8, 2001.

———, "Holy Writ," *Atlantic Monthly*, April 2003.

Samuel P. Huntington, "The Clash of Civilizations?" *Foreign Affairs*, Summer 1993.

Youseef M. Ibrahim, "Democracy: Be Careful What You Wish For," *Washington Post*, March 23, 2003.

Robert Killebrew, "Al Qaeda, the Next Chapter," *Washington Post*, August 8, 2004.

N. R. Kleinfield, "Hijacked Jets Destroy Twin Towers and Hit Pentagon in Day of Terror," *New York Times*, September 12, 2001.

Patrick Lang, "Wahhabism and Jihad: A Challenge to Religious Tolerance," *America*, March 10, 2003.

Ann M. Lesch, "Osama Bin Laden: Embedded in the Middle East Crises," *Middle East Policy*, June 2002.

Bernard Lewis, "License to Kill: Usama bin Ladin's Declaration of Jihad," *Foreign Affairs*, December 1998.

———, "The West and the Middle East," *Foreign Affairs*, February 1997.

Robert Marquand, "The Tenets of Terror: A Special Report on the Ideology of Jihad and the Rise of Islamic Militancy," *Christian Science Monitor*, October 18, 2001.

Ken Menkhaus, "Political Islam in Somalia," *Middle East Policy*, March 2002.

Augustus Richard Norton, "Activism and Reform in Islam," *Current History*, November 2002.

David B. Ottaway, "Pressure Builds on Key Pillar of Saudi Rule," *Washington Post*, June 8, 2004.

Margo Patterson, "Islamic Fundamentalism Feared, Misunderstood," *National Catholic Reporter*, October 8, 2004.

Daniel Pipes, "Jihad and the Professors," *Commentary*, November 2002.

Salman Rushdie, "Yes, This Is About Islam," *New York Times*, November 2, 2001.

Andrew Sullivan, "This Is a Religious War," *New York Times*, October 7, 2001.

Fareed Zakaria, "The Extremists Are Losing," *Washington Post*, September 3, 2002.

Web Sites

Islam.com, www.islam.com. A categorized listing of useful links on Islam, its beliefs, and practices; includes Salafi- and Arab-owned Islamic resources.

Islam Page—Islam, Muslims, Allah, Muhammad, Salvation, Jesus, www.islamworld.net. This Web site has many links to pages explaining Islamic history and doctrine, including links to the writings of some Islamic fundamentalist writers such as Hasan al-Banna and Sayyid Qutb. The site actively attempts to convert readers to Islam and attempts to refute the tenets of other religions.

Middle East Web (Palestinian-Israeli Conflict) Balanced News, Facts, History, Opinions, Peace Education, www.mideastweb. org. This Web site has numerous links to articles on the subject of the Palestinian-Israeli conflict, including overviews, a general introduction, and a great many primary source documents.

Ted Thornton/Department of History and Social Science, Northfield Mount Hermon School—History Middle East, www.nmh school.org/tthornton/mehistorydatabase/mideastindex.htm. This Web site, prepared by a history teacher, has links to many pages on the subject of Middle Eastern history and current events.

Index